FUNCTIONAL ENGLISH for COMMUNICATION

Ujjwala Kakarla
Leena Pundir Agarwal
Tanu Gupta

ATLANTIC
PUBLISHERS & DISTRIBUTORS (P) LTD

ATLANTIC
PUBLISHERS & DISTRIBUTORS (P) LTD
7/22, Ansari Road, Darya Ganj, New Delhi
Tel.: +91-11-4077 5252, 2327 3880
E-mail: orders@atlanticbooks.com
Web: www.atlanticbooks.com

Reprinted in 2026

Published by Atlantic Publishers & Distributors (P) Ltd 2024

Previously Published by SAGE Publications in 2019

Printed & bound in India by Atlantic Print Services

Contents

Preface

Functional English for Communication serves as a guide to teachers and learners focusing not only on traditionally acknowledged skills such as listening, speaking, reading, and writing but also on vocabulary, lexis, and communicative grammar. Although this book has been designed as per All India Council for Technical Education guidelines, it will appeal to students across all streams apart from professional students of engineering and management. The book attempts to help the learners enrich their communication through exercise-drill approach and specimen studies in the academic and professional environs. The textbook is meant to teach as well as aid in self-learning English in a competent and creative manner with a wide range of practical activities. The modules aim at improving professional writing skills conducive to business and industrial contexts, and also train the students to use English language appropriately in spoken form with clarity and confidence enhancing their communication skills and employability skills.

The textbook has been divided into six units.

Unit 1 emphasizes vocabulary building, covering concepts such as word formation, root words from foreign languages, derivatives, and lexical relations, thereby developing and improving the skill of students in the area of vocabulary.

Unit 2 highlights the basic writing skills for professional communication covering various aspects such as sentence structures, use of phrases and clauses, proper punctuation, and paragraph development in documents fostering practice of grammatical concepts in various contexts.

Unit 3 dwells on the importance of essential grammatical concepts such as subject–verb agreement, noun–pronoun agreement, articles, and prepositions. Moreover, the unit focuses on common errors such as misplaced modifiers, redundancies, and clichés, so that students may develop their linguistic competency.

Unit 4 introduces nature and various styles of sensible writing such as describing, defining, and classifying with a wide range of examples to use the language effectively in written forms.

Unit 5 covers writing practices which include comprehension, precis writing, essay writing, composing business memos, letter writing, and technical report writing. Many samples have been provided for analysing and practising.

Unit 6 focuses on oral communication, enabling the students to develop their listening and speaking skills through various activities in various contexts such as conversations, situational dialogues, oral presentations, and group discussions. In addition, the students will be trained to develop their interview skills through effective tips and role plays.

Taking into account various competitive examinations such as CAT, TOEFL, GMAT, IELTS, and TEFL, a wide range of practice exercises are provided at the end of each unit to help the learners acquaint with the test patterns and to prepare well in advance to face the exams with confidence.

We sincerely hope that the text breaks a new ground in teaching of English in the most interactive, interesting, and productive way, enriching the teachers and learners to think critically and practically to use English language in the best possible way in academic, social, and professional contexts to serve different purposes.

ACKNOWLEDGEMENTS

We express our gratitude to our family members, friends, and colleagues for their support and cooperation.

About the Authors

Dr. Ujjwala Kakarla is an award-winning writer, researcher, trainer and educationist based in Hyderabad. She holds her doctorate in Indo-Anglian Literature and is an expert in Technical Communication, Soft Skills, Gender Sensitization, Human Values and Professional Ethics. She has lectured and taught intensive courses in various technical institutions and universities. She has been the resource person in imparting holistic education for various companies, schools and colleges. Moreover, she rendered her services to the aviation sector as Senior Linguist Expert in affiliation to DGCA and UKCAA. Currently, she teaches at VNRVJIET, an autonomous technical institution in affiliation to JNTUH. She has to her credit twelve patents and numerous research papers, articles and poetry published in literary journals, holistic magazines, Scopus, SCI and UGC-indexed scientific journals. As an ardent writer and passionate educator, she has been honoured with 50 Aspiring Authors and Researchers Award by Fox Story News Magazine and Nation Choice Award by Glantor X News Magazine.

Dr. Leena Pundir Agarwal is currently working as Assistant Professor of English at Omkarananda Saraswati Government Degree College, Devprayag, Tehri Garhwal. She holds sixteen years of teaching experience and completed her doctorate in English Literature from Chaudhary Charan Singh University, Meerut.

Dr. Tanu Gupta is currently working as Professor and Head, Department of English, Chandigarh University. With 23 years of teaching experience, she has many publications including six books and around eighty papers in national and international peer reviewed journals. She has been credited with five best research paper awards. She has guided nine doctorates and six M.Phil research scholars. She has been the member of the editorial board for many reputed national and international journals indexed in Web of Science and UGC care.

1

UNIT

Vocabulary Building

1.1 THE CONCEPT OF WORD FORMATION

English is a flexible language and one can build on one's vocabulary and learn how to make new words. The expression *word building* means the process of creating or forming words out of sequences of morphemes or words. Word formation is the formation of words in a language by the processes of derivation and composition. The resources of English language have been enriched by the phenomenon as well as by borrowings from other languages. New words have continued to be made from old ones, and have thus added to the existing store of words or vocables.

1.2 ROOT WORDS FROM FOREIGN LANGUAGES AND THEIR USE IN ENGLISH

In English, a root is a word or a portion of a word from which other words originate. Most words in the English language are based on roots from ancient Greek and Latin. Knowing the meaning of these root words can help one decipher the meaning of the new words that we encounter.

Root	*Meaning*	*Words in English*
ab-, a-, abs-	away from	abnormal, abrasion, absent, abstain, abstract, abstraction, aversion, avulsion
acer-, acri-	bitter, sharp, sour	acerbic, acrid, acrimonious, acrimony, exacerbate
acr-	height, summit, tip	acrobat, acronym, acrophobia
aer-	air, atmosphere	aerobic, aerodynamic, aeronautics
aesth-	feeling, sensation	aesthesia, aesthesis, aesthete, aesthetics
ag-, act-	do, go, move	act, action, actor, agenda, agent, agile
ali-, alter-	other	alias, alibi, alien, alter, alternate
alt-	high, deep	altimeter, altitude
ambi-, am-, amb-	both, on both sides	ambidexterity, ambient, ambiguous, ambit, ambition, ambivalent
arbit-	judge	arbitrary, arbitration
ard-	heat, glow, passion	ardent, ardour, arson
audac-	daring	audacious, audacity
aug-, auct-	grow, increase	augment, augmentation, augur
ben-	good, well	beneficence, benefit, benevolent, benign
calum-	trick, lie, deceive	calumnious, calumny
carn-	embodied in	carnate, incarnation
ced-	move, yield, go, surrender	accede, cede, concede, precede
clam-	cry out	acclaim, claim, clamour
contra-	against	contraband
cred-	believe, trust	accreditation, credence, credentials, credibility
dic-, dict-	say, speak, proclaim	benediction, condition, contradict, dictate
err-	stray	aberrance, aberrancy, aberrant, aberration
eu-	well, good	euphony, euphoria, euphoric
ferv-	boil, glow	ferment, fervent, fervid, fervour
idi-	own, peculiarity	idiolect, idiom, idiosyncrasy, idiosyncratic
irasc-, irat-	be angry	irascible, irate, ire
judic-	judge	adjudicate, prejudicial, quasi-judicial
laps-	slide, slip	collapse, collapsible, elapse
nihil-	nothing	annihilate, annihilation, annihilator, nihilistic, nil

Root	*Meaning*	*Words in English*
nom-	arrangement, law, order	agronomy, antinomy, astronomy, autonomous
nunci-	announce	annunciation, denounce, enunciate
omni-	all	omniscient, omnivore
oner-	burden, load	exoneration, onerous, onus
opt-	choose	adopt, adoptee, adoption, adoptive, co-option
optim-	best	optimal, optimum
ora-	pray, plead	exorable, inexorable, oracle
ordin-	order	coordinator, disorder, extraordinary
orn-	decorate	adornment, ornament
pac-	peace	appease, pacify
pact-	fasten	compact, impact
path-	feel	pathetic, apathy, empathy
pati-, pass-	suffer, feel, endure, permit	compassionate, compatible, dispassionate, impassion
pell-, puls-	drive, push	compel, compulsory, dispel, expel, expulsion, impel
pet-	strive towards	compete, competition, impetus
phon-	sound	symphony, telephonic
plac-	calm	implacable, placable, placate
pon-, posit-	put	component, depose, deposit, exponent, expose, expound
port-	carry	deport, export, import, port, portable
rid-, ris-	laugh	deride, derision, ridicule, ridiculous
rudi-	unskilled, rough, unlearned	erudition, rude, rudiment, rudimentary
sacr-, -secr-	sacred	consecrate, desecrate, sacrament
san-	healthy	sanatorium, sane, sanitarium, sanitary
sep-	rot	antiseptic, sepsis, septic
sequ-, secut-	follow	consecutive, consequence, ensue, obsequious, prosecute, pursue, second, sequel, sequence, subsequent
ser-	attach, join	assert, assertion, assertive
serv-	save, protect, serve	conserve, deserve, observe, preserve, reserve, servant
soci-	group	associate, society
sol-	comfort, soothe	consolation, console, solace
tac-, -tic-	be silent	reticent, reticence, tacit, taciturn

Root	*Meaning*	*Words in English*
en-, -tin-, tent-	hold, keep	abstain, discontent, discontinuous
termin-	boundary, limit, end	determine, interminable, terminal, termination
terr-	earth	subterranean, terracotta, terrain, terrestrial, territory
test-	witness	attest, contest, detest, protest, testament, testify, testimony
tract-	draw, pull	abstract, attract, contract, detract, retract
trepid-	tremble	intrepid, trepid, trepidation
turb-	disturb	disturb, perturb, trouble
vac-	empty	evacuate, vacancy, vacation
vigil-	watchful	invigilate, surveillance, vigil
voc-	call, voice	advocacy, avocation, avouch, avow, evocative, vouch
vol-	will	benevolent, involuntary, malevolence, volunteer

PRACTICE EXERCISE A

Look at the following sentences and identify the meanings of the words highlighted by associating them with their roots:

a. Negotiations between both partners of the company have been very **amicable**.
b. One should be **circumspect** about giving too much personal information on the Internet.
c. Scientists were **euphoric** at the success of the test.
d. He delivered a moving **eulogy** at his friend's funeral.
e. He **maliciously** damaged his neighbour's car with a cricket bat.
f. The police tried to **placate** the little boy with a cookie.
g. A string of victories had made the Indian cricket team **complacent**.
h. The cult leader led his followers to believe that he was **omnipotent**.
i. The Venus Fly Trap is a **carnivorous** plant.
j. We must be thankful for our **intrepid** soldiers guarding our borders.
k. After an **interminable** wait of six hours, the passengers were asked to board the aircraft.
l. The city markets were filled with **contraband** goods.
m. He was not popular among the students because of his **idiosyncratic** behaviour.
n. She was a **benevolent** woman, volunteering all of her free time to charitable organizations.

o. The **turbid** water clogged the pipes.
p. There was a **tacit** agreement that he would pay off the loan.
q. The Prince had **obsequious** servants who showered him with attention.
r. This battlefield is **consecrated** to the memory of soldiers who died here.
s. The kids erupted in **derision** when the old man fumbled in the classroom.
t. The public is enraged by the **inexorable** rise in petrol prices.

1.3 ACQUAINTANCE WITH PREFIXES AND SUFFIXES FROM FOREIGN LANGUAGES IN ENGLISH TO FORM DERIVATIVES

Words exist in clusters in that several words derived from a single word form a group or family. There are many ways of word formation in English.

1.3.1 Affixation

Prefixes and Suffixes

One of the commonest word formation processes is affixation. Affixes are bound morphemes attached to the root or stem of a word. Suffixes and prefixes together are called affixes. Many English words are also formed by taking root words and adding combinations of prefixes and suffixes to them.

Prefixes are words added to the beginning of a word to make a new word with a different meaning. Some of the common prefixes in English are:

Prefix	*Meaning*	*Example*
circum-	around	circumference, circumscribe
co-, com-, con-	with	companion, concurrent
de-	down, undo, not	degenerate, depress
di-, dis-	lack of, not, apart	disadvantage, displacement
hypo-	under, insufficient	hypodermic, hypothetical
il-, im-, in-, ir-	in, into, not, against	illegitimate, inadequate
inter-	among, between	interpose, intervene
intra-	within	intramural, intravenous
semi-	half, partially	semi-annual, semi-conscious
sub-, sup-, sus-	under	submarine, subtropical
super-, supra-	above, excessive	superlative, supranationalism

Prefix	*Meaning*	*Example*
trans-	across, beyond	transform, transportation
ultra-	beyond, excessive	ultraliberal, ultrasonic
un-	not	undeserved, unhappy
uni-	one	uniform, unilateral

Foreign Words Used in English

Over the centuries the English language has assimilated words and phrases from foreign languages.

ab initio	*Latin* from the beginning
a cappella	*Italian* sung without instrumental accompaniment (literally 'in chapel style')
à deux	*French* for or involving two people
ad hoc	*Latin* made or done for a particular purpose (literally 'to this')
ad infinitum	*Latin* endlessly; forever (literally 'to infinity')
ad interim	*Latin* for the meantime
ad nauseam	*Latin* to a tiresomely excessive degree (literally 'to sickness')
a fortiori	*Latin* more conclusively (literally 'from a stronger [argument]')
agent provocateur	*French* a person who tempts a suspected criminal to commit a crime so that they can be caught and convicted (literally 'provocative agent')
à huis clos	*French* in private (literally 'with closed doors')
al dente	*Italian* (of food) cooked so as to be still firm when bitten (literally 'to the tooth')
Alfresco	*Italian* in the open air (literally 'in the fresh')
amour propre	*French* self-respect (literally 'own love')
annus mirabilis	*Latin* a remarkable or auspicious year
a posteriori	*Latin* based on reasoning from known facts or past events rather than on assumptions or predictions (literally 'from what comes after')
a priori	*Latin* based on deduction rather than experience (literally 'from what is before')
au courant	*French* well informed; up to date (literally 'in the [regular] course')
au fait	*French* having a good or detailed knowledge (literally 'to the point')
au fond	*French* basically; in essence (literally 'at the bottom')
au naturel	*French* in the most simple or natural way

beau geste	*French* a noble and generous act (literally 'fine gesture')
beau ideal	*French* the highest standard of excellence (literally 'ideal beauty')
beau monde	*French* fashionable society (literally 'fine world')
beaux arts	*French* the fine arts
bête noire	*French* a person or thing one particularly dislikes (literally 'black beast')
belles-lettres	*French* literary works written and read for their elegant style (literally 'fine letters')
billet-doux	*French* a love letter (literally 'sweet note')
Blitzkrieg	*German* an intense, violent military campaign intended to bring about a swift victory (literally 'lightning war')
bona fide	*Latin* genuine; real (literally 'with good faith')
bon mot	*French* a clever or witty remark (literally 'good word')
bon vivant	*French* a person with a sociable and luxurious lifestyle (literally 'person living well')
Brasserie	*French* an informal or inexpensive restaurant (literally 'brewery')
carpe diem	*Latin* make the most of the present time (literally 'seize the day!')
carte blanche	*French* complete freedom to act as one wishes (literally 'blank paper')
cause célèbre	*French* a controversial issue attracting much public attention (literally 'famous case')
caveat emptor	*Latin* the buyer is responsible for checking the quality of goods before purchasing them (literally 'let the buyer beware')
c'est la guerre	*French* used as an expression of resigned acceptance (literally 'that's war')
chacun à son gout	*French* everyone to their own taste
chef-d'œuvre	*French* a masterpiece (literally 'chief work')
cherchez la femme	*French* there is certain to be a woman at the bottom of a problem or mystery (literally 'look for the woman')
comme il faut	*French* correct in behaviour or etiquette (literally 'as is necessary')
compos mentis	*Latin* sane; in full control of one's mind
Cognoscenti	*Italian* people who are well informed about something (literally 'people who know')
cordon sanitaire	*French* a guarded line placed around an area infected by disease to prevent anyone from leaving (literally 'sanitary line')
Cosa Nostra	*Italian* a US criminal organization related to the Mafia (literally 'our thing')
coup de foudre	*French* love at first sight (literally 'stroke of lightning')
coup de grâce	*French* a blow by which a mortally wounded person or thing is mercifully killed (literally 'stroke of grace')
coup de main	*French* a sudden surprise attack (literally 'stroke of hand')

coup d'état	*French* a sudden violent seizure of power (literally 'blow of state')
cri de cœur	*French* a passionate appeal or protest (literally 'cry from the heart')
cui bono?	*Latin* who stands to gain? (implying that whoever does may be responsible for a crime; literally 'to whom (is it) a benefit?')
de facto	*Latin* in fact, whether by right or not
Dei gratia	*Latin* by the grace of God
déjà vu	*French* the sense of having experienced the present situation before (literally 'already seen')
de jure	*Latin* rightful; by right (literally 'of law')
de nos jours	*French* contemporary (literally 'of our days')
Deo gratias	*Latin* thanks be to God
Deo volente	*Latin* God willing
de profundis	*Latin* expressing one's deepest feelings (literally 'from the depths')
de rigueur	*French* obligatory; required by etiquette or current fashion (literally 'of strictness')
dernier cri	*French* the very latest fashion (literally 'the last cry')
de trop	*French* not wanted; superfluous (literally 'excessive')
deus ex machina	*Latin* an unexpected event that saves an apparently hopeless situation (literally 'god from the machinery')
dolce far niente	*Italian* pleasant idleness (literally 'sweet doing nothing')
dolce vita	*Italian* a life of pleasure and luxury (literally 'sweet life')
doppelgänger	*German* an apparition or double of a living person (literally 'double-goer')
double entendre	*French* a word or phrase with two possible interpretations (from obsolete French, 'double understanding')
dramatis personae	*Latin* the characters in a play (literally 'persons of the drama')
embarras de richesse	*French* more options or resources than one knows what to do with (literally 'embarrassment of riches')
éminence grise	*French* a person who has power or influence without holding an official position (literally 'grey eminence')
en famille	*French* with one's family; in an informal way (literally 'in family')
enfant terrible	*French* a person whose behaviour is unconventional or controversial (literally 'terrible child')
en masse	*French* all together (literally 'in a mass')
en passant	*French* by the way (literally 'in passing')
entente cordiale	*French* a friendly understanding between states
entre nous	*French* between ourselves
esprit de corps	*French* a feeling of pride and loyalty uniting the members of a group (literally 'spirit of body')

ex gratia	*Latin* (of payment) given as a favour rather than because of any legal obligation (literally 'from favour')
ex officio	*Latin* by virtue of one's position or status (literally 'out of duty')
fait accompli	*French* a thing that has been done or decided and cannot now be altered (literally 'accomplished fact')
faute de mieux	*French* for want of a better alternative
faux pas	*French* an embarrassing blunder or indiscretion (literally 'false step')
femme fatale	*French* a seductive woman (literally 'disastrous woman')
fête champêtre	*French* an outdoor entertainment; a garden party (literally 'rural festival')
fin de siècle	*French* relating to the end of a century
force majeure	*French* superior strength
folie de grandeur	*French* delusions of grandeur
gîte	*French* a small furnished holiday house in France
grande dame	*French* a woman who is influential within a particular sphere (literally 'grand lady')
haute couture	*French* the designing and making of clothes by leading fashion houses (literally 'high dressmaking')
haute cuisine	*French* high-quality cooking (literally 'high cookery')
haut monde	*French* fashionable society (literally 'high world')
hors de combat	*French* out of action due to injury or damage (literally 'out of the fight')
ideé fixe	*French* an obsession (literally 'fixed idea')
in absentia	*Latin* while not present (literally 'in absence')
in camera	*Latin* in private (literally 'in the chamber')
in extremis	*Latin* in an extremely difficult situation; at the point of death
in loco parentis	*Latin* in the place of a parent
in medias res	*Latin* in or into the middle of things
in propria persona	*Latin* in his or her own person
in situ	*Latin* in the original or appropriate position
inter alia	*Latin* among other things
in toto	*Latin* as a whole
ipso facto	*Latin* by that very fact or act
je ne sais quoi	*French* a quality that is hard to describe (literally 'I do not know what')
jeu d'esprit	*French* a light-hearted display of wit (literally 'game of the mind')
jeunesse dorée	*French* wealthy, fashionable young people (literally 'gilded youth')
joie de vivre	*French* exuberant enjoyment of life (literally 'joy of living')

katzenjammer	*German* a hangover or a severe headache accompanying a hangover (literally 'cats' wailing')
laissez-faire	*French* a non-interventionist policy (literally 'allow to do')
locum tenens	*Latin* a temporary deputy or stand-in (literally 'one holding a place')
locus classicus	*Latin* the best known or most authoritative passage on a subject (literally 'classical place')
magnum opus	*Latin* the most important work of an artist, writer, and so on (literally 'great work')
manqué	*French* having failed to become what one might have been (from *manquer* 'to lack')
mea culpa	*Latin* an acknowledgement that something is one's fault (literally 'by my fault')
memento mori	*Latin* something kept as a reminder that death is inevitable (literally 'remember [that you have] to die')
ménage à trois	*French* an arrangement in which a married couple and the lover of one of them live together (literally 'household of three')
modus operandi	*Latin* a way of doing something (literally 'way of operating')
modus vivendi	*Latin* an arrangement that allows conflicting parties to coexist peacefully (literally 'way of living')
mot juste	*French* the most appropriate word or expression
ne plus ultra	*Latin* the best example of something (literally 'not further beyond')
nil desperandum	*Latin* do not despair
noblesse oblige	*French* privilege entails responsibility
nolens volens	*Latin* whether one wants or likes something or not (literally 'not willing, willing')
non sequitur	*Latin* a conclusion or statement that does not logically follow from the previous statement (literally 'it does not follow')
nouveau riche	*French* people who have recently become rich and who display their wealth ostentatiously (literally 'new rich')
objet d'art	*French* a small decorative or artistic object
on dit	*French* a piece of gossip (literally 'they say')
papabile	*Italian* worthy or eligible to be elected pope
par excellence	*French* better or more than all others of the same kind (literally 'by excellence')
parti pris	*French* a preconceived view; a bias (literally 'side taken')
per annum	*Latin* for each year
per capita	*Latin* for each person (literally 'by heads')
per se	*Latin* by or in itself or themselves
persona non grata	*Latin* a person who is not welcome somewhere

pièce de résistance	*French* the most important or impressive item (literally 'piece [i.e., means] of resistance')
pied-à-terre	*French* a small flat or house kept for occasional use (literally 'foot to earth')
pis aller	*French* a last resort (literally 'worse to go')
plat du jour	*French* a special dish prepared by a restaurant on a particular day (literally 'dish of the day')
plus ça change	*French* used to express resigned acknowledgement of the fact that certain things never change (from *plus ça change, plus c'est la même chose* 'the more it changes, the more it stays the same')
pococurante	*Italian* careless or nonchalant (literally 'little caring')
prima facie	*Latin* accepted as so until proved otherwise (literally 'at first face')
primus inter pares	*Latin* the senior or representative member of a group (literally 'first among equals')
pro rata	*Latin* proportional; proportionally (literally 'according to the rate')
proxime accessit	*Latin* the person who comes second in an examination or is runner-up for an award (literally 'came very near')
quid pro quo	*Latin* a favour or advantage given in return for something (literally 'something for something')
raison d'être	*French* the most important reason for someone's or something's existence (literally 'reason for being')
reductio ad absurdum	*Latin* a method of disproving a premise by showing that its logical conclusion is absurd (literally 'reduction to the absurd')
roman-à-clef	*French* a novel in which real people or events appear with invented names (literally 'novel with a key')
sangfroid	*French* the ability to stay calm in difficult circumstances (literally 'cold blood')
savoir faire	*French* the ability to act appropriately in social situations (literally 'know-how to do')
sine die	*Latin* (of proceedings) adjourned indefinitely (literally 'without a day')
sine qua non	*Latin* a thing that is absolutely essential (literally 'without which not')
soi-disant	*French* self-styled; so-called (literally 'self-saying')
sotto voce	*Italian* in a quiet voice (literally 'under voice')
sub judice	*Latin* being considered by a court of law and therefore not to be publicly discussed elsewhere (literally 'under a judge')
sub rosa	*Latin* happening or done in secret (literally 'under the rose')
sui generis	*Latin* unique (literally 'of its own kind')
table d'hôte	*French* a restaurant meal offered at a fixed price, with few if any choices (literally 'host's table')

tant mieux	*French* so much the better
tant pis	*French* so much the worse; too bad
terra firma	*Latin* dry land; the ground (literally 'firm land')
terra incognita	*Latin* unknown territory
tête-à-tête	*French* a private conversation (literally 'head-to-head')
tour de force	*French* a thing accomplished with great skill (literally 'feat of strength')
tout de suite	*French* at once (literally 'quite in sequence')
unheimlich	*German* uncanny or weird
verboten	*German* forbidden
via media	*Latin* a compromise (literally 'middle way')
victor ludorum	*Latin* the overall champion in a sports competition (literally 'victor of the games')
vis-à-vis	*French* in relation to; as compared with (literally 'face-to-face')
vox populi	*Latin* public opinion (literally 'the voice of the people')
zeitgeist	*German* the characteristic spirit or mood of a particular historical period (literally 'time spirit')

PRACTICE EXERCISE B

Look at the following sentences and identify the meanings of the words highlighted by associating them with their prefixes:

a. Jake's teachers called him an **incorrigible** child who was always getting into trouble.
b. Security at the Red Fort for Independence Day celebrations is **impregnable.**
c. Archaeological evidence has **demythologized** some parts of the Bible.
d. Once the pilot turns off the seat belt sign, travellers may prepare to **disembark** from the plane.
e. Only about one in three couples who **cohabit** end up getting married.
f. The judge gave the convicted man two **concurrent** sentences to be served at the same time.
g. The **transcontinental** railroad provided fast, safe, and cheap travel to passengers.
h. **Ultrasonic** waves cannot be heard by the human ear.
i. **Intramural** fighting within the political party is the reason of its defeat in elections.
j. A few months later **discord** arose among the three partners of the company.

PRACTICE EXERCISE C

Complete these sentences choosing from the list of foreign words:

croissant	café	ballet	faux pas	patio	entrepreneurs
rendezvous	renaissance	kindergarten	waltz		

a. My friends say that dancing the ________ is easy.
b. Our daughter is going to turn 5 next year, so we've been trying to find a good ____________ for her.
c. Michelangelo and Raphael were two of the most famous artists from the ______________.
d. It was very hot today, so we decided to go out to the _________ to drink a cold glass of lemonade.
e. It's 2:00 now, so let's _____________ back here at 6:00.
f. If you make a _____________, then the mistake usually isn't very big, but it can make people uncomfortable.
g. A ____________ is a type of pastry or bread that is light and flaky.
h. I've only got about 20 minutes for lunch, so I'll just stop at a ________ for a quick sandwich.
i. My niece and nephew are in _________ class.
j. Elon Musk is one of the most famous _______________ in the world.

Suffixes are words added at the end of a word to make a new word with a different meaning. Suffixes can be classified into two types: *inflectional* and *derivational.* Inflectional suffixes do not generally change the meaning or word class status of a stem or root. Derivational suffixes, on the other hand, change the word class status and to some extent the meaning of the stem also.

Examples of Inflectional Suffixes

The plural ending -s/-es, the past ending -ed in words such as *books, nouns, cities, stories, liked,* and *wanted* are inflectional suffixes.

Examples of Derivational Suffixes

The nominal endings -hood, -tion, and such others; the adjectival endings -ive, -ly, and the like in words such as *motherhood, construction, active,* and *hardly* are derivational suffixes.

Some of the common suffixes in English are:

Suffix	*Meaning*	*Example*
-acy	state or quality	privacy, fallacy, delicacy
-al	act or process of	refusal, recital, rebuttal

Suffix	*Meaning*	*Example*
-ance, -ence	state or quality of	maintenance, eminence, assurance
-dom	place or state of being	freedom, kingdom, boredom
-ism	doctrine, belief	communism, narcissism, scepticism
-ity, -ty	quality of	inactivity, veracity, parity, serenity
-ment	condition of	argument, endorsement, punishment
-sion, -tion	state of being	concession, transition, abbreviation
-ate	become	regulate, eradicate, enunciate, repudiate
-en	become	enlighten, awaken, strengthen
-esque	reminiscent of	picturesque, statuesque, burlesque
-ic, -ical	pertaining to	musical, mythic, domestic

PRACTICE EXERCISE D

Add the correct suffixes to make the sentences complete:

a. He has taken (approve) for his leaves well in advance.
b. Restaurant utensils must be able to withstand rough (use).
c. One needs to be (courage) in order to admit his or her mistakes.
d. He was an intellectual (scholar) man.
e. Nobody thought the (argue) over car parking would lead to bloodshed.
f. We (ready) agreed in spite of the late Friday night hour.
g. As her (excite) grew, she spoke faster.
h. The lush (green) of the Doon Valley brought him back every year.
i. Her teacher gave her a letter of (refer).
j. She was last seen (hurry) out of the house and looked frightened to death.

Derivational Suffixes

All the derivational suffixes are interchangeable. A word may be basically:

- Noun
- Verb
- Adjective
- Adverb

Formation of Adjective from Noun

Noun	*Adjective*
Ancestor	Ancestral
Debt	Indebted
Earth	Earthen
Hypocrite	Hypocritical
Industry	Industrious
Justice	Just
Miracle	Miraculous
Quarrel	Quarrelsome
Race	Racial
Zeal	Zealous

Formation of Verb from Noun

Noun	*Verb*
Authority	Authorize
Blood	Bleed
Circle	Encircle
Economy	Economize
Fraud	Defraud
Origin	Originate
Prison	Imprison
Throne	Enthrone
Utility	Utilize
Victim	Victimize

Formation of Abstract Noun from Noun

Noun	*Abstract Noun*
Coward	Cowardice
Cunning	Cunningness
Creature	Creation
Hero	Heroism
Machine	Mechanism
Royal	Royalty
Servant	Service
Witch	Witchery

Formation of Verb from Adjective

Adjective	*Verb*
Abundant	Abound
Bitter	Embitter
Equal	Equalize
Fresh	Refresh
Large	Enlarge
Little	Belittle
Mean	Demean
Rich	Enrich
Specific	Specify
Various	Vary

Formation of Noun from Verb

Verb	*Noun*
Acquit	Acquittal
Betray	Betrayal
Deny	Denial
Expel	Expulsion
Laugh	Laughter
May	Might
Oblige	Obligation
Precise	Precision
Rely	Reliance
Vary	Variety

Formation of Adverbs from Other Words

Words	*Adverbs*
Back	Backwards
Cheer	Cheerfully
Glory	Gloriously
Head	Headlong
Length	Lengthwise
Poor	Poorly
Shore	Ashore
Side	Sideways
Three	Thrice
True	Truly

PRACTICE EXERCISE E

Rewrite the following sentences using the highlighted words as indicated. The meaning must not change. Look at the example first.

We waited in the **queue** for half an hour. (verb)
We **queued** for half an hour.

a. I'll **ring** him this evening. (noun)
b. I wrote a **reply** to his letter yesterday. (verb)
c. It **rained** a lot yesterday. (noun)
d. The corrupt politician faces **exposure**. (verb)
e. You should not **quarrel** with anybody. (noun)
f. Heavy rains brought **calamity** to the village. (adjective)
g. She was accused of being a **witch**. (abstract noun)
h. The visitor **frightened** the child. (adjective)
i. I'm headed to the **coast** this weekend. (adjective)
j. Her investments in the share market have made her **rich**. (verb)

1.3.2 Compounding

Word formation in English also takes place by compounding words. Compounding takes place when two or more words are put together to form a new word with a new meaning. Some examples of compound words include:

Noun–noun compounds: blackbird, coalman, pigtail, motorcycle
Noun–verb compounds: finger-pointing, breastfeeding, rainfall, haircut
Verb–noun compounds: killjoy, crossword, washing machine, driving licence
Verb–verb compounds: go and do, up and leave, look forward, wear away
Verb–adverb compounds: drop out, pick out, camp out, drawback
Adverb–verb compounds: foreground, intake, output, input
Adjective–verb compounds: dry cleaning, public speaking, shortchange, blacklist
Adjective–noun compounds: hardware, software
Double prepositions: into, within, without, from behind
Reflexive pronouns: myself, herself, himself, itself
Conjunctions: wherever, whatever, however, whenever
Compound conjunctions: not only but also, either or, even if, neither nor
Indefinite pronouns: somebody, nobody, anything, everyone

1.3.3 Blending

Word formation also takes place by blending words. Blending is a combination of two or more words to create a new one, usually by taking the beginning of one word and the ending of the other word.

Examples:
Information and commercial = infomercial
Britain and exit = Brexit
Documentary and drama = docudrama
Education and entertainment = edutainment
Situational and comedy = sitcom
Biography and epic = biopic
Electronic and mail = e-mail
Malicious and software = malware
Web and log = blog
Picture and element = pixel
Internet and citizen = netizen
Network and etiquette = netiquette
Web and seminar = webinar

1.3.4 Clipping

Word formation also takes place by cutting or clipping of words. Clipping is the reduction process to create new words by shortening polysyllable words.

Examples:
Telephone = phone
Teenagers = teens
Refrigerator = fridge
Public house = pub
Popular music = pop
Gasoline = gas
Laboratory = lab
Influenza = flu

1.3.5 Back Formation

It is a reduction process in which a noun is reduced to form a verb.

Examples:
Television = televise
Option = opt
Editor = edit
Emotion = emot
Automation = automate
Beggar = beg

Attrition = attrit
Cohesion = cohese

1.3.6 Conversion

It is the process of gaining new words in different parts of speech without adding derivative elements. A word of one form is converted into another form by simply relabelling it. It is also called zero derivation.

Verbs and nouns: guess, spy, printout
Nouns and verbs: bottle, butter, chair
Verbs and adjectives: see through, leaf through
Adjectives and nouns: the poor, the rich, the good
Singular and plural forms: sheep–sheep, deer–deer
Present and past forms: put–put, shut–shut, cut–cut

1.3.7 Process Morpheme

This process does not involve any affixation but shows phonological changes in the word. Words formed this way are instances of process morpheme.

Examples:
Bring–brought
Speak–spoke
Tooth–teeth
Mouse–mice
Breath–breathe

PRACTICE EXERCISE F

Which of the following are cases of process morpheme and which are cases of conversion?

1. Cut–cut
2. Thrust–thrust
3. Beat–beat
4. Spit–spat
5. Man–men
6. Louse–lice
7. Criterion–criteria
8. Buy–bought
9. Bet–bet
10. Advice–advise

1.4 SYNONYMS, ANTONYMS, AND STANDARD ABBREVIATIONS

Words exhibit different kinds of relationship: it can be a relationship of meaning; it can be a relationship of form (written, spoken, spelling, and pronunciation); or they can exhibit a relationship which is neither a relation of meaning nor a relation of form. The third relationship can be collocational relation. These relationships are lexical relations.

1.4.1 Synonyms

Synonym is a word that means almost the same as another word. But these words are not necessarily interchangeable. Synonyms are used to make dull writing more interesting and imaginative. Similarity does not mean total sameness. Two synonymous words cannot replace each other in all contexts. The terms *wide* and *broad* are very close in meaning but substituting 'wide' for 'broad' in the expression 'broad-minded' will result in odd and unacceptable expression. For example:

When she turned on the light in the kitchen, she saw a mouse *hasten* under the refrigerator.
When she turned on the light in the kitchen, she saw a mouse *scutter* under the refrigerator.

By learning synonyms of various words, we can increase our vocabulary.

PRACTICE EXERCISE G

Each question gives a word followed by four choices. Select the most suitable synonym. (CAT model)

1. **Abstract**
   a. peculiar b. summary c. normal d. diagnostic
2. **Complacent**
   a. disappointed b. evasive c. satisfied d. flimsy
3. **Famished**
   a. agricultural b. hungry c. prestigious d. feasible
4. **Exterminate**
   a. evict b. dissociate c. accuse d. annihilate
5. **Stalwart**
   a. watchful b. sturdy c. delicate d. encomium

6. **Embargo**
a. challenge b. restraint c. departure d. quarrel

7. **Bizarre**
a. bookish b. odd c. tasty d. jubilant

8. **Abysmal**
a. shameless b. dangerous c. profound d. horrible

9. **Ovation**
a. applause b. growth c. abuse d. attraction

10. **Panacea**
a. wonder b. elixir c. placebo d. honey

11. **Resilient**
a. stretchable b. spirited c. rigid d. buoyant

12. **Zest**
a. humour b. keen interest c. attitude d. liking

13. **Impetuous**
a. cat-like b. rash c. impertinent d. jovial

14. **Morbid**
a. dry b. ethereal c. inflatable d. macabre

15. **Taciturn**
a. obstinate b. introvert
c. uncommunicative d. unapproachable

PRACTICE EXERCISE H

Each question has a sentence with one word underlined. Identify the meaning of the underlined word from the four alternatives. (CAT model)

1. The students' agitation was kept in **abeyance** by the police action.
a. postponed b. kept suspended
c. alleviated d. invigorated

2. His mental **aberration** accounts for this kind of work.
a. deviation from normality b. firmness
c. tight grip d. alertness

3. The **sedentary** job made him obese and led to diabetes.
a. hard b. detestable c. irregular d. inactive

4. Politicians **extol** their leaders for self-aggrandizement.
a. praise highly b. accuse c. indict d. encourage

5. The actor's sitting room was luxurious and **flamboyant**.
a. costly b. congested c. ostentatious d. elevated

6. The minister got an overwhelming **encore** when he finished his song.
   a. stone pelting b. garlanding
   c. call for repetition d. financial help

7. The **luxuriant** growth of flowers in our garden surprised the visitors.
   a. showing luxury b. abundant
   c. multicoloured d. sweet smelling

8. His **officiousness** was disliked by one and all among his colleagues.
   a. in the manner of an officer b. haughty look
   c. interference in a dominating way d. efficiency in doing work

9. What she did was a **manifestation** of her frustration.
   a. expression b. desire c. wishes d. aim

10. Many people were **trampled** in the stampede.
    a. injured b. crushed c. run over d. twisted

11. The ship arrived at a previously **uncharted** island.
    a. unsure b. unknown c. unseen d. unmapped

12. She had no need to **flaunt** her beauty.
    a. express b. boast c. show off d. flout

13. The nights are clear but **suffused** with sloth and sullen expectation.
    a. covered b. coloured c. filled d. spread over

14. At present, he is in **pecuniary** difficulties.
    a. monetary b. business c. minor d. professional

15. The **cautious** are not always cowards.
    a. thrifty b. anorexic c. circumspect d. vigilant

1.4.2 Antonyms

Antonym is a word which is opposite in meaning to the given word. Antonyms can be formed by adding or removing (or both) a prefix and suffix to the given word. For example:

Satiable = insatiable
Introvert = extrovert

Knowledge of antonyms can also increase your word power. Antonyms include both opposites and reversives. For example, consider the following pairs:

Do = undo
Learn = unlearn

These pairs do not mean 'not do' and 'not learn'. They mean 'do the reverse of do and of learn'. Such pairs are called reversives.

PRACTICE EXERCISE I

Look at the following highlighted words and suggest the correct antonym from the given options. (CAT model)

1. Because of the **paucity** of our oil supply, we need to seek out other fuel resources
   a. overflow b. inflow c. plenty d. glut
2. Her attorneys claim there is no **conclusive** evidence that any murders took place.
   a. powerful b. indecisive c. exclusive d. partial
3. Do not let your depressive emotions **trigger** a craving for food when you are not hungry.
   a. choke b. taper off c. dilute d. ignite
4. They walked **parallel** to an abandoned highway for a couple of hours until they reached the telephone booth.
   a. divergent b. difficult c. similar d. dissimilar
5. Both sides have **manifested** a stubborn unwillingness to compromise.
   a. displayed b. concealed c. suppressed d. marked
6. He **embellished** his speech with a few quotations.
   a. dishonoured b. demolished c. spoiled d. sufficed
7. People hoped that the new government would **inaugurate** a period of change.
   a. terminate b. inculcate c. facilitate d. ameliorate
8. Anna didn't get paid to work at the old people's home, but she felt it was **rewarding** work because it brought her happiness.
   a. lucrative b. disappointing c. thrilling d. nail-biting
9. I am in a rather **unique** position, as my job is different from anyone else's.
   a. unoriginal b. serious c. melody d. correct
10. His sister, normally so talkative, was **strangely** quiet throughout the evening.
    a. familiarly b. fearfully c. negatively d. excitedly

PRACTICE EXERCISE J

Each question has a word followed by four choices. Identify the antonym. (CAT model)

1. **Immaculate**
   a. unclean b. immobile c. motherly d. accumulated

2. **Aggravate**
a. segregate b. adulterate c. ameliorate d. accommodate

3. **Fragrant**
a. malodorous b. utopian c. capricious d. ulterior

4. **Haphazard**
a. cumbersome b. concocted c. orderly d. zigzag

5. **Robust**
a. sturdy b. feeble c. muscular d. ridiculous

6. **Grouchy**
a. cantankerous b. grumpy c. contented d. surly

7. **Salubrious**
a. hale b. robust c. unhealthy d. hygienic

8. **Traitorous**
a. perfidious b. recreant c. devoted d. treacherous

9. **Disparage**
a. evolve b. expose c. appreciate d. converge

10. **Impudent**
a. rude b. courteous c. impertinent d. insolent

11. **Novice**
a. adept b. dilettante c. amateur d. greenhorn

12. **Fortitude**
a. benefit b. eruption c. chivalry d. cowardice

13. **Callous**
a. careful b. wrinkled c. bloated d. emaciated

14. **Pedestrian**
a. mobile b. regular c. exciting d. imaginative

15. **Capricious**
a. greedy b. mutable c. resolute d. suppressive

1.4.3 Standard Abbreviations

Often frequently used short phrases or word sets are reduced, either to their initial letters or the first and last letters of the word. These are called abbreviations.

Abbreviation is useful in making word sets easier and quicker to remember, write, and say. They add power to communication by reducing long phrases to something we can quickly refer. If we are unable to shorten things we may well not even bother talking about them. Abbreviations therefore help us communicate when we might otherwise be silent or less eloquent.

Some abbreviations are read as individual letters

USA	United States of America
PM	Prime Minister
UN	United Nations
TPS	Thermal Power Station
SPCB	State Pollution Control Board
RSDO	Research Designs and Standards Organisation
MLF	Multilateral Funding
OGL	Open General License
NGO	Non-governmental Organization

Acronyms

Acronyms are alphabet-based formations. The initial letters of several words are combined to form a single word. These abbreviations are read as words in themselves. Acronym is also a blanket term that encompasses 'initialisms' but pronounced by uttering each letter of the word individually as singular acronym.

OPEC	Organization of Petroleum Exporting Countries
VAT	Value Added Tax
UNESCO	United Nations Educational, Scientific and Cultural Organization
SARS	Severe Acute Respiratory Syndrome

Common acronyms used in appreciation

LOL	Laughing out Loud
LYLAB	Love You Like a Brother
LYLAS	Love You Like a Sister
GMTA	Great Minds Think Alike
ROFL	Rolling on Floor Laughing
TY	Thank You
TYVM	Thank You Very Much

Common acronyms used in chat

Acronyms are used across every industry. The world of texting and instant messaging has given rise to a whole series of acronyms. For example:

AFK	Away from Keyboard
BRB	Be Right Back
BBIAB	Be Back in a Bit
BBL	Be Back Later
TTFN	Ta Ta for Now
BBS	Be Back Soon

BTW	By the Way
HAGN	Have a Good Night
KISS	Keep It Simple Stupid
KIT	Keep in Touch
EG	Evil Grin
BEG	Big Evil Grin
NYOB	None of Your Business
OMG	Oh My God
PM	Private Message
POS	Parents over Shoulder
TTYL	Talk to You Later
LTNS	Long Time No See
IDK	I Don't Know

Common acronyms used in business

Acronyms are often used in the business world to identify a business or to create shorthand communication between co-workers.

AKA	Also Known As
DBA	Doing Business As
DND	Do Not Disturb
MBA	Masters of Business Administration
OT	Overtime
POS	Point of Service
DAEMON	Disk and Execution Monitor
HR	Human Resources
EDS	Electronic Data Systems
NASDAQ	National Association of Securities Dealers Automated Quotation
POP	Post Office Protocol
TBC	To Be Continued
SD card	Secure Data card
EOD	End of Day
ETA	Estimated Time of Arrival
IAM	In a Meeting
IMO	In My Opinion
SWOT	Strengths, Weaknesses, Opportunities, Threats
TED	Tell me, Explain to me, Describe to me
SMART	Specific, Measurable, Attainable, Realistic, Time-Bound

Common informative acronyms

Sometimes an acronym can be very useful at giving you advice or essential information. Informative acronyms are used in the medical field, but they certainly aren't exclusive to health-related subjects, as the following list shows.

DOA	Dead on Arrival
AIDS	Acquired Immunodeficiency Syndrome
HIV	Human Immunodeficiency Virus
DARE	Drug Abuse Resistance Education
ADD	Attention Deficit Disorder
ADHD	Attention Deficit Hyperactivity Disorder
CDC	Centers for Disease Control and Prevention
AMA	Against Medical Advice
MD	Medical Doctor
OTC	Over the Counter
EST	Eastern Standard Time
PST	Pacific Standard Time
CST	Central Standard Time
PPV	Pay Per View
SSN	Social Security Number
ADL	Activities of Daily Living
SUV	Sports Utility Vehicle
ABS	Anti-lock Braking System
ASAP	As Soon as Possible
JIT	Just in Time
FYI	For Your Information
DOB	Date of Birth
UFO	Unidentified Flying Object

Some abbreviations are written forms only; they are still pronounced as full words

Mr	Mister
Ms	Miss
Dr	Doctor

Some abbreviations are used as a part of language

etc.	et cetera
e.g.	for example
i.e.	that is to say
abr.	Abridged
acc.	according (to)
betw.	Between
ft.	foot, feet
gen.	general, genesis
est.	established, estimated
hr	hour(s)
inc.	incorporated
inst.	institution

Jr.	junior
Jan.	January
Lib.	Library
long.	longitude
Ltd	Limited
km	kilometre(s)
M	minute(s)
m	metre(s)
mt	mount
no.	number
mts	mountains
pub.	published
rev.	revised
pop.	population

PRACTICE EXERCISE K

Complete these sentences with suitable abbreviations:

a. Many factors are important, ____________, class, gender, age, and ethnicity.
b. Tennis, soccer, baseball, ____________, are outdoor games.
c. He works in the morning shift, ____________, from 6 AM to 1 PM.
d. The church of ____________ Mary and All Saints is a large and beautiful building.
e. Lydia lived in a newly constructed flat on Oak ____________.

PRACTICE EXERCISE L

Give the full forms of the following acronyms:

1. TESOL	2. TOEFL	3. IELTS	4. GRE
5. AIDS	6. LASER	7. RADAR	8. NASA

PRACTICE EXERCISE M

Complete the following sentences choosing the appropriate word or affixes based on the hints given in the brackets:

un-, in-, post, less, ful, AIDS, chauffer, en masse, status quo, organic farming, infotainment, flu

1. I have a _________ card. (paid)
2. Could you _________ the thread? (tie)
3. Acronym of Acquired Immunodeficiency Syndrome _________.
4. The misery has become _____________. (tolerable)
5. The celebrity's ______________ has been caught driving under the influence of alcohol.
6. The people marched ____________.
7. We need measures to change the ____________ of education system.
8. Maria is a ___________ daughter. (duty)
9. The police officer was ____________ to arrest the criminal. (clue)
10. __________________ is the dire need to conserve earth's natural resources.
11. Education and entertainment is ________________.
12. The clipping word for influenza ______________.

FURTHER READING

1. Redman, Stuart. *English Vocabulary in Use*. Cambridge, MA: Cambridge University Press, 1997.
2. Kumar, Sanjay, and Pushp Lata. *Communication Skills*. New Delhi: Oxford University Press, 2018.
3. O'Dell, Felicity. 'English Teaching Essentials: Vocabulary'. In *English Teaching Professional*, 31. London: 2004.
4. Yule, George. *Study of Language*. Cambridge, UK: Cambridge University Press, 1996.
5. MacCarthy, Michael, and Felicity O'Dell. *English Vocabulary in Use*. Cambridge, UK: Cambridge University Press, 1994.
6. Infoplease. https://www.infoplease.com/common-abbreviations (accessed on 26 September 2018)
7. FluentU. https://www.fluentu.com/blog/english/english-words-from-other-languages/ (accessed on 26 September 2018)

2

UNIT

Basic Writing Skills

The Speech and the Sentence

Human beings express themselves through speech. This speech consists of words which are spoken or written in groups. Since every human being wants to make himself intelligible, he uses these words in a specific, well-arranged manner. This well-arranged group of words is the sentence. Thus a sentence is a group of words arranged in a pre-intended, specific order which makes complete sense. The word 'sentence' comes from the Latin word 'sentro' which means speech.

Types of Sentences (Semantic)

Based on the meaning and depending upon each particular situation we express ourselves in five different ways. Thus we make use of five kinds of sentences, which are being discussed as follows.

1. **Assertive/Statement/Declarative Sentences**

   Sentences which make simple assertions such as stating facts, describing things, or reporting events are called assertive sentences. These are in turn divided into two types, namely (a) positive and (b) negative.

   Examples:

   I will agree with you. (Positive statement)
   I will not agree with you. (Negative statement)

2. **Interrogative/Question Sentences**

   Sentences in which some questions are asked or some enquiries made are called interrogative sentences. These are divided into four types, namely:

1. Yes/No Type Questions
   (a) Positive
   (b) Negative
2. WHO Type Questions
   (a) Positive
   (b) Negative

Examples:
Type 1
Do you teach English? (Positive question)
Do you not teach English? (Negative question)

Type 2
When shall I meet you? (Positive question)
What doesn't he write? (Negative question)

3. Imperative Sentences
Sentences which express an order, command, request, advice, direction, or suggestion are called imperative sentences. These sentences begin with the verb, and the subject (you) is understood. These are of four types, namely:

Type 1: (a) Positive (You-V_0 whom/what/where/how/when/why)
(b) Negative (Don't V_0 whom/what/how/when/why)

Examples:
You meet me in the class tomorrow.
Don't go to bazaar in auto.

Type 2: (a) Positive and (b) Negative ('Let' is used at the beginning of these sentences but subject is not omitted but expressed.)

Examples:
Let's start at once.
Let the boys not meet the director.

When we use comma after the subject it expresses irritation or intolerance.

Examples:
You, vacate the house.
You, don't make so much fuss before others.

4. Exclamatory Sentences
Sentences that express some strong feelings such as joy, sorrow, surprise, regret, applause, or contempt in an empathetic way are called exclamatory sentences.

Examples:
How fast time flies!
What a tragedy!

5. **Optative Sentences**
   Sentences which express an ardent wish, prayer, boon, or curse are called optative sentences.

   Examples:
   May God help you!
   May you live long!

Transformation of Sentences
Transformation of a sentence refers to changing its form without altering its sense.

I. Changing exclamatory sentence into assertive sentence
Examples:
1. What a wonderful idea!
   It is a wonderful idea.
2. O that I were a kid again!
   I wish I were a kid again.
3. What a great surprise it is!
   This is indeed a great surprise.

PRACTICE EXERCISE A

Transform the following exclamatory sentences into assertive sentences:

1. How cool it is today!
2. What a pleasant morning!
3. What a pity you can't attend the function!
4. What an insult for the family!
5. Shame on you to abuse your parents like this!

II. Changing interrogative sentence into assertive sentence
Examples:
1. Is not knowledge better than money?
   Knowledge is better than money.
2. Is there any sense in talking so rude?
   There is no sense in talking rude.
3. Why worry about what others say?
   It is foolish to worry about what others say.

PRACTICE EXERCISE B

Transform the following interrogative sentences into assertive sentences:

1. Is that the way one should behave?
2. Have you seen such a marvellous monument as the Charminar?
3. Who does not know about him?
4. What does it matter whether we win or lose?
5. Can you change your attitude?

III. Changing imperative sentence into interrogative sentence

Examples:

1. Stop playing games.
   Will you stop playing games?
2. Tell her to come here.
   Will you tell her to come here?
3. Open the door.
   Open the door, will you?

PRACTICE EXERCISE C

Transform the following imperative sentences into interrogative sentences:

1. Post the letter.
2. Speak politely.
3. Please take me to the principal.
4. Please get me a glass of milk.
5. Keep quiet.

PRACTICE EXERCISE D

Change the following statements into questions and negatives:

1. I have a lot of work to do.
2. Plenty of people want to buy cars.
3. There is a great deal of controversy about the language problem.
4. The sea is a long way off.
5. A great deal of research has been done on the subject.
6. A lot of money has been spent on the project.

2.1 SENTENCE STRUCTURES

2.1.1 Parts of a Sentence

The parts of a sentence can be categorized as the subject, verb, object/complement, phrase, and clause.

Subject

The doer of an action is called the subject.

Verb/Predicate

It is the doing word which indicates the action performed by the subject.

Examples:
Rama ate a mango yesterday.
S V
He met the collector last month.
S V
That he has come pleases me.
S V

Object

It is the word which receives the action performed by the subject. These are of two types:

Direct object (DO)/Complement of the verb
It refers to a thing affected by the action of the verb.

Indirect object (IO)
It usually refers to a person who receives the direct object.

Examples:
He gave me a book
IO DO
He has presented him a pen
IO DO

Complement

It is the word which completes the sense left incomplete by the copulative (or linking) verbs expressing the state of being, seeming, appearing, and feeling.

Such verbs are be, seem, appear, taste, feel, become, grow, act, sound, and the like. They actually do not indicate any action but only the state of being or existing. There are two common types of complements: **subject complements** (which follow the verb 'be' and other linking verbs) and **object complements** (which follow a direct object).

Examples:
I felt strong. ('felt' as a copulative verb)
Honey tastes sweet. ('tastes' as a copulative verb)

Subject Complements

Subject complements rename or describe the subjects of sentences. In other words, they *complement* the *subjects.*

Many of these complements are nouns, pronouns, or other nominals that rename or provide additional information about the subject of the sentence.

They always follow linking verbs. A less contemporary term for a noun, pronoun, or other nominal used as a subject complement is *predicate nominative.*

He is the *boss.*
Nancy is the *winner.*
This is *she.*
My friends are *they.*

In the first example, the subject complement *boss* explains the subject *he.* It tells what 'he' is.

In the second example, the subject complement *winner* explains the subject *Nancy.* It tells what Nancy is. In the third example, the subject complement *she* renames the subject *this.* It tells who 'this' is. In the final example, the subject complement *they* identifies the subject *friends.* It tells who the 'friends' are.

Other subject complements are adjectives that modify the subjects of sentences. They also follow linking verbs. A less contemporary term for an adjective used as a subject complement is *predicate adjective.*

My co-workers are *friendly.*
This story is *exciting.*

In the first example, the subject complement *friendly* modifies the subject *co-workers.* In the second example, the subject complement *exciting* modifies the subject *story.*

Object Complements

An object complement always follows the direct object and either renames or describes the direct object. Consider this sentence:

She named the baby Bruce.

The verb is *named.* To find the subject, ask, 'Who or what named?' The answer is *she*, so *she* is the subject. Now ask, 'Whom or what did she name?' She named the baby, so *baby* is the direct object. Any word following the direct object that renames or describes the direct object is an *object complement.*

She named the baby Bruce, so *Bruce* is the *object complement.*

The *object complement* characterizes the object in the same way as the subject complement characterizes the subject: it identifies, describes, or locates the object (as in *We chose Bill as* group leader; *We consider him a fool; She laid the baby in the crib*), expressing either its current state or resulting state (as in *They found him in the kitchen* vs. *She made him angry*). It is not possible to delete the object complement without either radically changing the meaning of the sentence (e.g., *She called him an idiot–She called him*) or making the sentence ungrammatical (e.g., *He locked his keys in his office–He locked his keys*).

2.2 USE OF PHRASES AND CLAUSES IN SENTENCES

2.2.1 Phrase

Phrase is a group of words which neither consists of a subject, predicate, and object nor does it make a complete sense.

Examples:
She is a woman <u>of great beauty</u>.
Tell me <u>how to wind the watch</u>.
He is a man <u>of great strength</u>.

Types of Phrases

The function of a phrase depends on its construction (words it contains). On the basis of their functions and constructions, there are nine common types of phrases in English grammar.

Noun Phrase

In a noun phrase, one or more words work together to give more information about a noun.

- all my dear **children**
- the information **age**

- seventeen hungry **lions** in the rocks
- 'Buy a big bright green pleasure machine!'

Adjective Phrase

In an adjective phrase, one or more words work together to give more information about an adjective.

- so very *sweet*
- *earnest* in her desire
- very *happy* with his work
- It is always the *best* policy to speak the truth—unless, of course, you are an exceptionally *good* liar.

Verb Phrase

In a verb phrase, one or more words work together to give more meaning to a verb. In English, the verb phrase is very complex, but a good description of its many forms can be found here.

- Your father may be going away for a little while.
- They auctioned the palace for five crores of rupees.
- You must go right now.
- You can't eat that!

Adverb Phrase

In an adverb phrase, one or more words work together to give more information about an adverb.

- especially *softly*
- *formerly* of the city of Perth
- much too *quickly* to see clearly
- Movements born in hatred very *quickly* take on the characteristics of the thing they oppose.

Prepositional Phrase

In a prepositional phrase, one or more words work together to give information about time, location, possession, or condition. The preposition always appears at the front of the phrase (preposition = pre-position). Prepositional phrases differ from the other four types of phrases in that a preposition cannot stand alone as the head word of a phrase.

Examples: The cupcake *with sprinkles* is yours.
The cupcake *with colourful sprinkles* is yours.

Although a preposition is still the head word in a prepositional phrase, it has to be accompanied by another element—or prepositional complement—if the phrase is to be complete. Most typically, the prepositional complement will be a noun phrase.

- *after* a very long walk
- *behind* the old building
- *for* all the hungry children

Infinitive Phrase

An infinitive phrase consists of an infinitive (to + simple form of verb) and modifiers or other words associated to the infinitive. An infinitive phrase always works as an adjective, adverb, or a noun in a sentence.

Examples:

She likes to read novels.	(As noun/object)
To earn money is a desire of everyone.	(As noun/subject)
He shouted to inform people about fire.	(As adverb, modifies the verb 'shout')
He made a plan to buy a flat.	(As adjective, modifies noun 'plan')

Gerund Phrase

A gerund phrase consists of a gerund (verb + -ing) and modifiers or other words associated with the gerund. A gerund phrase works as a noun in a sentence.

Examples:

I like writing good essays.	(As noun/object)
She started thinking about the future.	(As noun/object)
Sleeping late night is not a good habit.	(As noun/subject)
Crying of a baby woke him up.	(As noun/subject)

She was waiting for her mother, her eyes on the clock.
John is painting a wall, his shirt dirty with paint.

Complex Structures

Noun phrases and prepositional phrases can have particularly complex structure in written texts, with several layers of phrase embedding. In fact, the complexity of phrases is a very striking measure for comparing the complexity of syntax in different contexts, that is, formal or informal, used for different purposes and for different audiences. The simplest structures occur in conversation and the complexity increases through fiction and newspaper writing, with academic writing showing the greatest complexity of phrase structure.

- *in case* it should happen again
- Ran away home quickly to his mother
- Out from under the kitchen table
- From behind the desk
- In the morning

Participle Phrase

A participle phrase consists of a present participle (verb + -ing), a past participle (verb ending in -ed or other form in case of irregular verbs), and modifiers or other associate words. A participle phrase is separated by commas. It always works as an adjective in a sentence.

Examples:

The kids, making a noise, need food.	(Modifies 'kids')
I received a letter, mentioning about my job.	(Modifies 'letter')
The chair, made of steel, is too expensive.	(Modifies 'chair')
We saw a car, damaged in an accident.	(Modifies 'car')

Absolute Phrase

A group of words including a noun or pronoun and a participle as well as any associated modifiers is called absolute phrase (also called nominative phrase). Absolute phrase describes (give information about) the entire sentence. It resembles a clause but it doesn't have a true finite verb. It is separated by a comma or pair of commas from the rest of the sentence.

Examples:
She looks sad, her face expressing worry.
He, having anger in his eyes, met his enemy.
He, having books in his hand, was going to college.

2.2.2 Clause

A clause is a group of words which has a subject and a predicate of its own and forms part of a larger sentence. There are three kinds of clauses:

Principal Clause

This clause is the main part of a sentence which consists of a subject, a predicate, and an object to make a complete sense which does not depend on any other clause.

Examples:
I love my country.
She is the best girl in the class.
We shall set out for the journey.

Subordinate Clause

It always depends on the main clause to give a complete sense.

Examples:
That he is honest is known to all.
SC PC
Wherever you go I shall follow you.
SC PC
We shall set out for a journey when the sun rises.
PC SC

Types of Subordinate Clause

The subordinate clause is of three types: noun clause, adjective clause, and adverb clause.

a. Noun Clause

A noun clause is a group of words that act as a noun in a sentence. They begin with relative pronouns such as how, which, who, or what, combined with a subject and predicate. For example:

The dog can eat what he wants.

Here, 'what he wants' stands as a noun for what the dog can eat. It's a noun clause because it has a subject (he) and a predicate (wants). Here's another:

Whoever gave the dog popcorn is in trouble!

'Whoever gave the dog popcorn' is the noun in the sentence, meaning the person who gave the dog popcorn.

To be sure of the noun clause in a sentence, you can switch it with a single noun and the sentence will still make sense, like this:

The dog can eat popcorn.
Sally is in trouble!

The noun clause can have several functions in a complex sentence.

Subject of a verb

Examples:
What he said is true.
How on earth he manages is a mystery.
Where he has gone is not known to anybody.

Object of a verb

Examples:
I wonder *why there is a strike today.*
Take *whatever you want.*
Nobody knows *who did this mischief.*

Complement of a verb

Examples:
He is not *what he seems.*
Life is *what we make of it.*
The problem is *how the poor can be helped.*

Object of a preposition

Examples:
He had to manage with *whatever he got.*
He paid no attention to *what I said.*
This is addressed to *whomsoever it may concern.*

In apposition to a noun or pronoun

Examples:
I accept the principle *that all men are equal.*
Do you know the maxim *that health is wealth?*
Isn't it a pity *that she should have met with an accident?*

b. Adjective Clause

Adjective clauses have a subject and a verb (or predicate). They will start with a relative pronoun, such as that, who, whom, whose, or which, or a relative adverb such as why, where, or when. Adjective clauses function as an adjective and modify nouns and pronouns. They are also called relative clauses.

Just as the other dependent clauses, the adjective clause does not express a complete thought. It does not need commas separating it from the rest of the sentence if it has essential information in it, that is, if you need the information it provides. If it gives additional information, then you use commas. A good way to test for this is to leave out the clause, read the sentence, and see if the meaning of the two sentences is different.

Here are some examples of adjective clauses. The adjective clause is underlined.

- Chocolate, which many of us adore, is fattening.
- People who are smart follow the rules.
- I can remember the time when there were no computers.
- Charlie has a friend whose daughter lives in China.
- Wine that is produced in Tuscany is not cheap.

Adjective clauses perform four grammatical functions within sentences in the English language. The four functions of adjective clauses are:

- Noun phrase modifier
- Verb phrase modifier
- Prepositional phrase modifier
- Noun clause modifier

For example:

- The map *you sent me last week* seems outdated. (noun phrase modifier)
- The neighbour *whose car you hit* mowed over my flowers. (noun phrase modifier)
- Hunting tigers, *which many people still consider sport,* should be outlawed internationally. (verb phrase modifier)
- Employees must arrive between 7:00 and 9:00, *which is a reasonable time frame.* (prepositional phrase modifier)
- That the museum cancelled the lecture, *which is quite surprising,* disappoints me. (noun clause modifier)

PRACTICE EXERCISE E

Look at the following sentences and put a X in front of the sentences that contain adjective clauses. Then underline the whole adjective clause.

1. ______ Tom, who is always late, arrived late for his wedding.
2. ______ His bride was angry with him for arriving late.
3. ______ We replaced the window, which we had accidentally broken with a baseball.
4. ______ The broken window was in the living room.
5. ______ The cat with the injured paw limped on three legs.
6. ______ The cat that won the fight got injured.
7. ______ Irvin played on the team that won the tournament last week.

PRACTICE EXERCISE F

Study the sentences below and place a X in front of the ones that include adjective clauses. Underline the adjective clauses and relative pronouns.

1. ______ Yesterday I saw a man. The man was picking his nose.
2. ______ Yesterday I saw a man who was picking his nose.
3. ______ Yesterday I saw a house. The house was painted turquoise.
4. ______ Yesterday I saw a house which was painted turquoise.
5. ______ Yesterday I saw a woman. I knew the woman.
6. ______ Yesterday I saw a woman whom I knew.
7. ______ Yesterday I saw a dog. I chased the dog down the street.
8. ______ Yesterday I saw a dog which I chased down the street.
9. ______ Yesterday I saw a dog. The dog's collar was studded with spikes.
10. ______ Yesterday I saw a dog whose collar was studded with spikes.
11. ______ Yesterday I saw a man. The man's hair was green.
12. ______ Yesterday I saw a man whose hair was green.

PRACTICE EXERCISE G

Read each sentence and put an asterisk in front of the sentences that are ungrammatical.

1. ______ Yesterday I saw a man who was picking his nose.
2. ______ Yesterday I saw a man that was picking his nose.
3. ______ Yesterday I saw a man was picking his nose.

4. ______ Yesterday I saw a house which was painted turquoise.
5. ______ Yesterday I saw a house that was painted turquoise.
6. ______ Yesterday I saw a house was painted turquoise.

7. ______ Yesterday I saw a woman whom I knew.
8. ______ Yesterday I saw a woman who I knew.
9. ______ Yesterday I saw a woman that I knew.
10. ______ Yesterday I saw a woman I knew.

11. ______ Yesterday I called a man whom I worked for.
12. ______ Yesterday I called a man who I worked for.
13. ______ Yesterday I called a man that I worked for.
14. ______ Yesterday I called a man I worked for.

15. ______ Yesterday I called a man for whom I worked.
16. ______ Yesterday I called a man for who I worked.

17. ______ Yesterday I called a man for that I worked.
18. ______ Yesterday I called a man for I worked.

19. ______ Yesterday a player made derogatory statements which he was suspended for.
20. ______ Yesterday a player made derogatory statements that he was suspended for.
21. ______ Yesterday a player made derogatory statements he was suspended for.
22. ______ Yesterday a player made derogatory statements for which he was suspended.
23. ______ Yesterday a player made derogatory statements for that he was suspended.
24. ______ Yesterday a player made derogatory statements for he was suspended.

25. ______ Insolence is a behaviour which I won't put up with.
26. ______ Insolence is a behaviour that I won't put up with.
27. ______ Insolence is a behaviour I won't put up with.

c. Adverbial Clause

Adverbial clause is used as an adverb. Besides, it modifies only verbs or verb phrases that are in the main clause. Adverbial clauses perform the functions of an adverb.

i. Adverbial Clause of Time

Adverbial clause of time usually begins with when, after, before, while, and the like. This answers the question 'when'.

Examples:

i. He was provoked when the man asked for a bribe. (Modifies the verb phrase 'was provoked')
ii. When I saw him, I was perplexed. (Modifies the verb phrase 'was perplexed')
iii. Before we responded, they had run away. (Modifies the verb phrase 'had run')
iv. As at the time I was an undergraduate, she was not yet born. (Modifies the verb phrase 'was not')

ii. Adverbial Clause of Place

Adverbial clause of place is used with where and wherever. This answers the question 'where'.

Examples:

i. Nobody knows <u>where Nigeria is heading for</u>. (Modifies the verb 'knows')

ii. I am ready to sleep wherever you give me. (Modifies the verb phrase 'am ready to sleep')
iii. Where I will be tomorrow nobody can tell. (Modifies the verb phrase 'can tell')

iii. Adverbial Clause of Reason

Adverbial clause of reason is used with why, because, and so on. It answers the question 'why'?

Examples:

i. Because I did well they were happy. (Modifies the verb 'were')
ii. She cried because she was jilted. (Modifies the verb 'cried')
iii. Never leave an idea because nobody believes in it. (Modifies the verb 'leave')
iv. I will make it because God is on my side. (Modifies the verb phrase 'will make')

iv. Adverbial Clause of Concession

Adverbial clause shows contrast between the main clause and the subordinate clause. The markers of this clause include although, though, even though, and so on. However, *but* does not co-occur in a construction where these markers occur.

Examples:

i. Although he prepared, he did not do well in the test. (Modifies the verb phrase 'did not do')
ii. Even though I know it, I won't tell you. (Modifies the verb phrase 'won't tell')
iii. He stays where the gods meet. (Modifies the verb 'stays')

v. Adverbial Clause of Manner

Adverbial clause of manner can be identified with words such as how, as, as if, and the like. This answers the question 'how'.

Examples:

i. He talks as if he knows everything. (Modifies the verb 'talks')
ii. She dances as an insect does. (Modifies the verb 'dances')
iii. They prayed as if only prayer could solve their problem. (Modifies the verb 'prayed')
iv. Sheela thinks the way her father wants. (Modifies the verb 'thinks')

vi. Adverbial Clause of Condition

Adverbial clause of condition can be identified with words such as unless, if, except, unless, until, and the like. This gives the condition under which something or an event will happen.

Examples:

i. Unless you are rightly connected, you may not make headway.
(Modifies the verb phrase 'may not make')

ii. If you think you are the wisest person, you are the king of the fools. (Modifies the verb 'are')

iii. Unless the masses voice out, the government may do nothing about their plight. (Modifies the verb phrase 'may do')

iv. Until we believe in the sanctity of human life, this society may not witness peace. (Modifies the verb phrase 'may not witness')

vii. Adverbial Clause of Degree of Comparison

The chief conjunctions used are *as*, *as...as*, *so...as*, and *than*. It answers the questions 'how much', 'how little', or 'how many'.

Examples:

i. She is as pretty as a rose.
ii. She is not so brilliant as her brother.
iii. She is not shorter than her sister.
iv. He is much elder than her.

List of Adverb Clauses

When creating adverb clauses, feel free to be creative. The following examples will help you get started:

Even when I'm sick...
When you have finished working...
Whenever you like...
Wherever we prefer...
Since I returned from vacation...
As she was not there...
Since you always do well...
Before entering high school...
After I return...
So that he would understand...

PRACTICE EXERCISE H

The following exercise will help you gain greater understanding about how adverb clauses work. Choose the best answer to complete each sentence.

1. The women took notes ________________________.
   a. while being taught to cook
   b. steadily
   c. noisily
   d. for their children

2. We will go to the game ________________.
   a. Friday b. even if it rains
   c. Saturday d. sometime

3. You can put the package ________________.
   a. outside b. inside
   c. wherever you like d. somewhere

4. ________________, you will not be punished.
   a. Since you have apologized b. We decided
   c. He told me d. You are lucky

5. She was so tired ________________.
   a. she left b. she cried
   c. today d. that she could not stand

Coordinate Clause

It has also an equal rank as principal clause but it is connected to the principal clause by a coordinating conjunction to make a complete sense.

Examples:

I went to Delhi (PC) but I could not find time enough to see your brother (CC).

I take my breakfast (PC) and I leave for the school (CC).

PRACTICE EXERCISE I

Identify the phrases and clauses in the following sentences:

1. The sun rises in the east.
2. I caught him by the collar.
3. Work hard lest you should fail.
4. She sang a sweet song.
5. Where there is a will there is a way.
6. The birds are resting in their nests.
7. Please tell me whom you want to see
8. This is the whole story in a nutshell.
9. It is no use crying for the moon.
10. He arrived after the meeting was over.

PRACTICE EXERCISE J

Name the kind in each of the following sentences:

1. Are you sure of your success in the examination?
2. Alas! My friend is no more
3. Beauty is nine days' wonder.
4. A man is known by the company he keeps.
5. May god help you in your venture!
6. Look before you leap.
7. How pleasant the weather is!
8. Kindly give me a piece of paper.
9. Do not pluck flowers.
10. Books should be studied carefully.

PRACTICE EXERCISE K

Indicate the subject, verb, direct object/complement:

1. We should not hate anybody.
2. Scholars love books.
3. Ram seems happy.
4. It has grown dark.
5. She felt brave at the time of crisis.
6. Kiran is a good player of hockey.
7. I ran a five-mile race.
8. He called me a liar.
9. The boy was beaten black and blue.
10. Sweet are the uses of adversity.

Sentence Structure
According to the clause structure, sentences can be divided into four different kinds: simple, compound, complex, and compound-complex.

Simple Sentences
A simple sentence contains a subject and a verb, and it may also have an object and modifiers. However, it contains only *one* independent clause.

Examples:
- She read.
- She completed her literature review.
- He organized his resources by theme.

Compound Sentences

A compound sentence contains at least *two* independent clauses. These two independent clauses can be combined with a comma and a coordinating conjunction or with a semicolon.

Examples:

- She completed her literature review and she created her reference list.
- You can go by bus or by train.
- He went to Chennai, got his visa, and came back.

Complex Sentences

A complex sentence contains at least *one* independent clause and at least *one* dependent clause. Dependent clauses can refer to the subject (*who, which*), the sequence/time (*since, while*), or the causal elements (*because, if*) of the independent clause. If a sentence begins with a dependent clause, note the comma after this clause. If, on the other hand, the sentence begins with an independent clause, there is no comma separating the two clauses.

Examples:

- Although she completed her literature review, she still needed work on her methods section.
- I shall do as I like.
- When we went there, we found that he had gone.

Compound-Complex Sentences

A compound-complex sentence contains at least two independent clauses and at least one dependent clause.

Examples:

- While the man played the harmonium, the boys sang and the girls danced.
- I knew that he was ill, but I did not that he suffered from cancer.
- As long as it was dry, we climbed up the steep hillsides and ran races on their level tops.

PRACTICE EXERCISE L

Change the following complex sentences into simple sentences:

1. After he had learned his lessons, he went out to play.
2. While I was walking along the street, I saw a dead cobra.
3. Although he was wealthy and educated, he never made a name.
4. If you follow my advice, you will win your object.
5. As he was driven out of his country, he sought asylum in a foreign land.
6. A gypsy who was wandering across the fields found the baby.

PRACTICE EXERCISE M

Rewrite the following simple sentences as compound sentences:

1. The old man being weak could not walk properly.
2. His father in spite of being poor is a contended man.
3. She must work hard to be successful in the examination.
4. Our teacher is popular among students for his diligence.
5. But for his faults he would have progressed immensely.
6. Visualizing a danger ahead, the traveller became cautious.
7. The student must accept his fault to escape his punishment.
8. The culprit ran away to escape his arrest.
9. Taking off their clothes the children jumped into the river.
10. In the event of being late you will not be allowed entry.

PRACTICE EXERCISE N

Change the following sentences (without changing their meaning) as directed:

1.	What a piece of work is man!	(Change into assertive form)
2.	O that I could fly high in the sky!	(Change into simple sentence)
3.	There is no greater feeling than love.	(Change into an interrogative sentence)
4.	This is not the way to talk to your elders.	(Change into interrogative sentence)
5.	Will anybody forget those happy days spent here?	(Change into an assertive sentence)
6.	If you do not hurry, you will be late in the office.	(Make use of the word 'unless')
7.	But for your help, we would have been ruined.	(Make use of the word 'if')
8.	No one but a fool would trust him.	(Change into an affirmative sentence)
9.	What a delicious food we had yesterday!	(Change into an assertive sentence)
10.	The child is very pretty.	(Change into an exclamatory sentence)

PRACTICE EXERCISE O

Rewrite the following complex sentences as compound sentences:

1. I am confident that he is innocent in this matter.
2. Unless he works hard, he cannot pass the examination.
3. However hard work she may do, she cannot pass the examination.
4. She is sure that he has stolen her purse.
5. As the shopkeeper quarrels with every customer, nobody likes him.
6. If he does not improve his behaviour, he will lose all his friends.
7. Unless the culprit accepts his fault, he will not be spared.
8. She did not attend the office because she felt unwell today.
9. She has lost the book that she had purchased.
10. If you do not attend the class, you will not be allowed to sit in the examination.

PRACTICE EXERCISE P

Rewrite the following compound sentences as complex sentences:

1. Let me reach my office and then I shall talk to him.
2. Spare the rod and spoil the child.
3. The thief saw the policeman, so he ran away.
4. She is feeling unwell so she cannot attend her office today.
5. The child felt hungry, so he started weeping.
6. The news is very good but it is not true.
7. Eat less and you will remain healthy.
8. The old man is very rich but he is a miser.
9. Children put on new clothes and went to see the fair.
10. Keep quiet or you will repent.

2.3 IMPORTANCE OF PROPER PUNCTUATION

Purpose and Examples

Punctuation	*Purpose*	*Examples*
Period [.]	End a sentence	Most sentences end in a period.
Question mark [?]	Indicate a question	'What time is it?' she asked. 'How much longer?' he asked.
Exclamation point [!]	Express emotion	'I hate you!' he shouted. 'I love you!' she shouted.

Punctuation	*Purpose*	*Examples*
Semicolon [;] or comma [,]+conjunction [and, or, nor, for, so, but, yet]	Connect complete sentences (two independent clauses)	It is raining; the dog is wet. *Or* It is raining, and the dog is wet.
Comma [,] but if one or more items in that list already have a comma, use a semicolon [;]	Connect items in a list	My lunch is a sandwich, an apple, and a bag of pretzels. *But* My dinner is a salad of spinach, carrots, and tomatoes; a bowl of pasta; and two breadsticks.
Quotation marks [' ']	Indicate a quotation	'To be or not to be' is one of the most famous lines from *Hamlet.*
comma [,] or, less commonly, colon [:]	Introduce a quotation (words directly spoken)	She yelled, 'Let's get out of here!' The president declared, 'We will prevail.'
Apostrophe [']	Show possession or contraction	Why is Lisa's wallet in Ben's backpack?
Colon [:] if what precedes the colon is a complete sentence	Introduce a list of three or more items	There are three things I want to do before I die: go on a cruise, go skydiving, and learn to surf.
Commas [,]	Separate a word or phrase that is relevant but not essential information	Elaine, my roommate, is from Chicago. Her nickname as a child, her mother told me, was 'Boo-boo'.
Parentheses [( )]	Separate a word or phrase that is relevant but secondary information	There is an exception to every rule (including this one).
Colon [:]	Introduce an explanation (what follows 'explains' or 'answers' what precedes)	You know what they say about real estate: Location is everything.
Ellipsis [...]	To show information is omitted	'... was really good at public speaking.'
Brackets [[ ]]	To show information was added	'[Winston Churchill] was really good at public speaking.'
Hyphen [-] unless the first word is an adjective ending in -ly	Connect two words that work together as one object or modifier	Mother-in-law, five-year-old son, highly rated
En dash [–]	Show the span between two numbers or the scores of a game	The score is 14–21. He lived from 1953–2016.
Em dash [—]	Separate a word or phrase for emphasis	Never steal from that store—never. It's not just a bad idea—it's illegal.

Punctuation is one of the most important aspects of written English. It is, in fact, this feature of writing that gives meaning to the written words much like pauses and changes in tone of the voice while speaking. An error in punctuation can convey a completely different meaning to the one that is intended.

2.3.1 Rules and Examples

Commas or Semicolons

1. **Use commas to separate two or more things in a list.**

   Example: London, New York, and Tokyo are some of the largest cities in the world.

2. **Use comma before 'and'**

   When using commas to separate items in a list, place a comma before 'and' that precedes the last separate item in the list. For example:

   The menu included a large variety of vegetables—green beans, cabbage, tomatoes, peas, eggplant, and spinach.

   However, in the following example, the comma has not been used. It ends with '... eggplant and spinach'.

   The menu included a large variety of vegetables—green beans, cabbage, tomatoes, peas, eggplant and spinach.

   This can be misinterpreted to mean that 'eggplant and spinach' is one dish on the menu, while in fact, 'eggplant' and 'spinach' are two separate items. Hence, a comma avoids ambiguity.

3. **Commas with an appositive**
   Place commas around the appositive (noun, noun phrase, or series of nouns placed next to another word or phrase to identify or rename it) only if the information given is not essential. If the information is essential, do not place the commas. For example:

   Her husband, John, is very intelligent.

   (Here commas are used before and after John because it is assumed that she has only one husband. Hence, if the word 'John' was removed, the meaning would not change.)

   Her friend Steve lives in France.

   (Here commas are *not* used because Steve is essential information telling us which friend lives in France.)

4. **Comma in an indirect quote**
   Do not use a comma in an indirect quote.
   For example: You said, that you would come. (Incorrect)
   You said that you would come. (Correct)

5. **Double or single quotation marks to enclose quotes**
   Use double quotation marks to enclose direct quotes, and single quotation marks to enclose a quotation within a quotation, and vice versa.
   For example:

   "We were just entering the building when someone called us from behind," explained Sarah; and

   "We were just entering the building when someone yelled 'Stop!' from behind," explained Sarah.

6. **Use semicolon to separate two or more items in a list that already has commas.**

   Example: London, England; New York, USA; and Tokyo, Japan, are some of the largest cities in the world.

7. **Use a semicolon between independent clauses not joined by *and, but, for, yet,* or *so*.**

   Example: I like reading; my friend likes watching movies.

8. **Use a semicolon between two independent clauses that are connected by conjunctive adverbs or transitional phrases.**

   Example: However they choose to write, people are allowed to make their own decisions; as a result, many people swear by their writing methods.

9. **Use a semicolon between items in a list or series if any of the items contain commas.**

   Example: There are basically two ways to write: with a pen or pencil, which is inexpensive and easily accessible; or by computer and printer, which is more expensive but quick and neat.

Period or No Period

1. **Periods/full stops are used for**
   - Initials in names (examples: J. F. Kennedy, Robert E. Lee)
   - Latin abbreviations that need no explanation (examples: e.g., i.e.)
   - Contraction (examples: Dr, Ltd)
   - Abbreviations end in lower case/small letters (example: Dec. for December)
2. **Periods/full stops are not used for**
   - Abbreviations in upper case/capital letters (examples: UNESCO, CNN)
   - Abbreviations of countries (examples: the USA, the UK)
   - Abbreviations of compass directions (examples: NW, SSE)
   - Metric abbreviations (examples: kg, cm)

3. **Use a single space after a period**
Two spaces after a period, exclamation, or question mark have been used since the beginning of typing. This rule has since expired. In this era only one space is necessary.

Capitalization

1. **Capitalization of person's title or rank**
Do not capitalize the title or rank of a person when it follows the name. Capitalize only when it precedes a name.

Example 1: John Doe, *colonel* in the army, was the chief guest at the function.

Example 2: *Colonel* John Doe was the chief guest at the function.

2. **Compass points and capitalization**
Capitalize points of the compass (north, south, eastern, western, and so on) only when they designate geographical parts of a region, and NOT when used to indicate parts of regions.
For example: *Western* Hemisphere, but *western* United States.

3. **Capitalize academic titles**
Capitalize all academic titles when preceding a name.

Examples: Doctor Jones, *Professor* Smith, *Judge* Fitzgerald.
Do not capitalize them when they stand alone (i.e., without a person's name).

Examples: doctor, professor, judge.

4. **Capitalization of abbreviations**
Capitalize abbreviations only if the words they stand for are to be capitalized.

Examples: UK (United Kingdom), but *p.* (page).

5. **Resumed quotations within sentences**
Do not capitalize quotations resumed within a sentence.

Examples: 'I am not going', he said, 'because I have an assignment to complete.'

6. **Capitalization of family relationships**
Family relationships are capitalized only when used as proper names.

Example: My favourite ***uncle*** is ***U***ncle Jack.
In the first instance, the 'u' is small as the word 'uncle' has been used as a common noun. In the second case, 'U' has been capitalized because here the word 'uncle' is a proper noun specifying a particular uncle.

7. **Question within a sentence**
   Always capitalize an independent question within a sentence.

   Example: The question is, ***Who*** is the protagonist of the story?

8. **Capitalize the word 'Government'**
   Capitalize the word 'Government' when referring to the government of a specific country.

   Example: Japan's Imperial Government; The US Government's decision to; The Government raised taxes, and so on.

Exclamation Mark

1. **Use exclamation marks sparingly in your writing. Its overuse reduces its impact. Use it only to express**

   - A strong command (Get out of here!)
   - An excitement (Let's celebrate!)
   - Anger or contempt (What a rude person!)
   - Surprise (It's you!)
   - A rhetorical question (How could he do it!)

   These are all emotional situations. No emotions are involved in formal writing; therefore, do not use exclamation marks in formal writing.

Colons

1. **Use a colon to introduce an item or a series of items. Do not capitalize the first item after the colon (unless it's a proper noun).**

   Examples:

   You know what to do: practice.

   You may be required to bring many things: sleeping bags, pans, utensils, and warm clothing.

   I want the following items: butter, sugar, and flour.

   I need an assistant who can do the following: input data, write reports, and complete tax forms.

2. **A capital letter generally does not introduce a word, phrase, or incomplete sentence following a colon.**

   Examples:

   He got what he worked for: a promotion.

   He got what he worked for: a promotion that paid a higher wage.

3. **When listing items one by one, one per line, following a colon, capitalization and ending punctuation are optional when using single words or phrases preceded by letters, numbers, or bullet points.**

   Examples:
   I want an assistant who can do the following:
   a. input data
   b. write reports
   c. complete tax forms

4. **If each point is a complete sentence, capitalize the first word and end the sentence with appropriate ending punctuation. Otherwise, there are no hard and fast rules, except be consistent.**
   The following are requested:
   a. Wool sweaters for possible cold weather.
   b. Wet suits for snorkelling.

Apostrophes

1. **Use the *apostrophe* to show possession. To show possession with a singular noun, add an apostrophe plus the letter *s*.**

   Examples:
   a woman's hat
   the boss's wife
   Mrs Chang's house

2. **Add only an apostrophe to all nouns ending in *s*. And some add an apostrophe+*s* to every proper noun, be it *Hastings's* or *Jones's*. One method, common in newspapers and magazines, is to add an apostrophe+*s* (*'s*) to common nouns ending in *s*, but only a stand-alone apostrophe to proper nouns ending in *s*.**

   Examples:
   the class's hours
   Mr Jones' golf clubs
   the canvas's size
   Texas' weather

3. **To show plural possession, simply put an apostrophe after the *s*.**

   Examples:
   Correct: guys' night out (guy + s + apostrophe)
   Incorrect: guy's night out (implies only one guy)
   Correct: two actresses' roles (actress + es + apostrophe)
   Incorrect: two actress's roles

4. **With a singular compound noun (for example, *mother-in-law*), show possession with an apostrophe + *s* at the end of the word.**

   Example: my mother-in-law's hat

   If the compound noun (e.g., brother-in-law) is to be made plural, form the plural first (brothers-in-law), and then use the apostrophe + *s*.

   Example: my two brothers-in-law's hats

5. **Show possession when a noun ending in *y* becomes plural, write *ies*. Do not write *y's*.**

   Example:
   Correct: three companies' policies.
   Incorrect: three company's policies.

6. **There are various approaches to plurals for abbreviations, single letters, and numerals. With groups of two or more capital letters, apostrophes seem less necessary.**

   Examples:
   There are two new MPs on the base.
   He learnt his ABCs.
   She consulted with three MDs. *Or* She consulted with three MD's.
   Some write M.D.'s to give the *s* separation from the second period.

   Single-digit numbers are usually spelt out, but when they aren't, you are just as likely to see *2s* and *3s* as *2's* and *3's*.

   Examples:
   the 1990s
   the 1990's
   the '90s
   the 90's

7. **Amounts of time or money are sometimes used as possessive adjectives that require apostrophes.**

   Examples:
   Incorrect: three days leave
   Correct: three days' leave

   Incorrect: my two cents worth
   Correct: my two cents' worth

8. **Use an apostrophe with *contractions*. The apostrophe is placed where a letter or letters have been removed.**

   Examples: doesn't, it's, 'tis, can't, you'd, should've, rock 'n' roll
   Incorrect: does'nt
   Correct: doesn't

9. **If two people possess the same item, put the apostrophe+*s* after the second name only.**

   Example: Cesar and Maribel's home is constructed of redwood.
   Incorrect: Maribel and my home
   Incorrect: Mine and Maribel's home
   Correct: Maribel's and my home

   Incorrect: he and Maribel's home
   Incorrect: him and Maribel's home
   Correct: his and Maribel's home

   Incorrect: you and Maribel's home
   Incorrect: yours and Maribel's home
   Correct: Maribel's and your home

Ellipses

An ellipsis (plural: ellipses) is a punctuation mark consisting of three dots. Use an ellipsis when omitting a word, phrase, line, paragraph, or more from a quoted passage. Ellipses save space or remove material that is less relevant. They are useful in getting right to the point without delay or distraction.

1. **Use an ellipsis whether the omission occurs at the beginning of a sentence, in the middle of a sentence, or between sentences.**

   Example: '… [A]fter hours of careful thought, we vetoed the bill.'

2. **Ellipses can express hesitation, changes of mood, suspense, or thoughts trailing off.**

   Examples:
   I don't know … I'm not sure.
   Pride is one thing, but what happens if she …?
   He said, 'I … really don't … understand this.'

Question Mark

1. **Use a question mark only after a direct question.**

   Example:
   Correct: Will you go with me?
   Incorrect: I'm asking if you will go with me?

2. **Avoid the common trap of using question marks with indirect questions, which are statements that contain questions. Use a period after an indirect question.**

   Example:
   Incorrect: I wonder if he would go with me?
   Correct: I wonder if he would go with me.

3. **Some sentences are statements—or demands—in the form of a question. They are called rhetorical questions because they don't require or expect an answer. Many should be written without question marks.**

   Examples:
   Why don't you take a break.
   Would you kids knock it off.
   What wouldn't I do for you!

4. **Use a question mark when a sentence is half statement and half question.**

   Example:

   You do care, don't you?

   If a question is within the quoted material, a question mark should be placed inside the quotation marks.

   Examples:
   She asked, 'Will you still be my friend?'
   The question *Will you still be my friend?* is part of the quotation.

   Do you agree with the saying, 'All's fair in love and war'?
   The question *Do you agree with the saying?* is outside the quotation.

Hyphens

1. **Generally, hyphenate two or more words when they come before a noun they modify and act as a single idea. This is called a *compound adjective.***

   Examples:
   an off-campus apartment
   state-of-the-art design

2. **When writing out new, original, or unusual compound nouns, writers hyphenate to avoid confusion.**

   Example:
   I changed my diet and became a no-meater.
   No-meater *is too confusing without the hyphen.*

3. **Hyphens are often used to tell the ages of people and things.**
   With hyphens:

   Examples:
   We have a two-year-old child.
   We have a two-year-old.

4. **When using numbers, hyphenate spans or estimates of time, distance, or other quantities. Remember not to use spaces around hyphens.**

   Examples:
   3:15–3:45 PM.
   1999–2016
   300–325 people

5. **Hyphenate all compound numbers from *twenty-one* to *ninety-nine*.**

   Examples:
   thirty-two children
   one thousand two hundred twenty-one dollars

6. **Hyphenate prefixes when they come before proper nouns or proper adjectives.**

   Examples:
   trans-American
   mid-July

7. **Hyphenate all words beginning with the prefixes *self-*, *ex-* (i.e., *former*), and *all-*.**

   Examples:
   self-assured
   ex-mayor
   all-knowing

8. **Hyphenate all spelt-out fractions. But do not hyphenate fractions introduced with *a* or *an*.**

   Examples:
   More than one-third of registered voters oppose the measure.
   More than a third of registered voters oppose the measure.

Parentheses and Brackets

1. **Use parentheses to enclose information that clarifies or is used as an aside.**

   Example: He finally answered (after taking five minutes to think) that he did not understand the question.

2. **If material in parentheses ends a sentence, the period goes after the parentheses.**

   Example: He gave me a nice bonus ($500).

3. **Periods go inside parentheses only if an entire sentence is inside the parentheses.**

   Example: Please read the analysis. (You'll be amazed.)

4. **Punctuate correctly both inside and outside parentheses. The period after the parentheses is necessary to bring the entire sentence to a close.**

   Example:

   You are late (aren't you?).

   Brackets are far less common than parentheses, and they are only used in special cases. Brackets (like single quotation marks) are used exclusively within quoted material.

5. **Brackets are interruptions. They are used to explain or comment on the quotation.**

   Example:
   'Four score and seven [today we'd say eighty-seven] years ago ...'

Dash

The dash typically typed as two hyphens or as one long bar functions almost as a colon does in that it adds to the preceding material, but with extra emphasis. Like a caesura (a timely pause) in music, a dash indicates a strong pause, then gives emphasis to material following the pause.

Examples:

1. Jill Emery confirms that Muslim populations have typically been ruled by non-Muslims—specifically Americans, Russians, Israelis, and the French.
2. The dissolution took 20 minutes—much longer than anticipated—but measurements were begun as soon as the process was completed.

Finally, the dash we typically use is technically called the *em dash,* and it is significantly longer than the hyphen. There is also an *en dash*—whose length is between that of the hyphen and the em dash, and its best usage is to indicate inclusive dates and numbers:

July 6–September 17
pp. 48–56.

No spaces should appear on either side of the punctuation mark when hyphen, en dash, and em dash are used.

PRACTICE EXERCISE Q

Use appropriate punctuation marks in the following sentences.

1. We had a great time in France the kids really enjoyed it
2. Some people work best in the mornings others do better in the evenings
3. What are you doing next weekend
4. Mother had to go into hospital she had heart problems
5. Did you understand why I was upset
6. It is a fine idea let us hope that it is going to work
7. We will be arriving on Monday morning at least I think so
8. A textbook can be a wall between teacher and class
9. The girls father sat in a corner
10. In the words of Murphy's Law Anything that can go wrong will go wrong

PRACTICE EXERCISE R

Put appropriate punctuation marks in the following sentences:

1. A grandparents job is easier than a parents
2. It looks as if the sun goes around the earth but of course the earth really goes round the sun
3. He neither smiled spoke nor looked at me
4. Long ago in a distant country there lived a beautiful princess
5. It was my aunt who took Peter to London yesterday not my father.
6. Ruth was invited to the party but she was ill so Jane went instead of her
7. Sorry to disturb you could I speak to you for a moment
8. Is it any use expecting them to be on time
9. Johns going to sleep during the wedding was rather embarrassing
10. Having lost all my money I went home

2.4 CREATING COHERENCE

Written communication is more often than not well-structured. The words are carefully chosen to suit the message and the context. Letters, memos, notes, contracts, agreements, documents, reports, and the like often carry time value and need to be stored and preserved. Most businesses rely on records rather than verbal contracts. Good writing is simple, clear, exact, straightforward, well-informed, and lively. Coherence is one of the prerequisite elements of good writing. It is necessary to use words, phrases, and clauses clearly so as to form balanced sentences. Coherence seeks to establish proper relationship and links sentences to make the intended message clear. It brings consistency and orderliness to the encoded message.

Coherence is a procedure to ensure conceptual connectivity which includes logical relations, organization of events, objects and situations, and continuity in human experience. It deals with basic relations such as cause–effect, problem–solution, and temporal sequence of events.

Coherence between Words

Coherence between words can be created by parallelism. Parallel structure means using similar grammatical constructions between words in sentences. Parallelism is particularly important for words in lists. If you're writing a list of things someone likes to do, then each activity in the list should take the same grammatical form. For instance, if one verb in the list takes on the '-ing' gerund form, like 'running', then the other verbs in the list should also be in the gerund form. An incoherent structure would be to say:

Incorrect: Sarah likes to jump, running, and skate.

Instead, the list should be parallel like this:

Correct: Sarah likes jumping, running, and skating.

Coherence between Sentences

To achieve cohesion—the link of one sentence to the next—consider the following techniques:

1. **Repetition:** In sentence B (the second of any two sentences), repeat a word from sentence A.
2. **Synonymy:** If direct repetition is too obvious, use a synonym of the word you wish to repeat. This strategy is called 'elegant variation'.
3. **Antonymy:** Using the 'opposite' word, an antonym, can also create sentence cohesion, since in language, antonyms actually share more elements of meaning than you might imagine.
4. **Pro-forms:** Use a pronoun, pro-verb, or another pro-form to make explicit reference back to a form mentioned earlier.
5. **Collocation:** Use a commonly paired, expected or highly probable word to connect one sentence to another.
6. **Enumeration:** Use overt markers of sequence to highlight the connection between ideas. This system has many advantages: (a) it can link

ideas that are otherwise completely unconnected, (b) it looks formal and distinctive, and (c) it promotes a second method of sentence cohesion, discussed in (7) below.

7. **Parallelism:** Repeat a sentence structure. This technique is the oldest, most overlooked, but probably the most elegant method of creating cohesion.
8. **Transitions:** Use a conjunction or conjunctive adverb to link sentences with particular logical relationships.
   a. **Identity:** Indicates sameness.

      that is, that is to say, in other words, ...

   b. **Opposition:** Indicates a contrast.

      but, yet, however, nevertheless, still, though, although, whereas, in contrast, rather, ...

   c. **Addition:** Indicates continuation.

      and, too, also, furthermore, moreover, in addition, besides, in the same way, again, another, similarly, a similar, the same, ...

   d. **Cause and effect:**

      therefore, so, consequently, as a consequence, thus, as a result, hence, it follows that, because, since, for, ...

   e. **Indefinites:** Indicate a logical connection of an unspecified type.

      in fact, indeed, now, ...

   f. **Concession:** Indicates a willingness to consider the other side.

      admittedly, I admit, true, I grant, of course, naturally, some believe, some people believe, it has been claimed that, once it was believed, there are those who would say, ...

   g. **Exemplification:** Indicates a shift from a more general or abstract idea to a more specific or concrete idea.

      for example, for instance, after all, an illustration of, even, indeed, in fact, it is true, of course, specifically, to be specific, that is, to illustrate, truly, ...

Here is an example of sentences that create coherence through repetition:

The most important part of an essay is the thesis statement. The thesis statement introduces the argument of the essay. The thesis statement also helps to create a structure for the essay.

In this example, the repetition of the phrase 'thesis statement' helps to unify the three sentences. It is a phrase that ends the first sentence and transitions into the next sentence by starting with that same phrase.

Coherence between Paragraphs
Transitional words can also be used between paragraphs. Words such as:

- Therefore
- However
- Yet
- Thus
- First
- Later
- Then

Below is a list of some of the more common transitional words and phrases, grouped according to their function. But a word of warning here: Don't overdo it! Too many transitional words and phrases become tiresome and confusing—just as too many road signs do. But it is useful to be aware of them so that you can use them when necessary.

Adding information	again, also, and, and then, besides, equally important, finally, first, further, furthermore, in addition, in the first place, last, moreover, next, second, still, too
Comparing	also, in the same way, likewise, similarly
Conceding	granted, naturally, of course
Contrasting	although, and yet, at the same time, but at the same time, despite that, even so, even though, for all that, however, in contrast, in spite of, instead, nevertheless, on the contrary, on the other hand, otherwise, regardless, still, though, yet
Emphasizing	certainly, indeed, in fact, of course
Illustrating	after all, as an illustration, even, for example, for instance, in conclusion, indeed, in fact, in other words, in short, it is true, of course, namely, specifically, that is, to illustrate, thus, truly
Summarizing	all in all, altogether, as has been said, finally, in brief, in conclusion, in other words, in particular, in short, in simpler terms, in summary, on the whole, that is, therefore, to put it differently, to summarize
Giving a time sequence	after a while, afterward, again, also, and then, as long as, at last, at length, at that time, before, besides, earlier, eventually, finally, formerly, further, furthermore, in addition, in the first place, in the past, last, lately, meanwhile, moreover, next, now, presently, second, shortly, simultaneously, since, so far, soon, still, subsequently, then, too, until, until now, when

Other ways to create coherence between paragraphs include having a consistent paragraph structure and point of view. The structure of a coherent paragraph includes a topic sentence, which focuses on the main idea. The topic sentence usually comes first in a paragraph. The topic sentence is followed by supporting sentences that develop the idea, and finally, a concluding sentence to tie it all together. Transitional words then bridge the gap between paragraphs, and the structure starts anew with another topic sentence for the next paragraph.

Coherence is a product of many different factors, which combine to make every paragraph, every sentence, and every phrase contribute to the meaning of the whole piece. Coherence itself is the product of two factors—paragraph unity and sentence cohesion.

Example 1: Coherence in Paragraphs

The following paragraphs represent weak and strong examples of coherence. You can implement them by having your students read them and asking them which they like better and why.

Weak Example: For me, the worst thing about waiting tables is the uniform. All the waitresses had to wear this ugly brown striped jumper. The shirts were polyester. Sometimes someone you know comes in. Now I have a job in an office.

Strong Example: For me, the worst thing about waiting tables was the uniform. At the last place I worked, all the waitresses had to wear an ugly brown striped jumper. Underneath it we had to wear an even uglier polyester shirt. Sometimes someone I knew would come in and I'd feel embarrassed by my outfit. Now I have a job in an office where I can wear my own clothes.

Example 2: Coherence in Paragraphs

The hotel is famous. It is one of the most well-known hotels in the country. The latest international dancing competition was held at the hotel. The hotel spent a lot of money to advertise the event. Because the hotel wanted to gain international reputation. But not many people attended the event.
(The connection of ideas is not very good.)

The hotel, which is one of the most well-known hotels in this region, wanted to promote its image around the world by hosting the latest international dancing competition. Although the event was widely advertised, not many people participated in the competition. *(The connection of ideas is better than in the first example.)*

The latest international dancing competition was held at the hotel, which is one of the most well-known hotels in this region. The hotel spent a lot of money on advertising the event since it wanted to enhance its international reputation;

however, it failed to attract many people. *(The connection of ideas is better than in the first example.)*

Activity A

Combine the following sentences using suitable transitional words or phrases.

1. I prefer folk music. My girlfriend adores heavy metal.
2. He's received three threatening letters. He is continuing to investigate the case.
3. The referee blew his whistle to start the game. It began to pour with rain.
4. Her boyfriend is very good-looking. He's a damn good cook.
5. She was absolutely exhausted. She's just finished her final exams.
6. You don't like him. You want that job. You'll have to be nice to him.

Activity B

Read the paragraphs below carefully. Then sit in pairs or threes and discuss what you think is the topic sentence in each of them and how you think they could be improved without changing the content. Then, working individually, rewrite them using the changes you discussed.

1. The book I would choose to take on a desert island is a book called *Frankenstein*. It's an amazing book about a man called Frankenstein who is a scientist. He's obsessed with creating life. He creates this monster out of different body parts. He brings it to life using electricity. The monster escapes. Frankenstein wants to forget the whole experiment. The monster tracks him down. He wants revenge. He gets it.
2. Gordon Brown took over from Tony Blair as Prime Minister in 2007. It was not an enviable task. Tony Blair was a master of the media and a good speaker. Gordon Brown appeared rather clumsy and boring. He was left with Blair's unpopular policies like the war in Iraq.
3. For the Liberal Party the election system is a huge disadvantage. They have supporters in all parts of the country and in all social classes. They are the third-largest party. Most of the votes they get are wasted. Their representation in Parliament is far below their popularity among the electorate.
4. The electoral system is not without its advantages. It usually provides governments with workable majorities. That makes it easier to carry out policies. It provides stability. Extremist or special interest parties have little chance of getting elected. It ensures that each constituent in the country has a personal representative in Parliament.

2.5 ORGANIZING PRINCIPLES OF PARAGRAPHS IN DOCUMENTS

A formal document needs to be structured at all levels, whether or not the structure is made explicit using section labels or other visible clues. Just as a document generally has an introduction, body, and conclusion, so does a paragraph. Each paragraph has one idea, thought, or purpose that is stated in an introductory sentence. This is followed by one or more supporting sentences and concluded with a summary statement and transition or link to the next idea or paragraph.

- The topic sentence states the main thesis, purpose, or topic of the paragraph; it defines the subject matter to be addressed in that paragraph.
- Body sentences support the topic sentence and relate clearly to the subject matter of the paragraph and overall document. They may use an organizing principle similar to that of the document itself (chronology, contrast, spatial) or introduce a related organizing principle (point by point, process or procedure).
- The conclusion sentence brings the paragraph to a close; it may do this in any of several ways. It may reinforce the paragraph's main point, summarize the relationships among the body sentences, and/or serve as a transition to the next paragraph.

2.5.1 Each Paragraph Is One Relevant Subtopic

Each paragraph in a document should have *one* topic that is clearly evident early in the paragraph. Every paragraph should have a clear relationship to the main topic of your document; if not, either the paragraph should be eliminated, or the main topic should be revised.

2.5.2 Use Complete Sentences

Except in extraordinary circumstances, sentences in the main text must be complete, that is, they must have a subject and a verb, so that they express an entire thought, not just a fragment or the beginning of a thought. Note that most '-ing' words are not verbs. 'The light turning green' is just a fragment, that is, a start to a sentence or a part of one. To be a sentence that you could use on its own followed by a period, it would have to be 'The light turned green,' which has both a subject and a verb.

2.5.3 Mechanics

When drafting a paragraph we commit some keyboarding errors which might be grammar, usage, or errors of mechanics, or they could be omitted words or typos. Some of the errors of mechanics include *capitalization, punctuation, spellings, and other errors.*

Spellings

There are certain complex rules for spellings.

1. **Write *i* before *e* (fiery, friend, dried) except after *c* (receive) and when sounding like *a* as in neighbour (weigh, heir, foreign).**

   Examples: All applicants will receive a response within three weeks.
   The breakfast special is fried eggs and sausage.

Adding Endings to Words

2. **If a word ends with a silent *e*, drop the *e* when adding a suffix that begins with a vowel (for example, the -ing suffix). However, do not drop the *e* when the suffix begins with a consonant (for example, the -ful suffix).**

   Examples: I like to skate. I enjoy skating.
   I could use a dictionary. A dictionary is very useful.

3. **When *y* is the last letter in a word and the letter before *y* is a consonant, drop *y* and add *i* before adding a suffix.**

   Examples: The beaches in Thailand are extremely beautiful.
   They hurried to the gate because they were so late.

4. **When forming the plural of a word that ends with a *y* preceded by a vowel, just add *s*. But if the letter before *y* is a consonant, drop *y* and add *i* before adding the suffix.**

   Examples: FAO Schwartz is a famous toy store. It sells all kinds of toys.
   Ladies and gentlemen, please be seated.

5. **When a word ends in a consonant preceded by one vowel, double the final consonant before adding a suffix that begins with a vowel.**

   Examples: The children swim at the community pool. They love swimming.
   You should begin at the beginning. Start by writing the title.

Other Errors

Compound Words

A compound word is a word that has two or more parts. For example, the word 'everywhere' is made up of two distinct words: *every* and *where*. But as a compound word, everywhere has a new meaning that is different from the meanings of *every* and *where*.

Example: I work to support myself and my family.
You can learn from everything happening today.

Fused Words

Sometimes two words are fused together to form an incorrect compound word.

Example 1. Incorrect: some people say that highschool is the best time of your life.

Correct: Some people say that high school is the best time of your life.

2. Incorrect: I like to play soccer alot.
Correct: I like to play soccer a lot.

Duplicate Words

Sometimes one may write the same word twice because of thinking faster than one writes or types.

Example:

Incorrect: Sally's older sister can may help her pay for the college.

Correct: Sally's older sister can help her pay for college. (Means sister is able to help Sally)

Correct: Sally's older sister may help her pay for college. (Means sister might decide to help)

Section Titles

Section titles for an article should say exactly and succinctly what the reader will get out of that section. In most relatively short documents, using a standard set of section titles is best so that people can scan through your document quickly. Section standards vary in different fields, but a common set is Introduction, Background, Methods (for an experimental paper) or Architecture (for a modelling paper), Discussion, Future Work (often merged with Discussion), and Conclusion.

2.5.4 Word-level Issues

Try Hard to Avoid Ambiguous References

Conversations are replete with ambiguous words such as 'this', 'these', 'his', 'it', 'they', and so on. These words have no meaning in themselves, but in conversation the meaning is usually clear from the context. In written text, however, the intended meaning is quite often not evident to the reader, because there are and can be many possible interpretations of 'it' and 'this'.

For example, for the word 'he', were there two or three people being discussed? If so then state the actual name of each; 'he' would be ambiguous.

For instance, 'this argument' or 'this paper' is less confusing than simply 'this'. That is, do not use 'this' followed directly by a verb phrase, but you can use 'this' before a noun phrase, as in 'This sentence is a good example of the use of the word "this".'

Watch Out for Homonyms

Spellcheckers are wonderful, but they are absolutely useless for detecting misused homonyms or near-homonyms, that is, actual words whose meaning is confused with other actual words. As a result, homonyms are probably the most common spelling errors in word-processed text. Even if you are lazy and let the spellchecker fix all of your other words, make certain that you know the differences between words like:

- it's, its
- their, there, they're
- whether, weather
- to, too, two
- site, cite, sight
- waste, waist
- whole, hole
- fare, fair
- great, grate
- affect, effect
- discrete, discreet
- forth, fourth
- past, passed
- roll, role
- lead, led
- lie, lye
- throughout, through out
- seem, seam
- new, knew
- illicit, elicit
- complement, compliment
- extent, extend
- obtain, attain
- pair, pare
- personal, personnel
- suit, suite
- principal, principle
- bear, bare

If you do not know the difference, you must simply avoid using any of these words. Yet because the spellchecker takes care of all the other words you may misspell, learning to use these few words correctly is surely not much of a burden, and is crucial for convincing your readers that you are competent and trustworthy.

Avoid 'Comprise'

Apparently, the word 'comprise' has now been used incorrectly so many times to mean 'compose' that this usage is now becoming acceptable. But it is much safer simply to avoid 'comprise' altogether, as anyone who does know what it started out meaning will be annoyed when you use it to mean 'compose'.

'But' and 'However' Are Not Interchangeable

The words 'but' and 'however' have similar meanings, but they are not interchangeable. If you take a grammatically correct sentence containing 'but' and replace it with 'however', or vice versa, the result will almost always be incorrect, mainly because of comma punctuation.

Correct Examples:
'I like oranges, but I do not like tangerines.'
'I like oranges. However, I do not like tangerines.'
'I like oranges; however, I do not like tangerines.'
'I, however, do not like grapefruits.'
'I like oranges however they have been prepared.'

If you exchange any of these 'but's and 'however's, then the sentences would become incorrect, and in some cases meaningless.

A 'Point' Is a Single Item

The word 'point' can only be used for a single, atomic item. Thus it is not appropriate to discuss a 'subpoint', 'part of a point', the 'first half' of a point, and so on. Instead use 'topic' or 'section' and the like.

'A Research'

There is no noun phrase 'a research' in English. Use 'a study' or just 'research', never 'a research'.

Avoid Capitalization

When in doubt, use lower case. Capitalization is appropriate only for specific, named, individual items or people. For example, capitalize school subjects only when you are referring to a specific course at a specific school: math is a general subject, but Math 301 is a particular course. Similarly, Department of Computer Sciences vs. a computer science department, the president vs. President Bush. *When in doubt, use lower case.*

Avoid Contractions

Contractions are appropriate only for conversational use and for informal writing, *never* for technical or formal writing.

2.5.5 Additional Guidelines Specific to Academic Writing

Academic writing includes texts such as original research papers, research proposals, and literature reviews, whether published or not.

Formatting and Grammar Rules

When in doubt about grammar or page format, researchers in psychology and computer science generally follow the APA Style guide; biological fields use similar standards. Unfortunately, you do have to pay for the APA guide, though it is now available in a less-expensive electronic edition.

Pay Attention to How Your Document Looks

Use readable, clear fonts and reasonable margins, following the typical format used for similar documents.

If the word processor cannot make the spacing regular between words (e.g., most versions of Microsoft Word), turn off right justification. Poor spacing makes the page look jumbled and seem incoherent, even if the writing is not.

Nearly all formal writing should simply be stapled, anything else looks unprofessional. For instance, using a fancy cover and binding for a short paper or report is distracting and makes it difficult to photocopy the paper; such binding is necessary only for long papers that a staple would have trouble keeping together. At the opposite extreme, it should be obvious that folding one corner is not an acceptable substitute for a staple.

Authors Are Authors, Not Writers

The people who perform a scientific study are called 'authors', never writers, even though the results are presented in a written paper. Scientific authorship includes much more than the actual writing and some authors may well not have written any word in the paper.

Use Last Names

Never refer to the authors by their first names, as if they were your friends. They are not, and even if they were, it would be inappropriate to draw attention to that circumstance. Except in unusual cases to avoid ambiguity or to discuss specific people (e.g., the original founders of a field of research), first names are not even mentioned in the body of a scientific text; the last names are sufficient.

Author Names Are Keys, Spell Them Properly

In academic writing, an author's last name is like the key in a database lookup, if the name is misspelt (e.g., 'Davis' for 'Davies'), your reader will not be able to locate works by that author in the library or online. Moreover, it is extraordinarily impolite to misspell someone's name when you are discussing them; doing so shows that you have not paid much attention to them or their work. So you should make a special effort to spell author names correctly, double and triple checking them against the original source, and ensuring that you spell them the same way each time.

Use Appropriate Pronouns

Use appropriate pronouns when referring to the authors. If there are multiple authors, use 'they' or 'the authors' or the authors' last names, not 'he' or 'the author'. If there is only one author and you can determine the gender with great confidence, you may use 'he' or 'she'; otherwise use 'the author' or the author's last name.

Referring to Other Texts

Use double quotes around the title of an article when you refer to it in the text. Italics are reserved for books or other works of similar length. Avoid underlining altogether—underlining is just a way of indicating that handwritten or typewritten text should be typeset in italics, and is thus inappropriate when italics are available (as they are on any modern word processor).

Be Very Precise When Discussing an Author Discussing Another Author

For better or worse, academic writing often devolves into discussions of what one author said about another author. If commenting on such controversies, you should be extremely careful about using ambiguous terms such as 'his', 'the author', and so on. Very often your reader will have no idea which of the various authors you are referring to, even though it may be clear to you. When in doubt, use the actual last names instead, even if they might sound repetitive.

Avoid Footnotes

Footnotes should be used quite sparingly, and should never be used as a way to avoid the hard work of making your text flow into a coherent narrative. Only when something genuinely cannot be made to fit into the main flow of the text, yet is somehow still so important that it must be mentioned, does it go into a footnote.

Avoid Direct Quotes

In scientific (as opposed to literary or historical) writing, direct quotes should be used only when the precise wording of the original sentences is important, for example, if the work is so ground-breaking that the words themselves have driven research in this field. In nearly every other case, paraphrasing is more appropriate, because it lets you formulate the idea in the terms suitable for your particular paper, focusing on the underlying issue rather than the way one author expressed it.

Discussion/Future Work

In the discussion sections of a research paper, be sure to discuss all topics that the audience expected to see in the paper, even if you yourself do not believe them to be relevant. The reader is more likely to assume that you have been sloppy about your literature review than to assume you knew about the work but believed it not to be relevant. Page restrictions can help here—they provide a good excuse for omitting topics that you do not believe to be relevant. In a longer article or thesis without page limits you have no choice but to address the issue and explicitly state why the topic is not relevant despite the common belief that it is.

Bibliographies

In particular, every bibliography entry needs an author, date, and title; every journal article absolutely must have a volume number and page numbers; and every conference paper must have the title of the conference proceedings, the page numbers, and some indication of who published it.

Citations

The bibliography or reference list in an academic paper must consist of precisely those sources that you cite in the text, without any extra sources and without omitting any. Each citation must provide enough information for the reader to find the correct source in the bibliography.

2.5.6 Techniques for Paragraph Development

1. **Illustration**
   It provides examples to explain the main idea.

2. **Comparison and contrast**
   These bring out similarities and differences to develop the idea.
3. **Cause and effect**
   These refer to explaining the reasons for the end result.
4. **Classification**
   It refers to breaking the main idea into specific categories.
5. **Problem and solution**
   These refer to discussing the solutions to the problem posed.

Paragraph development is an organic process that makes intricate links between various ideas. These links, ultimately, create one single idea, a discussion of how it works, the explanation shown as an example and reiterate the final idea for better comprehension.

2.6 TECHNIQUES FOR WRITING PRECISELY

Precision refers to writing clearly and concisely choosing the words deliberately, constructing the sentences carefully, and using grammar properly. Writing clearly and concisely is one way to capture and retain reader's interest. Rambling on, conversely, may lose audience's attention. Several techniques can help to learn and write precisely for effective communication.

2.6.1 Choose Simple Words

Simplicity is the hallmark of good communication. It refers to ease of understanding. The words one chooses can either enhance or interfere with one's meaning and audience's comprehension. Choose the most effective words and have a clear insight into the structure of sentences and paragraphs.

Use simple words

Elaborate word	*Simple word*
ascertain	find out
commence	begin
constitute	make up
fabricate	build
initiate	begin
terminate	end
transmit	send
utilize	use

If the entire audience will understand technical terms, use them. If not, either substitute with simple terms instead, or if there are no substitutes, explain the meaning of the technical term using one of these methods:

- ***Use a synonym:*** 'memory' instead of 'RAM'.
- ***Describe the term:*** 'RAM allows your computer to run more quickly and efficiently.'
- ***Compare the term with a common concept:*** 'RAM is like having a large desk with numerous drawers for storage. You can quickly and efficiently access your files at a moment's notice.'
- ***Define the term:*** 'RAM, or random access memory, is one type of computer data storage systems. It allows your computer to quickly and efficiently access files.'

2.6.2 Replace Vague Words with Specific Ones

Vague words tend to be abstract and can conceal one's meaning. Specific words, on the other hand, precisely and shortly convey clear meaning.

For instance, in describing a new product one's company is developing:

- **Vague:** The Acme Corporation is developing *a new consumer device that allows users to communicate vocally in real time.*
- **Specific:** The Acme Corporation is developing *a new cell phone.*

Readers may not immediately understand what the first sentence describes. Is this a brand new kind of device? Or a device they've never heard of? The second sentence, on the other hand, says exactly what the product is, leaving little room for doubt.

2.6.3 Eliminate Unnecessary Words

Unnecessary words come in many forms. Like vague words, they can conceal instead of revealing the meaning.

- ***Excessive detail***
  - **Before:** I received and read the email *you sent yesterday* about the report *you're writing for* the project. I agree it needs *a thorough, close* edit *from someone familiar with your audience.*
  - **After:** I received your email about the project report and agree it needs an expert edit.
- ***Extra determiners and modifiers***
  - **Before:** *Basically,* the first widget *pretty much* surpassed the second one in *overall* performance.
  - **After:** The first widget performed better than the second.

- ***Repetitive words***
  - **Before:** The engineer considered the second monitor an *unneeded luxury.*
  - **After:** The engineer considered the second monitor a luxury.
- ***Redundant words***
  - **Before:** The test revealed conduction activity that was *peculiar in nature.*
  - **After:** The test revealed peculiar conduction activity.

2.6.4 Replace Multiple Negatives with Affirmatives

Multiple negatives require the readers to interpret the meaning conveyed. Affirmatives, instead, convey concise meaning that needs no interpretation.

- **Before:** Your audience *will not appreciate* the *details that lack relevance.*
- **After:** Your audience will appreciate relevant details.

2.6.5 Avoid Noun Strings

Noun strings can confuse readers, as they are difficult to understand.

- **Before:** The Acme Corporation continues to work on the *cell phone case configuration revision project.*
- **After:** The Acme Corporation is developing a redesigned cell phone case.

Sentences express and connect the meaning of one's ideas. Follow these guidelines to write clear and concise sentences for the audience to comprehend quickly and easily to bring about precision.

2.6.6 Pay Attention to Sentence Length

Use short sentences to emphasize a point; use longer sentences to connect ideas.

Example: 1. This report provides operational information about the electrical equipment the Acme Corporation recently installed at their headquarters in Los Angeles (*long sentence*).

2. The equipment will increase energy efficiency by 25 per cent (*short sentence*).

2.6.7 Use the Known-New Contract

The known-new contract refers to a sentence that will have known, or old, information as well as new and that the known information will precede the new. This contract allows users to easily connect what they already know to the new information.

- **Before:** Support higher data rates for non-voice communication (*new information*) with third-generation (3G) cell phone technology (*known information*).
- **After:** Third-generation (3G) cell phone technology (*known information*) supports higher data rates for non-voice communications (*new information*).

2.6.8 Use the Appropriate Voice

In the active voice, the subject performs the action of the verb. The focus of an active sentence is the subject:

Example: Gary (subject) threw (verb) the ball (object).
In the passive voice, the subject receives the action of the verb. The focus of a passive sentence is the action:

Example: The ball (object) was thrown (verb) by Gary (subject).
Each type of voice has its place in writing precisely. Use active voice by default; research shows readers comprehend it more quickly than passive voice. But use passive voice when

- The action is more important than the subject, such as when you're describing research or testing done: *Example:* The results generated from the test were telling.
- The subject is unknown.
  Example: Every year, hundreds of people are diagnosed with hearing problems caused by excessive cell phone use. *Or*
- In some contexts, identifying the subject would cause unnecessary embarrassment. Try to avoid.
  Example: The lights in the lab were left on for three nights in a row and the bulb burnt out as a result.

However, don't use passive voice to conceal serious responsibility:
Example: Mistakes *were made* that delayed the testing for weeks.

Use active voice instead:
Example: The team *made* mistakes that delayed the testing for weeks.

2.6.9 Use Transitions

Transitions are words and phrases that indicate connections between sentences. Use them at the beginning of sentences to connect ideas by:

- time: before, after, during, while, until
- space: above, below, inside
- cause and effect: as a result, because, since
- similarity: as, likewise, similarly
- contrast: although, however, on the other hand

2.6.10 Monitor Nominalizations

Nominalizations occur when a verb is used as a noun:

- occur—occurrence
- evaluate—evaluation
- execute—execution

Nominalizations work well as sentence transitions.

- Electrical signals *occur* naturally between devices. These *occurrences* happen only when the device is turned on.

However, nominalizations should be avoided when they hide the action of a sentence:

- **Before:** Employee achievement led to the *creation* of the Engineer of the Year award.
- **After:** The Acme Corporation *created* the Engineer of the Year award to recognize employee achievement.

2.6.11 Avoid Using Forms of the Verb 'Be'

Forms of the verb 'be' (is, am, are, were, was) indicate a state of being rather than an action. They can weaken an active sentence and, in some instances, may indicate passive voice. Use active verbs instead whenever possible.

- **Before:** The report *is waiting* for your approval.
- **After:** The report *awaits* your approval.

2.6.12 Reduce Prepositional Phrases

Prepositional phrases help establish relationships between people and things in a sentence:

- Frank drove his car *to work*.
- The lab closes *at 7:00* PM.
- Joy had to revise her presentation *for the conference*.

Unnecessary use of prepositional phrases interferes with the clarity of a sentence.

- **Before:** The opinion of the manager.
- **After:** The manager's opinion.
- **Before:** It is a matter *of* the gravest importance *to* the health *of* anyone who uses a microwave and has a heart condition to avoid standing *in front of* the microwave *while* it is running.
- **After:** Anyone *with* a heart condition should avoid standing *in front of* an operating microwave oven.

2.6.13 Revise Your Sentences Using the Paramedic Method

Use this popular method to make your writing precise. The first step is to concretely identify problems in the sentences:

- Underline prepositions (of, about, to, in, across, and the like).
- Circle forms of the verb 'be' (is, am, are, were, was).
- Put boxes around action words (verbs such as test, result, change, and the like; as well as nominalizations such as testing, resulting, changing, and the like).
- Highlight the person or thing performing the action.
- Bracket wind-up explanations.
- Cross out redundancies.

The next step is to revise the problem areas identified:

- Rewrite or delete unnecessary prepositional phrases.
- Replace forms of 'be' with action verbs.
- Put the action in the verb.
- Put the person or thing performing the action into the subject.
- Delete unnecessary wind-up explanations.
- Eliminate redundancies.

PRACTICE EXERCISE S

Put the following sentences in the correct order in order to produce well-organized paragraphs.

Paragraph 1

a. For a lightweight poster or sign, you can use either offset book stock or cover stock.
b. You'll probably have to take your publication to a commercial printer, however, since bristol won't feed through most desktop printers or copy machines.
c. The type of paper you choose for a poster or a sign depends on how it will be reproduced and how it is going to be used.
d. If you need to create a more durable poster or sign, or create packaging, bristol stock is your best choice.

Paragraph 2

a. It's rare, but not unheard of, for mail to go astray.
b. And many corporate mail servers have had growing pains too, experiencing holdups and the odd deletion.
c. On the whole though, you can assume e-mail will arrive.
d. However, during 1997, AOL and Microsoft Network—to name just the big players—had severe mail outages resulting in the delay, and in some cases loss, of e-mail.
e. In general, Internet e-mail is considerably more reliable than the postal service.

Paragraph 3

a. Time may indicate the importance of the occasion as well as on what level an interaction between persons is to take place.
b. The same applies for calls after 11:00 PM.
c. Different parts of the day, for example, are highly significant in certain contexts.
d. Our realization that time talks is even reflected in such common expressions as, 'What time does the clock say?'
e. In the United States, if you telephone someone very early in the morning, while he is shaving or having breakfast, the time of the call usually signals a matter of utmost importance and extreme urgency.
f. A call received during sleeping hours is apt to be taken as a matter of life and death, hence the rude joke value of these calls among the young.

PRACTICE EXERCISE T

Write the topic sentences for each of the following paragraphs.

Paragraph 1

First, they live in or on a host, and do it harm. The depth to which they penetrate the host varies as indeed does the damage. Fleas, leeches, and lice live on the surface and cause superficial injury. Athlete's foot is a skin disease caused by a fungus living in the surface layers of the foot. The parasite of sleeping sickness is found in the host's blood wriggling between blood corpuscles. Second, parasites show some simplification of body structures when compared with free-living relatives. Sacculina (a relative of the crab) shows loss of limbs and is reduced to a mass of reproductive tissue within the abdomen of its crustacean host. Dodder, a plant parasite, lacks leaves, roots, and chlorophyll. Third, although all organisms show adaptations to their way of life, in the case of parasites, they are often associated with a complex physiological response, for example, the ability to survive in regions almost devoid of available oxygen, such as adult liver flukes, or the hooks and suckers of adult tapeworm. Finally, parasites exhibit a complex and efficient reproduction, usually associated in some way with the physiology of the host, for example, rabbit fleas are stimulated by the level of sex hormone in their host.

Paragraph 2

In 1920 an average of 2.75 pounds of waste were produced each day by each individual in the United States. Today the quantity of waste produced is 53 pounds per person, and by 1980 it is estimated that this will rise to 8 pounds per person. One year's rubbish from 10,000 people covers an acre of ground to the depth of 10 feet. In one year Americans throw away 48,000 million cans, 26,000 million bottles, 430 million tons of paper, 4 million tons of plastic, and 100 million tyres, all of which together weigh almost a million tons.

Paragraph 3

That it might be experienced in any other way seems unnatural and strange, a feeling which is rarely modified even when we begin to discover how really differently it is handled by some other people. Within the West itself, certain cultures rank time much lower in overall importance than we do. In Latin America, for example, where time is treated rather cavalierly, one commonly hears the expression, 'Our time or your time?' '*Hora americana, hora mejicana?*'

PRACTICE EXERCISE U

Punctuate the connecting words in Paragraphs 1 and 2:

Paragraph 1

Although new technology creates new kinds of jobs it also usually makes many existing jobs disappear for example when trains started to be used as a primary form of transportation many jobs that depended on horses and oxen started to disappear later automobiles became the major form of transportation as a result railroad companies could no longer keep as many people employed another new kind of technology that is leading to job loss is the digital camera companies that make film are laying off workers because so many consumers are switching from cameras that use film to cameras that take digital photographs in the same way cell phones make public pay phones less profitable so telephone companies no longer need to employ as many technicians to install and maintain pay phones while it is true that technological change can produce new wealth and new jobs new inventions also tend to lead to the loss of jobs

Paragraph 2

Mark loves to travel but Amy doesn't so they often argue about where to spend their vacation time one summer they decided to try something different Mark went to Thailand but Amy stayed home Mark's brother, Alex, and sister-in-law, Jennifer, went with him they knew that they could only spend one week in Thailand so they had to decide what to do they could all go scuba diving in Southern Thailand or Mark could go by himself on an elephant trek in Northern Thailand and Alex and Jennifer could meet him later in Bangkok Mark chose the elephant trek and he had an exciting time Amy was also having a good time back home sometimes she went out with her friends at night and sometimes her mother would visit her during the day she also liked to spend time by herself practising her piano Mark and Amy learned that they could spent their vacations separately yet they both could have a good time

Paragraph 3

Complete the story choosing the words in brackets in right order:

Kamala lived ________________ (in the heart of the city/in a small flat/alone/ in Lawrence Enclave). She liked the neighbourhood _____________ and had been living ____________ (ever since she came to work in the city/there/very much/two years ago). She ____________ missed her parents, brother, and sister ____________ for she __________ went home ________________________ (every three or four months/usually/only/a lot/sometimes). Kamala worked ___________, but she relaxed ______________ and went out with her friends ________________ (from Monday to Friday/completely/at weekends/hard). One night, when she was reading ____________________, she heard someone knocking ________________on her door (after dinner/urgently/quietly/in her bedroom). Kamala ignored the knocking ________________, but it __________ became ________ louder (much/for a while/soon). She tiptoed ______________ to the door and looked ______________ the peephole (fearfully/noiselessly). There was no one outside! But ___________ as Kamala turned back ______________ her bedroom, the knocking started ______________ (towards/just/again/with a sense of relief). Not able to bear it ____________, She opened the door _____________ and ran out into the corridor, screaming (loudly/angrily/any longer). Kamala stopped ______________ when she saw, ________________________, her family standing ________________, laughing ____________________ (much to her surprise/suddenly/uncontrollably/near the staircase).

PRACTICE EXERCISE V

Fill in the blanks choosing the correct phrasal verbs in the brackets:

1. The boy felt __________ when none of his friends went to watch him play. (let up/let down/let in)
2. The people _____________ bravely during the famine. (carried out/carried on/carried away)
3. He has ________________ a wonderful idea for the picnic. (come into/come by/come up with)
4. Rishi is __________________ a bad time in office. (going through/going about/going into)
5. The children ______________ very well with each other. (get through/get on/get by)
6. She had no appetite and ______________________ the food on her plate. (picked at/picked on/picked up)
7. Admissions will __________ through the week. (go on/go about/go in)
8. A man came _____________ you. (asking about/asking for/asking of)
9. I hope we don't have to ___________ the trip. (call for/call off/call back)
10. I ______________ regularly to keep myself fit. (work in/work out/work at)
11. I would like to have coffee ___________ tea. (instead of/instead from/instead for)
12. _______________ the rains, we went out. (In spite of/Despite of/In spite)
13. ____________ fire, break glass to escape. (In case/In case of/In case with)
14. I am standing here _____________ my friends. (in behalf of/on behalf of/behalf of)
15. ______________, I had a happy childhood. (On the whole/In the whole/By the whole)

FURTHER READING

1. Goldstein, Barbara, Jack Waugh, and Karen Linsky. *Grammar to Go: How It Works and How to Use It*, 4th ed. Boston, MA: Wadsworth Publishing, 2013.
2. Strumpf, Michael, and Auriel Douglas. *The Grammar Bible: Everything You Always Wanted to Know About Grammar but Didn't Know Whom to Ask*. New York: Henry Holt & CO., 2004.
3. Simon, Paul. 'The Big Bright Green Pleasure Machine'. In Simon & Garfunkel album *Parsley, Sage, Rosemary and Thyme*. United States: Columbia Records, 1966.
4. Jerome, Jerome K. *The Idler*. London: Chatto & Windus, 1892.
5. Ellen Griswold in the movie *Vacation* (1983).
6. Habgood, J. S. *The Observer*, 4 May 1986.
7. Ballard, Kim. *The Frameworks of English: Introducing Language Structures*, 3rd ed. Houndmills: Palgrave Macmillan, 2012.
8. Biber, Douglas, Susan Conrad, and Geoffrey Leech. *Longman Student Grammar of Spoken and Written English*. London: Longman, 2002.
9. https://simple.wikipedia.org/wiki/Phrase (accessed on 19 September 2018)
10. www.alifseye.com/tutorials/single/10 (accessed on 19 September 2018)
11. www.linguisticsgirl.com/grammatical-functions-of-english-adjective-clauses/ (accessed on 19 September 2018)
12. https://nwaokebest.wordpress.com/2016/11/.../clauses-and-their-grammatical-function (accessed on 19 September 2018)
13. Brinton, Laurel J., and Donna M. Brinton. *The Linguistic Structure of Modern English*, 2nd ed. Amsterdam: John Benjamins Publishing Company, 2010.
14. Hopper, Paul J. *A Short Course in Grammar*. New York: W. W. Norton & Company, 1999.
15. Huddleston, Rodney. *Introduction to the Grammar of English*. New York: Cambridge University Press, 1984.
16. web.mnstate.edu/houtsli/tesl654/complex/adjective1.htm (accessed on 19 September 2018)
17. https://www.englishgrammar.org › Lessons (accessed on 19 September 2018)
18. https://www.lessonenglishgrammar.com › Knowledge Base › Solved Exercises (accessed on 19 September 2018)
19. https://www.lessonenglishgrammar.com › ... › Sentence Formation (accessed on 19 September 2018)
20. https://thewritecorner.wordpress.com/2009/11/14/the-importance-of-punctuation/ (accessed on 19 September 2018)
21. trio-solutions.com/the-importance-of-correct-punctuation/ (accessed on 19 September 2018)
22. https://www.grammarbook.com/punctuation_rules.asp (accessed on 19 September 2018)
23. https://www.englishgrammar.org › Punctuation (accessed on 19 September 2018)
24. https://www.englishpractice.com/punctuation/punctuation-exercise-2/ (accessed on 19 September 2018)
25. https://study.com/academy/lesson/coherence-in-writing-definition-examples.html (accessed on 19 September 2018)
26. https://papyr.com/hypertextbooks/comp1/coherent.htm (accessed on 19 September 2018)

27. https://writing.colostate.edu/guides/teaching/rhet-terms/pop3d.cfm (accessed on 19 September 2018)
28. https://access-socialstudies.cappelendamm.no/c365244/artikkel/vis.html?tid=365334 (accessed on 19 September)
29. https://www.uwb.edu/wacc/what-we-do/eslhandbook/coherence (accessed on 19 September 2018)
30. https://homepages.inf.ed.ac.uk/jbednar/writingtips.html (accessed on 19 September 2018)
31. Anderson, P. V. *Technical Communication: A Reader-Centered Approach.* Boston, MA: Thomson Wadsworth, 2007.
32. Henriquez, J. '10 Common User Questions—and Some Analogies That Help Clear Things Up'. *TechRepublic* [Online]. http://www.techrepublic.com/blog/10things/10-common-user-questions-and-some-analogies-that-help-clear-things-up/1261 (accessed on 19 September 2018)
33. Random access memory. *Wikipedia* [Online]. http://en.wikipedia.org/wiki/Random-access_memory (accessed on 19 September 2018)
34. Weber, R., and N. Hurm. 'Eliminating Words'. *Purdue Online Writing Lab* [Online]. http://owl.english.purdue.edu/owl/resource/572/02/ (accessed on)
35. Kolln, M., and L. Gray. *Rhetorical Grammar: Grammatical Choices, Rhetorical Effects.* Boston, MA: Pearson Education, 2010.
36. *Microsoft Publisher CD Deluxe Companion,* p. 185.
37. *The Internet and World Wide Web: The Rough Guide*, (1997), p. 15.
38. Edward Hall, (1973), *The Silent Language*, p. 2.
39. J. Hard, (1975). *Biology*, p. 57.
40. Klotz, John W. *Ecology Crisis: God's Creation & Man's Pollution*, 197. London: Concordia Press, 1972.
41. Hall, Edward. *The Silent Language*, 6. New York: Doubleday & Co., 1966
42. https://www.tacoma.uw.edu/sites/default/.../accs_Punctuation%20Chart_rev2016.pdf (accessed on 19 September 2018)
43. Azar, B. *Understanding and Using English Grammar*, 3rd ed. Toronto: Prentice Hall Regents. Chapters 16, 17, 19. Benson, B. and Byrd, P. (1989).
44. *Improving the Grammar of Written English: The Editing Process*, 49–74. Boston, MA: Heinle and Heinle.

3
UNIT

Identifying Common Errors in Writing

3.1 SUBJECT–VERB AGREEMENT

3.1.1 Verbs

A verb expresses what the subject of a sentence is, does, has, or what is done to it.

Examples:

1. He <u>is</u> a capable teacher.
2. She <u>has taught</u> the subject for 10 years.

Types of Verbs

1. Main verb   2. Auxiliary verb

A main verb is an action word which describes an action or movement. It is the important word in a sentence which gives a complete sense. These verbs can stand on their own in sentences. Main verbs are also called lexical verbs.

Examples:

The sun <u>rises</u> in the east.
She <u>sings</u> a song.
He <u>reads</u> a book.

A main verb usually has five forms:
For instance, let us take the verb 'speak'.

1. Base form: Speak
2. •S–es form: Speaks
3. Past form: Spoke
4. Past participle form: Spoken
5. Present participle form: Speaking

An auxiliary verb determines the mood, tense, voice, or aspect of another verb. Auxiliary verbs are also called helping verbs. They help the main verb in making a sentence negative and interrogative.

Auxiliary verbs are divided into two types:

Primary Auxiliaries
BE: am, is, are, were, was, been, being

HAVE: has, had, having
Do: does, did, done, doing

Modal Auxiliaries
will, shall, can, may, would, should, might, could, ought, must
daren't, needn't, used to

Verbs can be classified as
1. Finites 2. Non-finites

A finite verb is a verb that denotes tense and it is also limited by number or a person.

Examples:
He <u>goes</u> to school.
She <u>went</u> to market.

Non-finites are verb forms which do not give complete meaning. They have none of the tenses, have no number, and take no modals or auxiliary verbs. These are in turn divided into four types, namely:

1. Infinitive
2. Gerund
3. Present participle
4. Past participle

Examples:
She wants <u>to buy</u> a new car. (Infinitive)
<u>Buying</u> a new car needs money. (Gerund)
I found her <u>looking</u> for a new car. (Present participle)

Wounded in the car, she was brought to the medical hospital. (Past participle)

The infinitive has the following structures:

1. To + verb
2. To be + verb-ing (present participle)
3. To have + past participle
4. To have + past participle of *be* + verb-ing

Examples:
She wanted to learn music.
She is reported to be learning it.
She is reported to have learnt music already.
She is known to have been learning music for the past five years.

Use of Verbs

The verb must agree with its subject in number and person.

1. **When two subjects are joined by 'and', the verb is plural.**

   Examples:
   My friend and his father are in India.
   Sita and Geetha are reading.
   My brother and sister are arriving from London.
   Ram and Shyam are pursuing research on environmental pollution.

2. **When two singular nouns joined by 'and' refer to the same person or thing, the verb is singular.**

   Examples:
   The secretary and treasurer has been arrested.
   The district magistrate and collector is on leave today.
   The poet and artist is invited to the function.
   The academic and politician is establishing a new institute.
   The beggar and the criminal is imprisoned.

3. **If two different singular nouns express one idea, the verb should be in the singular form.**

   Examples:
   Bread and milk is good for breakfast.
   Rice and curry is my favourite dish.
   This is the long and the short of the matter.
   This is the beginning and ending of the drama.
   This is the length and breadth of the house.

4. **When two singular subjects are practically synonymous, the verb should be in the singular form**

   Examples:
   The law and order situation in the state is under control.
   His power and influence is on the decline.
   Power and position has no charm for my friend.
   Peace and prosperity is the need of the day.
   Intelligence and hard work is the key to success.

5. **When two singular subjects are preceded by 'each' or 'each and every' joined by 'and', the verb should be in the singular form.**

   Examples:
   Every boy and girl was present in the class yesterday.
   Every man and woman has the right to express his or her view.
   I am reading each and every book in the library.
   Each and every soldier is marching ahead.
   Each and every person has the right to fight for his rights.

6. **When the subjects joined by 'either-or' or 'neither-nor' are of different persons, the verb will agree in person and number with the noun nearest to it and the plural subject must be placed nearest to the verb.**

   Examples:
   Either Sheetu or Neetu has done this mischief.

   Neither Mohini nor Ragini is beautiful.

   Either the Chief Minister or the Cabinet Ministers are responsible for the problem.

   Neither you nor he is to take up this task.

   Either you or I am responsible for this mistake.

7. **When 'not only...but also' is used to combine two subjects, the verb should agree with the subject close to it.**

   Examples:
   Not only Harish but also his brothers were arrested.
   I drink not only milk but also tea.
   He not only speaks but also writes efficiently.
   I not only accept but also approve the proposal.

8. **'None' can take either a singular or a plural verb depending on the noun which follows it.**
   Note: In recent years, the SAT testing service has considered 'none' to be strictly singular. When 'none' is clearly intended to mean 'not one', it is followed by a singular verb.

Examples:
None of the counterfeit money has been found.
None of the students have finished the exam.
None of the rules have been implemented.
None of them were present.
None of the things belong to me.

9. **When the percentage or a part of something is mentioned with plural meaning, the plural verb is used.**

Examples:
30 per cent of the Indian women are literate.

Three quarters of the food has been eaten (reference of the food is as a whole).

Half of the students are more intelligent.

50 per cent of verbal communication accounts for listening.

90 per cent of the students are seeking admission in engineering colleges.

10. **When the expressions 'a lot of', 'a great deal of', 'plenty of', 'most of', and 'some of' refer to number, a plural verb is used. If the same expressions refer to an amount, the verb is in the singular number.**

Examples:
A lot of people were present in the gallery.
Some of the students were absent.
Most of the people are interested in politics.
A lot of work has to be completed before we go.
A great deal of work has been finished.

11. **When the word 'enemy' is used in the sense 'armed forces' of a nation with which one's country is at war, we have to use the plural verb.**

Examples:
The enemy were ready to fight.
The enemy are marching ahead in their encampments.
The army are being trained.

12. **In sports, while referring to the players, the name of the country is followed by plural verb.**

Examples:
England have won the World Cup.
India have won the tournament.
Pakistan have got defeated.

13. **Collective nouns indicating time, money, and measurements used as a whole are singular and take a singular verb.**

    Examples:
    Twenty-five rupees is not such a big amount for him.
    Two miles is too much for this man to run.
    Five metres of cloth is enough.
    Ten hours of study is necessary to be successful.

14. **'Doesn't' is a contraction of 'does not' and should be used only with a singular subject. 'Don't' is a contraction of 'do not' and should be used only with a plural subject.**

    Examples:
    He doesn't like it.
    They don't like it.

15. **If two infinitives are separated by 'and' they take the plural form of the verb.**

    Examples:
    To walk and to chew gum require great skill.
    To love and to be loved seem to be two sides of the same coin.

16. **Indefinite pronouns (someone, somebody, each, either one, everyone, or anyone) are considered singular and need singular verbs, although they convey plural meaning.**

    Examples:
    Anyone who wants to pursue higher education has to pass entrance exams.

    Everyone on the committee is welcome to express his/her ideas.

17. **If subjects are joined by 'or' or 'nor', the verb should agree with the closer subject.**

    Examples:
    Either the actors or the director is at fault.
    Either the director or the actors are at fault.

18. **A linking verb usually agrees with its subject, not with its complement.**

    Examples:
    Excessive *absences were* the reason for his failure.
    The reason of his *failure was* excessive absences.

19. **In sentences beginning with 'here' or 'there', the true subject follows the verb.**

Examples:
There are four hurdles to jump.
There is a high hurdle to jump.
Here are the keys.

20. The word 'were' replaces 'was' in sentences that express a wish or are contrary to fact:

Examples:
I wish it *were* Friday.
She requested that he *raise* his hand.

PRACTICE EXERCISE A

Fill in the blanks with a verb in agreement with its subject:

1. No news _______ good news.
2. He ______ read the whole of the book.
3. You as well as he _______ to blame.
4. The jury ______ divided in their opinions.
5. Each of the girls _______ to get a prize.
6. A black and a white cow _________ grazing in the field.
7. If I _______ you I would not do this.
8. The poet and the dramatist ______ dead.
9. Four-fifths of the book ______ been finished.
10. One of them ______made this mischief.

PRACTICE EXERCISE B

Correct the sentences where necessary:

1. Measles have broken out in the town.
2. The *Arabian Nights* are an interesting book.
3. The cost of all essential commodities have gone up.
4. Five miles are not a long distance for me to walk.
5. A pious man and a good neighbour have died.
6. Bread and milk are my only food for today.
7. The notorious dacoit with his followers have escaped.
8. The construction of these buildings have taken four years.
9. There is a bunch of keys on the table.
10. Sanjay as well as his brothers has gone home.

PRACTICE EXERCISE C

Choose the correct form of the verb that agrees with the subject:

1. Annie and her brothers (is/are) at school.
2. Either my mother or my father (is/are) coming to the meeting.
3. The dog or the cats (is/are) outside.
4. Either my shoes or your coat (is/are) always on the floor.
5. George and Tamara (doesn't/don't) want to see that movie.
6. Benito (doesn't/don't) know the answer.
7. One of my sisters (is/are) going on a trip to France.
8. The man with all the birds (live/lives) on my street.
9. The movie, including all the previews, (take/takes) about two hours to watch.
10. The players, as well as the captain, (want/wants) to win.
11. Either answer (is/are) acceptable.
12. Every one of those books (is/are) fiction.
13. Nobody (know/knows) the trouble I've seen.
14. (Is/Are) the news on at 5:00 or 6:00?
15. Mathematics (is/are) John's favourite subject, while civics (is/are) Andrea's favourite subject.
16. Eight dollars (is/are) the price of a movie these days.
17. (Is/Are) the tweezers in this drawer?
18. Your pants (is/are) at the cleaner's.
19. There (was/were) 15 candies in that bag. Now there (is/are) only one left!
20 The committee (debates/debate) these questions carefully.
21. We (is/are) going to go to the movies today after school.
22. Some of the boxes (was/were) opened and thrown in the trash.
23. Nobody near the trees (likes/like) the new game that they are playing.
24. Tilda (seems/seem) to think that Tom was not at home.
25. Few of the apples (is/are) still hanging on the tree.
26. I (disagree/disagrees) with the attitude of the author towards this new technology, 'the self-driving system'.
27. The best way to learn philosophy (am/is/are) to reflect on oneself every day.
28. The research (am/is/are) conducted to improve the lives of adolescents.
29. Pointing (am/is/are) one piece of evidence that (indicate/indicates) the ability of possessiveness and cognition.
30. In my home country, a lot of adults always (tell/tells) children that they should have a good attitude for everything because it (am/is/are) good for their lives.

3.2 NOUN–PRONOUN AGREEMENT

3.2.1 Nouns

A noun is a naming word which refer to people, animals, places, things, or feelings.

Naming People
It could be a name of any person, for example, *John, Fatima, Singh, Michael, Tom,* and so on.

Naming Places
It could be a name of any place, for example, America, China, Church, Taj Mahal, Paris, and so on.

Naming Things
car, hat, bottle, table, chair, ball, and so on.

Naming Animals
dog, rabbit, elephant, chicken, horse, and so on

Naming Feeling/Qualities/Ideas
joy, fear, beauty, strength, anger, and so on

Nouns are divided into two main classes: *concrete* and *abstract.*

Concrete nouns are the names of persons, or things we can touch and see. They exist physically and materially. These are subdivided into four groups:

Common Noun

A name given in common to every person, place, or thing of the same class is called a common noun.

Examples:
Newton is a scientist.
Hyderabad is a big city.

Proper Noun

The name of a particular person, place, or thing is called a proper noun.

Examples:
Kalidasa was a great poet.
India is my country.

Collective Noun

It is the name of a number of persons or things taken together and spoken of as whole.

Examples:
Give me a bunch of keys.
A herd of cattle is grazing in the field.

Material Noun

All those nouns which refer to metals and materials naturally obtained are called material nouns.

Examples:
Gold is a metal.
The house is built of brick.

Abstract Nouns

These are names of things that we can only think of, but cannot touch or see. They have no physical existence. They express quality (patience, beauty), a state (youth, death), a feeling of an action (pleasure, sorrow), or a general idea or system of thought (logic, astronomy).

Examples:
Honesty is the best policy.
Childhood is the happiest stage of one's life.

Types of Common Nouns

1. **Countable Nouns:** Countable nouns are the nouns that can be counted. Common nouns and collective nouns can be included in the larger class of countable nouns.

   Examples:
   Boy, table, troop, flock, and so on

2. **Uncountable Nouns:** Uncountable nouns are the nouns that cannot be counted. The classes of nouns known as material and abstract nouns can be included in this category.

   Examples:
   1. Things which are considered in mass or quantity and not in numbers, such as sugar, sand, hair, dust, and so on
   2. Materials: wood, cloth, silver, and so on

3. Liquids: water, milk, oil, ink, honey, and so on
4. Gases: steam, mist, nitrogen, air, and so on
5. Natural phenomena: heat, cold, lightening, electricity, and so on
6. Abstract nouns: joy, sorrow, freedom, attention, childhood, and so on
7. Branches of learning: economics, politics, physics, and so on

There are some uncountable nouns which we refer to in parts. When we do so, we use them with expressions such as a piece of, a grain of, a kilo of, and the like.

Examples:
A piece of chalk, a cake of soap, a block of ice, a loaf of bread, a log of wood, and so on.

These expressions also have their plural forms, for example, pieces of chalk and cakes of soap.

Use of Nouns

1. **A proper noun becomes a common noun when it is used in the plural form, or when an article is placed before it.**

   Examples:
   There are <u>five Gandhis</u> in our college.
   Vijay Kumar is <u>the Milton</u> of our college.
   Kalidas is <u>the Shakespeare</u> of India.
   Bombay is <u>the Manchester</u> of India.
   The young boy is indeed <u>a Newton</u>.
   Samudragupta was <u>the Napoleon</u> of India.

2. **A collective noun takes a singular verb when the whole group is considered one unit.**

   Examples:
   The committee consists of five members.
   The family living next door has come from Madras.
   The Indian Army defeated the Pakistan Army.
   A crew of sailors controlled the ship.
   The mob attacked the police station.
   The jury was unanimous in its opinion.

3. **An abstract noun can also be used as a common noun by placing an article before it.**

   Examples:
   Rajni is a beauty. (a beautiful girl)
   Childhood is a care-free period.

Cowardice flees away at the sight of bravery.
Honesty is the loyalty.
The childhood of Ram was full of misery.

4. **When a material noun denotes a mass of matter, it is not used in plural form.**

   Examples:
   The house is built of brick and stone.
   Gold is precious metal.
   Milk is good for health.
   The water of this well is cool.
   The cotton growing in the field has been sprayed with insecticides.
   Honey is sweet when tasted.

5. **Some nouns have the same form for the plural as well as for the singular.**

   Examples:
   Sheep, species, deer, aircraft, offspring, yoke, spacecraft, salmon, luggage, and so on

   Examples:
   The sheep is grazing in the field.
   The offspring is crying.
   The spacecraft is reaching the earth.
   The meat of the deer is venison.
   The aircraft is flying towards the north.

6. **Some nouns are used only in the singular form.**

   Examples:
   Advice, dust, grain, justice, clothing, information, poetry, scenery, machinery, furniture, hair, and so on

   Advice is the noun form, whereas *advise* is the verb form. Similarly, *practice* is noun, whereas *practise* is verb.

   Give me a piece of advice.

   The scenery is beautiful.

   The poetry is creative.

   The hair is black in colour.

   The corn is sweet.

7. **Some nouns are always used in plural form.**

   Examples:
   Scissors, tongs, pincers, trousers, pants, bowels, genitals, riches, thanks, premises, shorts, spectacles, bellows, earnings, outskirts, intestines, pantaloons, gymnastics, biceps, doldrums, nuptials, shears, and so on

Thanks for your compliment.

Give me a pair of tongs.

Wear your spectacles.

Your trousers are torn.

Riches give us fame.

8. **Some nouns are apparently plural in form but are singular in use.**

   Examples:
   News, economics, physics, mathematics, measles, mumps, ethics, orders, and so on

   What is the news?

   Physics is an interesting subject.

   He is afflicted with measles.

   Ethics builds up personality.

   Economics is difficult to understand.

   Note: 'Summons' is singular and 'summonses' is plural.

9. **Some nouns are used in singular and plural forms.**

   Examples:
   Cattle, poultry, people, vermin, clergy, youth, folk, and so on
   The cattle are chewing the grass.
   The people have to fight for their rights.
   The youth are curious about their future.
   The folk are performing mask dance.
   The vermin affects the crops.

10. **When a plural noun denotes a specific amount, length, weight, quantity, and so on considered as a whole, the verb must be in the singular form.**

    Examples:
    Ten thousand rupees is a large amount.
    Buy 10 dozen mangoes.
    Six kilometres is not a long distance.
    Pay me five hundred rupees.
    She bought two dozen eggs.

11. **The possessive case of nouns is formed when we put apostrophe ('s) to the noun. The possessive case is used with the nouns of living things but not with inanimate objects.**

    Examples:
    The girl's dress
    The boy's pen

Her uncle's property
My aunt's son
We won't say table's leg. (incorrect)
We say leg of the table. (correct)

12. **When the noun is plural but does not end in 's', the possessive case is formed by adding ('s).**

Examples:
Men's club
Women's Day
Children's Day

13. **When the noun is plural ending in 's', the possessive case is formed by adding only an apostrophe after 's'.**

Examples:
Girls' hostel
Birds' nests
Teachers' day

14. **If the last syllable of a singular noun ends in '-s' or '-ce' and the noun is followed by the word 'sake', the possessive case of the noun will be formed by adding (') only.**

Examples:
For goodness' sake
For conscience' sake
For justice' sake
For Jesus' sake

15. **The possessive case of a compound noun will be formed by adding ('s) to the last word.**

Examples:
Sister-in-law's house
Commander-in-chief's office
Brother-in-law's wife
Mother-in-law's parents
Vice chancellor's residence

16. **An inanimate noun refers to a place, thing, or idea that is non-living, such as the words 'rock', 'house', and 'love'. In the English language, these types of nouns do not typically take on a possessive form through the addition of ('s) that is commonly used with other types of nouns.**

Examples: Most English speakers simply say *The car door* instead of *The car's door.*

The roof of the house not *the house's roof*
The hood of the car not *The car's hood*
The tire of the bike not *The bike's tire*

PRACTICE EXERCISE D

Find out the nouns in the following sentences and identify the kind of nouns:

1. The book was lying on the table.
2. The jury gave its verdict.
3. Oxygen is essential for life.
4. Love begets love.
5. Smoking is a bad habit.
6. We cannot drink sea water.
7. All girls are not shy.
8. Bravery is the test of manhood.
9. Where there is a will, there is a way.
10. The use of alcohol is injurious to health.
11. Mankind should love nature.
12. We get wool from sheep.
13. Life is not a bed of roses.
14. Robbery is committed by robbers.

PRACTICE EXERCISE E

Correct the following sentences wherever necessary:

1. My friend gives me many advices regarding my future career.
2. The HMT factory has the latest machineries.
3. The beggar is begging for alms.
4. This scissor will not cut such a hard wire.
5. My hairs have turned grey recently.
6. The magistrate has issued a summon asking me to attend his court on Monday.
7. The magistrate has passed order for his release from prison.
8. He has lost all his luggages on his way home.
9. These scenaries of Kashmir are beautiful.
10. These golds have been brought from South Africa.

3.2.2 Pronoun

A pronoun is a word which is used instead of a noun.

Examples: he, she, it, they, and so on

Types of Pronouns

Personal Pronouns

Person	*Singular*	*Plural*
First person	I	we
Second person	you	you
Third person	he, she, it	they

Forms of Personal Pronouns

Nominative Case Subject	*Accusative CaseObject*	*Possessive Case*	
I	me	my	mine
we	us	our	ours
you	you	your	yours
he	him	his	his
she	her	her	hers
it	it	its	its
they	them	their	theirs

The forms 'my', 'our', 'your', 'her', and 'its' are determiners which can also be called possessive adjectives.

Possessive Pronouns

Examples:
This book is <u>his.</u>
This pen is <u>hers</u>.
The paper is <u>mine</u>.
The house is <u>theirs</u>.

Reflexive Pronouns

These are the pronouns which reflect the self. They are formed by the addition of the suffix 'self' or 'selves' to the simple pronouns.

Examples:
Myself, yourself, himself, herself, itself, themselves, and so on
They killed themselves for no reason.
The child cut itself.
She looked at herself.
We laughed ourselves.

Emphatic Pronouns

When the reflexive pronouns (with self or selves) are used to lay emphasis on a particular point, they are called emphatic pronouns.

Examples:
I offered to drive the car myself.
We ourselves saw the rainbow.
He himself told me about it.
They themselves left the place.
You yourself know better than anybody else.

Difference between Reflexive and Emphatic Pronouns
A pronoun is reflexive if the action of the doer (subject) returns to itself; but if it is used to just emphasize the action of the subject, it is an emphatic pronoun.

Demonstrative Pronouns

The pronouns which point out (or direct us straight away to) the objects which they refer to are called demonstrative pronouns.

Examples:
That is Dr Rao's house.
These are good mangoes.
This is your passport.
Those are some new buildings.
These are the golden rules of life.

Indefinite Pronouns

A pronoun which refers to a person or thing only in a general way is called indefinite pronoun.
Some, anyone, one, somebody, anybody, anything, something, other, others, another, nobody, nothing, somebody, none, all, and so on.

Examples:
Anyone can make her drink.

Some are born great.
All are mortal.
None knows where he lives.
Somebody will have to take the lead.
Anybody can attend the interview.
Nobody knows the fact.

Pronouns of Number

Examples:
Many of them are not good books.
Of the 10 guests, three were men.
The hotel has 20 rooms; all face the park.

Pronouns of Quantity

Examples:
More, much, little, few, most, and so on
There is a little water in the pot.
There are a few boys in the class.
There is much dust in the shelf.
We drink more water in summer.

Distributive Pronouns

These refer to persons considered individually. The distributive pronouns are in the singular number and are followed by singular verbs.

Examples:
Everyone, everybody, each, neither, either, and so on
Everyone has his own problems.
Each of these players deserves a prize.
David has two pens, but neither writes.
Either of these applicants can be employed.
Everybody will be given a chance to participate in this match.

Reciprocal Pronouns

These pronouns express mutual or reciprocal relationship and are considered to be single units. They are also referred to as compound personal pronouns.

Examples:
The two boys fought with each other. (refers to two persons)

The political parties quarrelled with one another. (refers to more than two persons)

The players congratulated <u>one another</u> on winning the match.

My sister and I hugged <u>each other</u>.

Interrogative Pronouns

These are used in framing questions to refer to people or things. The pronouns 'who', 'whom', and 'whose' are used to refer to people, 'which' is used to refer to both people and things, and 'what' is used in referring only to things.

Examples:
<u>Who</u> is the President of India?
<u>Whom</u> did she refer to?
<u>What</u> have you done?
<u>Which</u> is the road to the hospital?
<u>Whose</u> is this calculator?

Relative Pronouns

These pronouns stand for the nouns used before them. It performs two functions:

On one hand, it is used instead of a noun.
On the other hand, it connects two statements. Thus it does the work of a conjunction. Hence it is also called conjunctival pronoun.

Examples:
The girl <u>who</u> is speaking is my sister.
This is the gentleman <u>whose</u> guest I was in Bombay.
This is the book <u>which</u> I lost yesterday.
I have got <u>what</u> I wanted.
Do not reject anything <u>that</u> God gives you.

Use of Pronouns

1. **When two singular nouns joined by 'and' denote the same person or thing, the pronoun used must be singular in number.**

   Examples:

   The accounts officer and treasurer should be careful in his work of keeping accounts.

   The principal and professor is responsible in his dealings with the inspection committee.

   The director and administrator has his personal assistant.

   The judge and lawyer should be tactful in taking his final decision.

2. **When two singular nouns are preceded by 'each and every' joined by 'and', the pronoun must be in singular number.**

   Examples:
   Each and every teacher took his or her seat.
   Each and every student attended the ceremony.
   Each man and woman must attend to his or her work.
   Every Punjabi and every Bengali is proud of his country, India.

3. **Generally, singular pronoun is used when two or more singular nouns are joined by 'or', 'either-or', or 'neither-nor'.**

   Examples:
   Either Sita or Neeta has come to see Rini.

   Neither Dalbir nor Satbir was able to finish his work in time.

   Mohan, Sohan, or Manmohan has been sent to deliver the message.

   Either the manager or subordinate has failed in sending the official message.

4. **'One' can be used to talk about people in general and the pronoun that follows it should be 'one's' (not his/her).**

   Examples:
   One should love one's country.
   One should do one's duty.
   One should take care of one's parents in their old age.
   One should never tell one's secrets to anyone.
   One should love oneself.

5. **The personal pronouns—'yours', 'ours', 'hers', 'theirs', and 'its'—are written without the apostrophe (').**

   Examples:
   It is a mad dog which bites its tail.
   Yours faithfully
   The pen is yours.
   It is hers.
   The bike is theirs.

6. **While confessing a fault (or expressing a negative idea) the sequence of the personal pronouns for 'be' are as follows:**
   First person first, second person next, and the third person last

   Examples:
   I, you, and he are in the wrong and will be punished.

   I, you, and she are responsible for this terrible loss.

   I, you, and Bipin should not have offended the teacher by disobeying.

We and you are speaking lies.
I and she have committed a great blunder.

7. **While expressing a positive idea or praise, the sequence of the personal pronouns should be as follows:**
Second person, third person, and first person

Examples:
You, he, and I will get an award for the good work we have done.
You and he love mankind.
Vidya and I often go to shopping.
You, Shyam, and I are the best friends.
You and Ishwar must keep quiet.
You and I have to live as good neighbours.

8. **The pronouns who, whom, and whose are generally used for persons. 'Who' is used in the nominative case, 'whom' is used in the objective case, and 'whose' is used in the possessive case.**

Examples:
Sarita is the student who got an award.
They are the thieves whom the police caught.
This is the student whose certificates are lost.
She is the girl who lost her purse.
He is the person whom the boss suspended.
He is the boy whose parents were murdered.

9. **The pronoun 'each other' is used for two persons, places, or things and 'one another' is used for more than two persons or things.**

Examples:
These two students fought with each other.
Those four countries always disagree with one another.
We three should be united with one another.
Sita and Gita like each other.
The two boys resemble each other.

10. **A pronoun should be used in the objective case in a sentence beginning with 'let'.**

Examples:
Let him go to his office immediately.
Let her submit the records in time.
Let me speak to her.
Let him in.
Let them complete the task.

11. The relative pronoun 'which' is used for infants, small animals, and objects.

Examples:
This is the baby which was lost in the theatre.
This is the dog which my sister brought from the kennel's club.
This is the radio which I bought yesterday.
This is the child which met with an accident.

12. The relative pronoun 'that' is used for lifeless things and small animals in singular or in plural number

Examples:
This is the boy that failed in the exam.
The weather of Hyderabad is far better than that of Chennai.
I vividly remember the day that she came.
This is the kit that was found stolen.

13. As regards everybody, everyone, anybody, and the like, the pronoun of the masculine or feminine gender should be used according to the context.

Examples:
Everyone of the boys got his hall ticket.
She helped everyone of those boys in doing his work.
Everyone has to seek participation.
Anybody can do the service.
Everybody can seek the advice.

PRACTICE EXERCISE F

Fill in the blanks with suitable kinds of pronouns:

1. People love boys ________ respect their parents.
2. God helps those ________ help themselves.
3. I wash my clothes ________.
4. She ________ spoke these words to me.
5. We enjoyed ________.
6. ________ do you want to see?
7. ________ pen was stolen?
8. To ________ will you give your watch?
9. He is sitting by ________.
10. It is an ill wind ______ blows nobody good.

PRACTICE EXERCISE G

Correct the sentences wherever necessary:

1. One should do your duty honestly and sincerely.
2. You, he, and I are in the wrong direction.
3. The committee were divided in its opinion regarding this issue.
4. His problems are the same as my.
5. My opinion is the same as your.
6. Every teacher and every student should do their duty.
7. Those two companies always help one another.
8. Between you and I, the secretary is not a gentleman.
9. Only you and him can do the work fast.
10. Neither of the boys have submitted their records.

3.3 MISPLACED MODIFIERS

A misplaced modifier is a word, phrase, or clause that does not clearly relate to what it is intended to modify. In other words, a misplaced modifier makes the meaning of a sentence ambiguous or wrong. Misplaced modifiers make the sentence awkward and sometimes unintentionally humorous.

Example: Having finished the assignment, the TV was turned on. (incorrect)

'Having finished' is a participle expressing action, but the doer is not the TV set (the subject of the main clause): TV sets don't finish assignments. Since the doer of the action expressed in the participle has not been clearly stated, the participle phrase is said to be a dangling modifier.

Having finished the assignment, I turned on the TV. (correct)

The following principles of grammar will come in handy in avoiding the use of misplaced or dangling modifiers.

Rule 1: Related parts of a sentence should not be unnecessarily separated by other elements.

Example:
Not Good: As the car wound up the narrow road we found the trees becoming more scattered as we neared the top of the mountain. (Two subordinate clauses having the same rank and function are separated.)

Improved: As the car wound up the narrow road and neared the top of the mountain, we found the trees becoming more scattered.

Rule 2: It is particularly important to be careful about where you put limiting modifiers. These are words such as 'almost', 'hardly', 'nearly', 'just', 'only', and 'merely'. The entire meaning of a sentence changes if you place these modifiers before the verb.

Example:
Ambiguous: Randy has *nearly* annoyed every manager he has worked for.

Improved: Randy has annoyed *nearly* every manager he has worked for.

Rule 3: It is important to place the modifying phrase or clause as close as possible to the word it modifies.

Example:
Ambiguous: I heard that my wife intended to throw a surprise party for me while I was outside her bedroom window.

Improved: While I was outside her bedroom window, I heard that my wife intended to throw a surprise party for me.

Rule 4: A relative clause should be placed immediately after the noun it modifies.

Example:
Ambiguous: The reporter can occasionally pick up items from conversation with friends that will be of interest to readers of his paper.

Improved: From conversation with friends the reporter can occasionally pick up items that will be of interest to readers of his paper.

Rule 5: The infinitive form of the verb consists of the preposition 'to' followed by the base form of the verb such as 'to be', 'to serve', 'to chop', and so on. Inserting a word or words between 'to' and the verb of an infinitive creates what is known as a split infinitive. Avoid placing long, disruptive modifiers between 'to' and the verb of an infinitive.

Example:
Ambiguous: The marketing team voted to, before they launched the new software, run an anticipatory ad campaign. (The infinitive *to run* should not be split.)

Improved: The marketing team voted to run an anticipatory ad campaign before they launched the new software.

PRACTICE EXERCISE H

Restate the following sentences correctly:

1. Reaching the station, the sun came out. (Who reached the station? Obviously can't be the sun.)
2. Having been thrown in the air, the dog caught the stick. (Who has been thrown: stick or dog?)
3. I saw the trailer peeking through the window. (Who peeked through the window: I or trailer?)
4. Being in a dilapidated condition, I was able to buy the house very cheap. (Was the house in dilapidated condition or the person?)
5. Roaring down the track at 70 miles an hour, the train smashed the stalled car. (Was the car in high speed or the train?)
6. I was late for the school bus again. Running for the bus, my book fell in the mud. (Was the book running, or the person?)
7. Upon entering the doctor's office, a skeleton caught my attention. (Do you mean the skeleton entered doctor's office?)
8. Deciding to join the navy, the recruiter enthusiastically pumped Joe's hand. (Who decided to join the navy: Joe or recruiter?)
9. Though only 16 years old, the college accepted Martha's application. (Do you mean that the college is 16 years old?)
10. After a quick change into my hospital gown, the nurse told me to relax. (So did the nurse change into your hospital gown?)
11. Standing on the balcony, the ocean view was magnificent. (Who was standing on the balcony?)
12. At the age of 4, my grandma taught me to knit. (Do you mean your grandma is four years old?)

PRACTICE EXERCISE I

Choose whether each of the following sentences is correct, or whether it has a dangling modifier:

1. Unlike many other students, the financial aid office did not approve his application.
2. Unlike many other students, Jim didn't have any problems with his teachers.
3. Smoking my cigar, a fire engine came roaring around the corner.
4. Having learned French in just three months, Paul was as happy as he could be.
5. Drinking a beer, the feeling was a familiar one.
6. While watching a movie, people who talk loudly are really annoying.

7. While listening to the radio, one should always make sure that the volume is not too loud.
8. At the age of 16, I moved back to California.
9. Looking over the student's exam, several mistakes became evident right away.
10. Concerned about the rain, it was decided that the picnic should be cancelled.

PRACTICE EXERCISE J

In the following pairs, one sentence is correct, and the other sentence has a misplaced or dangling modifier. Mark the correct sentence.

1. A _____ Looking towards the south, a funnel-shaped cloud stirred up the dust.
   B _____ Looking towards the south, I saw a funnel-shaped cloud stir up the dust.
2. A _____ They saw a fence made of barbed wire behind the house.
   B _____ They saw a fence behind the house made of barbed wire.
3. A _____ After following the vision programme for two weeks, my doctor told me that my eyesight had improved.
   B _____ After I had followed the vision programme for two weeks, my doctor told me that my eyesight had improved.
4. A _____ We saw several birds looking out our window.
   B _____ Looking out our window, we saw several birds.
5. A _____ The four men eating lunch talked quietly in the corner.
   B _____ The four men talked quietly in the corner eating lunch.
6. A _____ Racing across the parking lot, the bus was reached before the door closed.
   B _____ Racing across the parking lot, I reached the bus before the door closed
7. A _____ Being only 5, the doctor did not know how to operate on me.
   B _____ Because I was only 5, the doctor did not know how to operate on me.
8. A _____ Mary nearly watched 200 movies last year.
   B _____ Mary watched nearly 200 movies last year.
9. A _____ To enter the contest, you must send an entry form with your slogan.

B _____ To enter the contest, an entry form must be sent with your slogan.

10. A _____ I remember seeing the picture of the firefighter who had been injured on the morning news.

 B _____ I remember seeing on the morning news the picture of the firefighter who had been injured.

3.4 ARTICLES

The articles are monosyllabic words which are called modifiers. They are placed before nouns which are modified just as adjectives which qualify nouns. Generally speaking, there are two types of articles:

1. The indefinite articles: a, an 2. The definite article: the

3.4.1 Uses of the Indefinite Articles

1. **'A' is used before the words commencing with a consonant sound while 'an' is used before the words commencing with a vowel sound.**

   Note: There are 44 sounds in English and each is given a symbol from the International Phonetic Alphabet. Out of 44 sounds, there are 20 vowel sounds and 24 consonant sounds. Strictly speaking, *a, e, i, o,* and *u* are just letters of the English alphabet.

   Examples: a boy, a man, a king, a girl, a woman, a child, a bird, and so on

   An armchair, an army, an idiot, an American, an enemy, and so on

2. **'A' is used before the words which begin with 'y'.**

   Examples: a yard, a yell, a yellow paper, a young man, a year, a youth, and so on

3. **'A' is used before the words which begin with 'u' or 'eu' giving the consonant sound 'yu'.**

   Examples: a university, a European, a union leader, a unique thing, a Unitarian, a uniform, and so on

4. **'A' is used before the words which begin with 'o' giving the consonant sound 'wa'.**

   Examples: a one-eyed man, a one-rupee note, a one-way traffic, such a one, and so on

5. **'A' is used before the words which begin with a pronounced 'h'.**

   Examples: a house, a human being, a historical place, a humorous story, a high wall, and so on

6. **'An' is used before words which begin with an unsounded 'h'.**

   Examples: an hour, an honour, an heir, an heirloom, an honest action, an exhausted opinion, and so on

7. **'A' and 'an' are used in the sense of one before singular countable nouns.**

   Examples:
   A stitch in time saves nine.
   It costs a rupee.
   We want a man for the job.

8. **'A' and 'an' are used in the sense of 'a certain'.**

   Examples:
   A boy of nine helped me.
   I hear a man knocking at the door.
   The police arrested a worker yesterday.

9. **'A' and 'an' are used in the sense of 'each' or 'every'.**

   Examples:
   He visits Taj Mahal once a year.
   You have to pay ₹20 a dozen.
   He gets a salary of ₹2,000/- a month.

10. **The indefinite articles are used with a singular noun to represent a whole class.**

    Examples:
    A dog is faithful to his master. (represents the whole genre of dogs)
    Only an infantry man knows what war is.
    A rose is a beautiful flower.

11. **The indefinite articles are used before abstract nouns when such nouns are used as common nouns.**

    Examples:
    A knowledge of science has become necessary nowadays.

The lecturer developed a love for poetry in the students.
She has a good knowledge of Sanskrit.

12. The indefinite articles are used when material nouns are used as common nouns.

Examples:
A glass of water
A tin of biscuits
A jar of oil

13. If the indefinite articles are used with proper nouns, they will become common nouns.

Examples:
He is a second Newton.
He feels he is a Nannayya.
He has become a Devdas.

14. The indefinite articles are used to indicate speed or price.

Examples:
Five rupees a kilo
Fifty miles an hour

15. The indefinite article 'a' is used with the words 'little' and 'few' when they mean 'some amount'.

Examples:
A few men attended the meeting.
There is a little sugar in the tin.
There is a little water in the pot.

16. The indefinite articles are used with a noun complement. This includes the names of professions.

Examples:
He is an actor.
She is a good dancer.
It was an accident.

17. 'A' is used before certain words such as noise, headache, hurry, distance, and walk.

Examples:
Don't make a noise.
I am in a hurry.
It is at a distance.
I go for a walk every day.
He is suffering from a headache.

18. When the person referred to is a stranger to the speaker.

Examples:
A Salim called for you while you were out.
A Mr Ram wants you on phone.

19. Before a noun that is introduced for the first time in speech and writing.

Examples:
I was born in a village in Assam.
I am an extraordinarily talented athlete.

20. 'A' is used to convey numerical sense 'one'.

Examples:
He has a million dollars in the Swiss Bank.
Give me a thousand rupees.

21. Before certain phrases

Examples:
To give a warning
To be in a temper
To catch a cold
To make a living
To make an effort
On an average
Make a mistake

22. 'A' is used after certain words such as such, rather, quite, and many.

Examples:
Such a show cannot be arranged now.
He is rather a fool.
Many a friend of mine is attending the party.
It is quite a sorrowful incident.

23. Before certain uncountable nouns preceded by noun + of

Examples:
A piece of advice
A bit of news
A drop of water
A piece of furniture

3.4.2 Uses of the Definite Article

1. **'The' is used before ordinals**

   Examples:
   The first
   The second
   The third

2. **Before musical instruments**

   Examples:
   The violin
   The guitar
   The flute

3. **To indicate directions**

   Examples:
   The east
   The west
   The south

4. **Before unique things**

   Examples:
   The sun
   The earth
   The moon

5. **Before oceans**

   Examples:
   The Atlantic Ocean
   The Pacific Ocean
   The Indian Ocean

6. **Before seas**

   Examples:
   The Dead Sea
   The Arabian Sea
   The Red Sea

7. **Before groups of islands**

   Examples:
   The Andamans
   The Maldives
   The Lakshadweep

8. Before historical or public buildings

Examples:
The Red Fort
The Taj Mahal
The Rashtrapati Bhavan

9. With certain adjectives indicating nationality

Examples:
The Dutch
The Spanish

10. Before parallel constructions or special comparatives

Examples:
The higher you go, the cooler you feel.
The more you earn, the more you spend.
The more they get, the more they want.

11. Before the names of rivers

Examples:
The Krishna
The Ganga
The Godavari

12. Before deserts

Examples:
The Sahara
The Thar

13. Before the names of political parties

Examples:
The Congress
The BJP
The TDP

14. Before adjectives in the superlative degree

Examples:
The tallest
The shortest
The cleverest

15. Before the names of missiles or rockets

Examples:
The Agni
The Prithvi
The Nag

16. Before the names of trains and airplanes

Examples:
The Air Force
The Jayanthi Express
The Sukhoi

17. Before the names of valleys

Examples:
The Kashmir Valley
The Nubra Valley
The Araku Valley

18. Before the names of epics

Examples:
The Gita
The Bible
The Ramayana

19. Before the dates of months

Examples:
The 23rd October of 1949
The 15th August of 1947

20. Before the names of newspaper and magazines

Examples:
The Hindu
The Frontline
The Indian Express

21. Before the names of certain countries that end in plural form

Examples:
The Netherlands
The West Indies
The Hagues

22. Before a noun when special emphasis is needed

Examples:
This is the novel I am talking about.
He mentions about the India when he was young.

23. Before names of countries each of which is a union of smaller units

Examples:
The United Kingdom
The USSR
The United Arab Republic

24. To change proper noun into a common noun or in comparing one person or place with another

Examples:
Kalidasa is the Shakespeare of India.
Mumbai is the Manchester of India.

25. Before plural nouns

Examples:
The boys are playing.
The children are reading.
The dogs are barking.

26. Used in changing adjectives into nouns

Examples:
Poor–the poor
Rich–the rich
Deaf–the deaf

27. Used before languages to represent people

Examples:
The Telugu
The Tamil

28. Before the names of plateaus

Examples:
The Deccan Plateau
The Tibet Plateau

29. To indicate a particular tribe

Examples:
The dog is a faithful animal.
The tiger is a ferocious animal.

30. Before 'monsoon'

Examples:
The southeast monsoon
The northwest monsoon

31. Before the names of certain chains of mountains

Examples:
The Alps
The Himalayas
The Vindhyas

32. Used before some nouns in the sense of visiting purpose

Examples:
He has gone to the hospital to see the patient.
The tourists visited the temple.

33. Before 'God'

Examples:
The God of love
The God of peace

34. To indicate historical events

Examples:
The First World War
The Waterloo Battle

35. Before the names of awards

Examples:
The Noble Prize
The Padma Bhushan
The Bharat Ratna

3.4.3 Omission of Articles

1. Before metals and things

Examples:
Gold is a metal.
Coffee is a fine drink.

2. Before proper nouns

Examples:
Hyderabad is the capital of Andhra Pradesh.
Delhi is a union territory.

3. Before plural nouns which denote a class

Examples:
Historians study old monuments for research purpose.
Camels are useful animals in deserts.

4. Before the words 'mother', 'father', 'aunt', 'uncle', and so on in general sense

Examples:
My mother is housewife.
My father is a doctor.

5. Before abstract nouns

Examples:
Honesty is the best policy.
Sincerity pays dividends.

6. Before the names of games and diseases

Examples:
Typhoid is a kind of fever.
Cricket is a good game.

7. Before the names of vehicles

Examples:
He came by train.
He came on motorcycle.

8. Before the names of meals used in general sense

Examples:
Lunch, dinner, supper, breakfast, dinner, and so on
I had lunch at 2.00 PM.
Let's have dinner at 9.00 PM.

9. Before the nouns such as school, bed, temple, prison, college, hospital, and so on when used in general sense

Examples:
We go to bed to sleep.
The doctor goes to hospital.
We go to university for higher studies.

10. Before the names of particular mountain

Examples:
Mount Everest
Mount Kailas

11. Before the words 'man' and 'nature' when used in a general sense

Examples:
Man is mortal.
Nature is beautiful.

12. Before the names of weeks, months, and years preceded by 'last' and 'next'

Examples:
Sunday is the last day of the week.
December is the last month of the year.

13. Before the word 'home'

Examples:
We went home.
She reached home late.

14. No article is used in certain expressions

Examples:
At night
To catch fire
In debt
At ease
To take offence
On demand
To lose heart
By air
To give ear
To send word
In hand
At sunrise
By land
On foot

15. In other time expressions, no article is used

Examples:
at night
at noon
at midnight
all day
all night
all month
every month
every year
last night
last Friday
yesterday
tomorrow

Note: But there are some expressions which can take both *a/an* and *the*:

Examples:
a/the whole day
a/the whole month
an/the entire year
an/the entire decade

PRACTICE EXERCISE K

Fill in the blanks with appropriate articles:

1. Who is cleaning _____ blackboard?
2. Twelve inches make _____ foot.
3. This is _____ historical novel.
4. English is not ______ easy language.
5. _____ poems he writes are good.
6. He is not _____ honourable man.
7. Have you read Vyasa's ______ Mahabharata?
8. Have you read _____ Gita?
9. Gavaskar is ______ second Bradman.
10. _______ Andamans are a group of islands.
11. The lion is ______ native of Africa.
12. He is ______ person I was speaking about.
13. It is not _____ good thing to advise fools.
14. She is ______ asset to her firm.
15. He is ______ better writer than clerk.
16. _____ Daniel came to judgement. Daniel is a wise man.
17. I saw _____ one-eyed beggar.
18. Of the two pens which is _____ better?
19. _____ bird in the hand is worth two in bush.
20. Violence is growing in ______ Punjab.
21. He is as stupid as _____ owl.
22. I found ______ animal wounded.
23. This novel is his ______ greatest work.
24. He took ______ unusual step.
25. ______ rose is the sweetest of all flowers.
26. The play is by _______ immortal Shakespeare.
27. We sell ____ best quality.
28. _____ Nelson is a British warship.
29. ______ English are fond of sports.
30. ______ wisdom of Solomon was famous

PRACTICE EXERCISE L

Insert articles where necessary:

1. I want ____ apple from that basket.
2. ____ church on the corner is progressive.
3. Miss Lin speaks ____ Chinese.
4. I borrowed ____ pencil from your pile of pencils and pens.
5. One of the students said, '____ professor is late today.'

6. Eli likes to play ____ volleyball.
7. I bought ____ umbrella to go out in the rain.
8. My daughter is learning to play ____ violin at her school.
9. Please give me ____ cake that is on the counter.
10. I lived on ____ Main Street when I first came to town.
11. Albany is the capital of ____ New York State.
12. My husband's family speaks ____ Polish.
13. ____ apple a day keeps the doctor away.
14. ____ ink in my pen is red.
15. Our neighbours have ____ cat and ____ dog.

PRACTICE EXERCISE M

Correct the following sentences:

1. The Beijing is the capital of China.
2. I first met your Dad at the Walmart.
3. He has failed in the English.
4. She died of the malaria.
5. She is best singer I have heard.
6. Rose is sweetest of all flowers.
7. A man is mortal.
8. You are in a trouble.
9. You are making a rapid progress.
10. There is a vast scope for improvement.
11. Your words are not worth penny.
12. Don't make noise.

3.5 PREPOSITIONS

A word used with a noun or a pronoun to show how the person or thing denoted by the noun or pronoun stands in relation to something else is called a preposition. It shows the relationship between a noun and a noun, a verb and a noun, and an adjective and a pronoun. The preposition is placed after the verb and before the noun, after the adjective and before the noun.

We can divide the prepositions into six categories:

3.5.1 Simple Prepositions

In, on, at, for, by from, of, off, out, till, up, down, though, past, with, since, via, after, under, per, as, but, round, than, and so on.

Examples:

1. Work in the college begins at 9 AM.
2. The professor gave a lecture on superconductivity.
3. The prize is given to her.
4. Mohan gave a lecture on patriotism.
5. He is fond of playing.

3.5.2 Compound Prepositions

These are formed by prefixing a preposition to a noun, an adjective, or an adverb. These include: About, across, along, among, beneath, beyond, before, below, behind, beside, between, aboard, amid, inside, outside, besides, toward, towards, against, upon, throughout, around, despite, until, alongside, opposite, unless, although, underneath, within, without.

Examples:

1. Go beyond your limitations.
2. Look before you leap.
3. I ran towards the river.
4. My home is opposite to yours.
5. He is against my decision.

3.5.3 Double Prepositions

Out of, from behind, from among, from under, from within, into, up to, and so on

Examples:

1. The student was sent out of class.
2. She ran into the park.
3. It's under a mile from here to the post office.
4. The noise seems to be coming from within the building.
5. He shot from behind as he ran away.

3.5.4 Participle Prepositions

Sometimes participles are used as prepositions. Sometimes they are used with the nouns expressed and sometimes with the nouns understood.

Considering (taking into account), according to, during (in the time of), concerning, regarding, owing to (because of), notwithstanding (in spite of), excepting, barring (apart from), following, including, pending (not considering), and so on

Examples:
1. Concerning your affairs, I have nothing to say.
2. Barring from accidents, she comes in time.
3. Considering the quality, the price is not high.
4. He succeeded not withstanding many obstacles.
5. Pending further orders, I will do as you like.

3.5.5 Phrase Prepositions

There are also phrases which do the work of prepositions and are called phrase prepositions.

Because of, in order to, on behalf of, according to, by means of, for the sake of, in the event of, in addition to, in favour of, instead of, in spite of, in course of, with reference to, in place of, in front of, on account of, in view of, in case of, by reason of, by way of, for the sake of, along with, with regard to, prefer to, apart from, and so on

Examples:
1. In case of need, please phone 89746.
2. He could not finish the work because of illness.
3. In order to get any work done, you have to bribe somebody.
4. In course of time, you will realize your mistake.
5. The soldier died fighting on behalf of his motherland.

3.5.6 Position of Prepositions

1. **A preposition usually precedes its object.**

   Examples:
   He has no taste for music.
   She is a great lover of books.
   Do not laugh at the poor.
   He is angry with me.

2. **A preposition is placed at the end of a sentence in the following cases:**
   a. **In the case of interrogative pronouns**

Examples:
What are you looking at?
Where is the boy you are complaining against?
Whom are you speaking of?
What are you searching for?

b. **In case of relative pronoun 'that' the preposition is always placed at the end.**

Examples:
Here is the watch that you searched for.
Here is the book that you were looking for.
This is a field that I am very much interested in.
This is the boy that I am waiting for

c. **In case of relative pronouns 'whom, which, what, or whose', the preposition is always placed at the end.**

Examples:
She is the girl whose mention I was making of
This is the person you spoke to.
This is the person whom I spoke about.
This is the house which I prefer to live in.

d. **When an emphasis on the object is desired, the preposition is placed at the end.**

Examples:
It is mischief he is bent upon.
His own achievements he always harps on.
This I insist on.
He is known all over the world.

3. **A preposition can also be used in the beginning of an interrogative sentence.**

Examples:
In which city do you live?
To whom are you referring?
In which direction is that?
For how many days are you availing leave?

4. **There are many words which can be used as prepositions or as adverbs.**

Examples:

	Preposition	Adverb
1.	He was here before 10.	He has done this before.
2.	She is sitting in the room.	Please come in.

3. He was behind us.	She is long way behind.
4. The shop is just round the corner.	Come round and see me today.
5. It has been raining since morning.	We have not met since.
6. She takes after her mother.	It rained after 3 o'clock.
7. The mother looks after her children.	He arrived the hall after me.

5. **There are some words with prepositions which require gerunds after them.**

Examples:
Refrain from hurting
Prevent from working
Pretext for delaying
Fond of playing
Bent upon doing
Insist on going
Expert in inventing
Disqualified from doing
Prohibit from entering
Knack of getting
Tired of writing
Addicted to gambling
Capable of teaching
Aid at doing
Abstain from drinking

3.5.7 Uses of the Most Commonly Used Prepositions

In

1. **With the names of countries and large towns and cities**

Examples:
My brother lives in Bombay.
My cousin settled in America.
My parents are in Calcutta.
I was born in Calcutta.

2. **To indicate time**

Examples:
In 1995 I took my degree.
The cloth shop was opened in May 1975.
In how many days will you be able to complete?
How long it takes in to go to Manas Sarovar?

3. To indicate circumstances, conditions, and surroundings

Examples:
Do not go out in the rain.
He is in great trouble.
My brother is in a hurry to go to office.
He is in a miserable condition.

4. To indicate activity

Examples:
She spends her time in reading books.
She is involved in doing her work.
She is engaged in performing a mask dance.
She is very attentive in drawing the graph.

5. To indicate dress

Examples:
The young baby is dressed in silk.
The cloth is white in colour.
Her frock is in pink.

6. To denote longer periods (months/years/seasons)

Examples:
In October
In winter
In the Middle Ages
In the 18th century
In the present

7. To indicate duration

Examples:
In the morning
In the evening
In the afternoon

8. To say how long it takes to do something

Examples:
I learned to drive in four weeks.
I will try to complete the work in four months.
I will complete the syllabus in three months.
I learned music in one year.

9. To say that somebody/something is:

Examples:
In a line

In a magazine
In the world
In a queue
In a letter
In the sky
In a photograph
In a newspaper
In a street
In bad weather
In the rain
In the dark
Fall in love
Been in love

10. We also say:

Examples:
Write in biro/pencil/ink.
Write in words/figures/block letters.

11. To indicate buildings or when we are thinking of the building itself

Examples:
You can eat in a restaurant.
I enjoyed the cinema but it was cold in cinema.
It is very warm in the hall.

12. We usually say in a car/taxi/cab

Examples:
I came in a car.
She went to the office in a taxi.
I came from the station in a cab.

13. To indicate when continuity is not intended but only a general action is to be expressed.

Examples:
We stayed in Delhi in 1995.
We stayed in hotel last night.
I stayed in the college four years.

14. It is used when we speak about the type of a place in general but not a particular place.

Examples:
Most Indians live in villages.
Most of the tribes live in the forests.

The poor people live in slum areas.
The Ladhakis live in snow-capped fields.

15. To denote a state of rest

Examples:
He is in bed.
He is lying in sofa.
The teacher is taking rest in the staff room.
He is sleeping in the rest room.

On

1. To indicate place

Examples:
He kept the book on the desk.
He sat on a chair.
He slept on a mat.

2. To indicate exact time

Examples:
He was born on 15 August 1947.
Republic Day is celebrated on 26 January.
Mahatma Gandhi was born on 2 October.

3. To describe a condition

Examples:
He is on probation this year.
He is on duty.
He is on a voyage this summer.
He has gone on business work.

4. In the sense of 'about/concerning'

Examples:
This is a book on grammar.
We are publishing a book on Indian history.
The article is based on journey in Ladakh.
I wrote a book on Sri Aurobindo.

5. To express the cause or basis for something

Examples:
She always acts on my advice.
She secured first rank on my suggestions.
She enrolled for PhD on my advice.

6. To indicate an objective or an aim

Examples:
I am bent on doing my PhD.
I am doing my research on a mystical poem.
He is studying on the problems of pollution.

7. To indicate a particular day, date, a special day of the year, important events, and anniversary

Examples:
On Independence Day
On 3 January
On the birth anniversary
On 16th birthday
On Sunday

8. To indicate punctuality. If something happens 'on time', it happens at the time which was planned.

Examples:
Be on time.
The work completed on time.
The construction of the lab was finished on time.
The meeting commenced on time.

9. We use 'on' in the expressions like:
On the ceiling, on the door, on the bike, on a motor, on a bus, on the plane, on a train, on holiday, on business, on duty, on a tour, on the phone, on a diet, on strike, on radio, on a cruise, on television, on a river, on the corner of a street, on the notice board, on the way, on the back, on a piece of paper, on the beach, on the ground, on her nose, on a page, on the floor, on an island, on the wall, on purpose (intentionally), on the whole, and so on

Examples:
I didn't do it on purpose.
On the whole (generally) I enjoy my job.
I came on bike.
I watched the news on television.

10. We also use 'on' with the following expressions like:
Depend on, rely on, put on, spend on, insist on, feed on (to make something stronger), concentrate on, live on, congratulate on, turn on, and so on

Examples:
Put on your coat.
Concentrate on your work.

Hatred feeds on jealousy.
His salary isn't enough to live on.
He turned on the light.
I congratulated on her success.

11. **'On' is also used in speaking of things at rest while 'upon' is used in speaking of things in motion.**

Examples:
He stood on the platform. (rest)
The dog sprang upon him. (motion)

12. **We should not use in/on/at before last/next/this/every.**

Examples:
I came last month.
I visit the ashram every month.

At

1. **To indicate point of time**

Examples:
At 4 o'clock in the evening I will meet you.
They set out at dawn.
The match will start at 3 PM.

2. **To denote a place or position**

Examples:
She is at school.
He is at hospital.
She is at college.
He is at party.

3. **With words denoting the rate or degree at which a thing is done**

Examples:
The car is going at full speed.
Sugar is selling at six rupees a kilo.
He is walking at full speed.

4. **To indicate aim or motion**

Examples:
She threw a stone at the cat.
She is pointing her arrow at the bird.
She aims at doing her postgraduation.

5. To indicate small towns and villages or locality

Examples:
I shall meet my friend at Naz Centre.
Let us meet at the club this evening.
He lives at Tanuku.
The President lives at White House.
He lives at Anandanagar at Baroda.

6. In the sense of being 'engaged in something'

Examples:
All my children are at play.
All the students are at work.
All the employees are at the meeting.

7. It is used with the following expressions:
Clever at, good at, bad at, shoot at, throw at, shout at, look at, smile at, point at, stare at, laugh at, fire at, aim at, glance at, presided at, at home, at the station, at college, at a concert, at a party, at cricket match, at the airport, at the station, and so on

Examples:
The Chief Guest presided at the function.
Everybody will laugh at you.
Look at these flowers.
Are you good at mathematics?
He is clever at playing tricks.
Don't point that knife at me.
Somebody threw an egg at the minister.

8. It is used with the expressions 'at the age of', 'km', 'at degree centigrade', and so on

Examples:
She married at 21.
The car was travelling at 50 km an hour.
Water boils at 100 degree centigrade.

<u>For</u>

1. To mean 'in place of' and 'in exchange for'

Examples:
Dalda is substitute for ghee.
I bought this book for 10 rupees.
She is a substitute for him.

2. To mean purpose and object

Examples:
She applied for a job.
Let us fight for peace.
Let us fight for our rights.

3. To mean destination and direction

Examples:
I am leaving for Hyderabad.
I am leaving for North India.
I am flying for Los Angeles.

4. In the sense of 'in spite of', 'despite', and 'not withstanding'

Examples:
For all his efforts he is unsuccessful.
For all his hard work he reaped a bad consequence.
For all his clever tricks he failed in deceiving his friend.

5. To express a period of time

Examples:
I am going away for the weekend.
I have been living here for four years.
She served her for two years.

6. To indicate that to which something is intended

Examples:
This is a letter for you.
This gift is for you.
He has bought a book for you.

7. Used in the expressions like:
Good for, like for, bought for, search for, care for, wait for, leave for, ask for, apply for, and so on

Examples:
The climate is good for your health.
He is good for nothing.
I am waiting for the rain to stop.
I am searching for the keys.

8. It is used to denote a space of future time in negative sentences.

Examples:
She will not read for an hour.
The sun will not rise for an hour.
She won't come for two hours.

To

1. **To indicate purpose**

   Examples:
   She came to meet me.
   She is studying to get a job.
   She is learning music to become a musician.

2. **To indicate place.**

   Examples:
   He came to his own house.
   He went to his native place.
   He is coming to Delhi on inspection.

3. **To indicate limit**

   Examples:
   We shall pay to the last pie.
   We will try to be in our limits.
   Try to spend the money only for essential things.

4. **To indicate things of motion**

   Examples:
   He ran to the picture house.
   He jumped into the canal.
   He ran to catch the squirrel.

5. **To indicate effect**

   Examples:
   To their utter surprise, she won the race.
   She is helping the poor to gain contentment.
   She is working hard to pass the exam.

6. **It is used in the expressions like:**
   Go to, return to, happen to, belong to, speak to, listen to, prefer to, superior to, walk to, write to, and so on

   Examples:
   Listen to the radio.
   Can I speak to Chris?
   What happened to it?
   Does this book belong to you?
   I want to go to Italy.
   I went to a party.

7. **It is also used in the expressions like:**
to hospital, to prison, to bed, to college, to the dentist, to university, to the city centre, to the airport, to work, and so on

Examples:
I am going to work now.
Are you going to the park?
I am going to bed.

Of

1. **To indicate relationship**

   Examples:
   The dramas of Shakespeare are charming forever.
   The results of the elections are not expected.
   The poetry of John Milton is related to theology.

2. **To form adjective phrases**

   Examples:
   He is a man of worth.
   She narrated to me a story of adventure.
   She is a woman of great beauty.

3. **To express division or measure**

   Examples:
   I wrote the story on a sheet of paper.
   He took one metre of cloth for his shirt.
   He bought two metres of cloth.

4. **To denote an objective relation**

   Examples:
   His love of English is very high.
   He has a good knowledge of Sanskrit.

5. **To denote subject relation**

   Examples:
   The love of mother is indeed great.
   The relation of her friend is indeed selfish.

6. **To express some cause**

   Examples:
   She died of malaria.
   My father did it of necessity.
   She was the cause of her illness.

7. **To indicate quality**

   Examples:
   He is man of noble character.
   He is man of good character.

8. **To indicate point of reference**

   Examples:
   He is blind of one eye.
   He is lame of one leg.

9. **To indicate material**

   Examples:
   The table is made of wood.
   The paper is made of pulp.
   The bag is made of plastic.

10. **To indicate contents**

    Examples:
    She sent me a basket of fruits.
    List of items
    List of contents

11. **To indicate possession**

    Examples:
    This is the factory of her uncle.
    She owns the college of her brother.
    She is the heir of the property.

12. **Used in the peculiar constructions like:**
    Afraid of, kind of, nice of, full of, take care of think of, complain of, and so on

    Examples:
    It is kind of you to help me.
    Are you afraid of dogs?
    The room was full of people.
    Take care of yourself.

<u>**After**</u>

1. **To indicate sequence in place**

   Examples:
   She is placed after you.
   You take after her place next.
   Take your seat after hers.

2. **To indicate sequence in time**

   Examples:
   He returned after night fall.
   He went home after the lunch.

3. **According to name**

   Examples:
   The college is named after him.
   Mother Teresa was named after Theresa.

4. **To indicate resemblance**

   Examples:
   The son takes after the father.
   Her qualities take after Newton.

5. **In the sense of 'not withstanding'**

   Examples:
   After all his promises he made, he joined the enemy camp.
   After all his efforts he failed.

6. **To overtake power**

   Examples:
   They are always after power.
   He is always after her property.

7. **Used in the expressions like**
   Tired after, after doing, leave behind, leaving after, work after, after eating/reading/playing/watching, and so on

   Examples:
   After reading the newspaper I will have my breakfast.
   Leave behind your compassion.

By

1. **To mean 'near', 'at the side of'**

   Examples:
   A house by the stream
   Stand by someone
   Sit by yourself

2. **Used in the sense of during**

   Examples:
   By day
   By night
   By afternoon

3. Used in the sense of not later than

Examples:
I shall finish the work by tomorrow.
By the end of this week the training will end.

4. In the sense of through the means of

Examples:
An engine driven by electricity.
A city destroyed by earthquake.

5. Used to refer to the agent or doer of an action

Examples:
The Ramayana was written by Valmiki.
The Mahabharata was written by Vyas.

With

1. To refer to the instruments with which action is done

Examples:
He cut the tree with an axe.
Cut the vegetables with a knife.
Cut the thread with scissors.

2. To denote cause

Examples:
He is down with fever.
The road blocked with rain water.

3. To denote association

Examples:
I shall be with you in a few minutes.
He was with his council of ministers to see the festival.

4. To denote the idea of mixing up

Examples:
She is with the crowd.
The teacher was with the students.
The judge was with his lawyers.

From

1. To denote starting point of an action

Examples:
Classes will run from 10 AM to 3 PM.
He will begin his lesson from next week.

2. **Used for the point of departure**

   Examples:
   He will go from Bombay to Calcutta.
   He will depart from Bangalore airport.

Across

1. **To mean from one side to another**

   Examples:
   He swam across the river.
   I was going across the road.

3.5.8 Common Misuse of Prepositions

Mistakes are often made by using the wrong preposition after certain words. Given below are the examples of misused prepositions:

1. Absorbed (i.e., very much interested) in, not at. Don't say: The man was absorbed at his work.
   Say: The man was absorbed in his work.
2. Accuse of, not for. Don't say: She accused the man for stealing.
   Say: She accused the man of stealing.
   Note: 'Charge' takes 'with': The man was charged with murder.
3. Accustomed to, not with. Don't say: I'm accustomed with hot weather.
   Say: I'm accustomed to hot weather.
   Note: Also 'used to': He is used to the heat.
4. Afraid of, not from. Don't say: Laura is afraid from the dog.
   Say: Laura is afraid of the dog.
5. Aim at, not on or against. Don't say: She aimed on or against the target.

   Say: She aimed at the target.

   Note: Use the preposition 'at' to denote direction, throw at, shout at, fire at, shoot at, and so on. 'Shoot' (without 'at') means 'to kill': He shot a bird (= he hit and killed it).
6. Angry with, not against. Don't say: The teacher was angry against him.
   Say: The teacher was angry with him.

   Note: We get angry with a person but at a thing. He was angry at the weather not with the weather.

7. Anxious (= troubled) about, not for. Don't say: They're anxious for his health.
   Say: They're anxious about his health.
   Note: 'Anxious for' means wishing very much: Parents are anxious for their children's success.
8. Arrive at, not to. Don't say: We arrived to the village at night.
   Say: We arrived at the village at night.
9. Ashamed of, not from. Don't say: He's now ashamed from his conduct.
   Say: He's now ashamed of his conduct.
10. Believe in, not to. Don't say: We believe to God.
    Say: We believe in God.
11. Boast of or about, not for. Don't say: James boasted for his strength.
    Say: James boasted of (or about) his strength.
12. Careful of, with, or about, not for. Don't say: Elke's very careful for her health.
    Say: Elke's very careful of/about her health. Or: You should be more careful with your money.
13. Travel by train, not with the train. Don't say: He travelled with the train yesterday.
    Say: He travelled by train yesterday.
    Note: We say, by train, by boat, by plane, by bike; also, by land, by sea, by air, by bus; in a bus or on a bus; by car or in a car, by taxi or in a taxi; on horseback, on a donkey, on a bicycle; on foot; and so on.
14. Complain about, not for. Don't say: Annette complained for the weather.
    Say: Annette complained about the weather.
    Note: When talking about illness we use complain of. We say she complained of a sore throat.
15. Conform to, not with. Don't say: We must conform with the rules.
    Say: We must conform to the rules.
16. Congratulate on, not for. Don't say: I congratulate you for your success.
    Say: I congratulate you on your success.
17. Consist of, not from. Don't say: A year consists from 12 months.
    Say: A year consists of 12 months.

18. Covered with, not by. Don't say: The mountains are covered by snow.
Say: The mountains are covered with/in snow.

19. Cure of, not from. Don't say: The man was cured from his illness.
Say: The man was cured of his illness.

20. Depend on or upon, not from. Don't say: It depends from her.
Say: It depends on (or upon) her.

21. Deprive of, not from. Don't say: Nelson Mandela was deprived from his freedom.
Say: Nelson Mandela was deprived of his freedom.

22. Die of an illness, not from an illness. Don't say: Many people have died from malaria.
Say: Many people have died of malaria.

23. Different from, not than. Don't say: My book is different than yours.
Say: My book is different from yours.

24. Disappointed by, about, or at, not from. Don't say: Phillipa was disappointed from the low marks she got in the test.

Say: Phillipa was disappointed by/about/at the low mark she got in the test.

Note: Before a person we use 'with' or 'in'. Don't say: Jane was disappointed from her son.

Say: Jane was disappointed with/in her son.

25. Divide into parts, not in parts. Don't say: I divided the cake in four parts.
Say: I divided the cake into four parts.
Note: A thing may be divided in half or in two.
Say: Paul divided the apple in half.

26. No doubt of or about, not for. Don't say: I've no doubt for his ability.
Say: I've no doubt of (or about) his ability.

27. Dressed in, not with. Don't say: The woman was dressed with black.
Say: The woman was dressed in black.

28. Exception to, not of. Don't say: This is an exception of the rule.
Say: This is an exception to the rule.

29. Exchange for, not by. Don't say: He exchanged his collection of matchboxes by some foreign stamps.
    Say: He exchanged his collection of matchboxes for some foreign stamps.
30. Glad about, not from or with. Don't say: Francis was glad from (or with) receiving your letter.
    Say: Francis was glad about receiving your letter.

3.5.9 Prepositions after Certain Words

Accuse of	Congratulate on
Guilty of	Repent of
Accustomed to	Consist of
Independent of	Satisfied with
Afraid of	Cure of
Indifferent to	Similar to
Aim at	Depend on
Interested in	Succeed in
Arrive at/in	Deprive of
Jealous of	Superior to
Ashamed of	Die of
Look at	Sure of
Believe in	Different from
Married to	Surprised at/by
Boast of	Dressed in
No doubt of/about	Suspect of
Careful of/with/about	Fail in
Complain about	Tired of
Prefer to	Full of
Composed of	Translate into
Proud of	Good at
Conform to	Warn of/about
Related to	Guard against

PRACTICE EXERCISE N

Fill in the blanks with appropriate prepositions:

1. Could I speak ____ Rama, please?
2. He started going ___ school ____ the age of 5.
3. The children are fond ___ swimming.
4. He is good ___ mathematics.
5. The father was angry ___ his son.
6. I have lived ____ the street ___ 10 years.
7. Aren't you coming ___ us?
8. I am very sorry ___ being late.
9. He goes to school ___ foot.
10. The dog ran _____ the road.
11. She has great affection ___ her children.
12. You should abstain ___ all bad habits.
13. He charges interest __ 6 per cent.
14. She has been ill ____ Wednesday.
15. Harish is _____ the top of the class.

PRACTICE EXERCISE O

Fill in the blanks with appropriate prepositions. Choose your answers from the options given in the brackets.

1. This material is different .... that. (from/to/with)
2. You should explain this .... them. (to/at/with)
3. He has been absent .... Monday. (since/for/from)
4. I haven't been to the theatre .... a long time. (since/for/from)
5. He goes .... school by car. (to/at/on)
6. This is a comfortable house to live .... (on/at/in)
7. They are called .... different names. (by/with/for)
8. We should not spend money .... luxuries. (for/on/with)
9. I gave him a chair to sit .... (on/at/in)
10. The new term begins .... 1 June. (on/in/from)
11. He poured the tea .... the mug. (into/on/in)
12. He said that he was very pleased .... my work. (with/on/at)

PRACTICE EXERCISE P

Fill in the correct prepositions: about, at, by, for, from, in, of, on, to, with.

1. She learned Russian ____________ the age of 45.
2. The book was written ____________ Mark Twain.
3. I'll show you the picture ____________ the palace.
4. We can only get to the camp ____________ foot.
5. He reminds me ____________ his old history teacher.
6. What are you talking ____________?
7. ____________ the end of next year we will have made over £100,000.
8. She always gets up early ____________ the morning and goes to bed late ____________ night.
9. I went to work ____________ Tuesday, but I didn't go ____________ Friday.
10. You'll have to wait. He'll be with you ____________ a minute.
11. Philip waited ____________ her at the movie theatre.
12. He started learning English ____________ 2005.
13. You have to pay ____________ the tickets on the day you order them.
14. We are very proud ____________ this company.
15. It's very kind ____________ you to help us.
16. The old man suffered ____________ a heart attack.
17. Please write ____________ pencil.
18. It's ____________ time you told him the truth.
19. The manager didn't take part ____________ the discussion.
20. He's very good ____________ telling jokes.

3.6 REDUNDANCIES

Redundancy means to use more words than are necessary to convey a meaning. Redundancy is related to wordiness, which is the use of too many words. The most important distinction is that redundancy uses words with the same meaning, while wordiness uses more words than are needed. Both redundancy and wordiness should be avoided.

For example, how often have you heard a friend say something like this: 'It was an unexpected surprise when pair of baby twins were born at 12 midnight?' What is a surprise if not unexpected? What are twins if not a pair? Who can be born but a baby? When is midnight if not at 12? The expressions we use are full of redundancy. Your friend could just as well have said: 'It was a surprise when twins were born at midnight' with far less repetition.

Redundancy typically takes the form of tautology: phrases that repeat a meaning with different though semantically similar words. Common examples are 'a variety of different items', 'an added bonus', 'to over-exaggerate', 'and etc.', 'end result', 'free gift', 'future plans', 'unconfirmed rumour', 'to kill, murder, or electrocute someone to death', 'past history', 'safe haven', 'potential hazard', 'completely surrounded', 'false pretence', and so on.

A more general classification of redundancy is pleonasm, which could be unnecessary words (or even word parts).

These redundant expressions are called *pleonasms*. Some common ones are in the list below. Remove the superfluous words (in brackets) and you will not subtract from the overall meaning of the expression.

- (actual) experience
- (advance) planning
- (advance) reservations
- (advance) warning
- all meet (together)
- (armed) gunman
- at (12) midnight
- at (12) noon
- autobiography (of my life)
- (awkward) predicament
- (baby) boy was born
- (basic) fundamentals
- cease (and desist)
- cheap (price)
- (close) proximity
- cold (temperature)
- commute (back and forth)
- consensus (of opinion)
- (difficult) dilemma
- each (and every)
- (empty) space
- (end) result
- estimated (roughly) at
- filled (to capacity)
- (free) gift
- (frozen) ice
- (general) public
- green (in colour)

- join (together)
- (natural) instinct
- never (at any time)
- (null and) void
- (pair of) twins
- (past) experience
- (poisonous) venom
- (pre-) recorded
- reason is (because)
- (regular) routine
- (small) speck
- (suddenly) exploded
- surrounded (on all sides)
- (unexpected) surprise

The following is a list of commonly used, redundant expressions and an example of the correct wording.

Redundant	*Factual and Precise*
Return back	return
Repeat again	repeat
Midway between	between
End result	result
Eye-witness	witness
Actual truth	truth
At this point of time	now
In the near future	soon
Have the capability of	can
In spite of the fact	although
Due to the fact that	because
Until such time as	when
Pair of twins	twins
Refer back	refer
Hot water heater	water heater
Pick and choose	select or choose
Surrounded on all sides	surrounded
Red in colour	red
Advance forward	advance
Absolutely complete	complete

Redundant	*Factual and Precise*
Until such time as	when
Trickle down	trickle
Final outcome	outcome
Month of January	January
Brief summary	summary
Collect together	collect
Collaborate together	collaborate
Follows after	follows
Dusk and nightfall	dusk or nightfall
CD-ROM disk	CD ROM
ATM machine	ATM
DVD disk	DVD
SARS syndrome	SARS
HIV virus	HIV
VIN number	VIN
PIN number	PIN
ISBN number	ISBN
Joint cooperation	cooperation
Lonely isolation	isolation
Wet rainy day	rainy day
Habitual custom	custom
Faster speed	speed
Pizza pie	pizza or pie
Adequate enough	adequate or enough

There is no denying the importance of redundancies in modern-day literary writing. However in the present, the use of tautological phrases and words has been cut down to avoid repetition and monotony. Despite the fact, writers use tautology as a tool to draw attention or emphasize an idea.

Here are some examples of redundant passages and how to fix them:
Passage I

- The United States Civil War began in 1861. On 12 April 1861, civil war broke out when battle broke out at Fort Sumter. The Civil War is the most deadly war (measured by per capita deaths) in American history, with at least 600,000 deaths caused by the war. The Civil War is also the first example of total war, which is so-called because of its totality. Total war touches all parts of societies. Total war had touched all parts of American society by 1865.

Words that are too close together include:

- The United States **Civil War** began in 1861. On April 12, 1861, **civil war** broke out when battle broke out at Fort Sumter. The **Civil War** is the most deadly **war** (measured by per capita deaths) in American history, with at least 600,000 deaths caused by the **war**. The **Civil War** is also the first example of **total war**, which is so-called because of its totality. **Total war** touches all parts of societies. **Total war** had touched all parts of American society by 1865.
- The United States Civil War began in 1861. On April 12, 1861, civil war **broke out** when battle **broke out** at Fort Sumter.
- The Civil War is the most **deadly** war (measured by per capita **deaths**) in American history, with at least 600,000 **deaths** caused by the war.
- The Civil War is also the first example of **total war**, which is so-called because of its **totality**. Total war touches all parts of societies. **Total war** had touched all parts of American society by 1865.
- Total war **touches all parts of societies**. Total war had **touched all parts of American society** by 1865.

The paragraph would read better if written:

- The United States Civil War began on 12 April 1861, when battle broke out at Fort Sumter. By 1865, there were more than 600,000 casualties. In terms of per capita deaths, the Civil War is the deadliest in American history. It is also the first example of total war, so-called because it touches all parts of societies. Certainly, by the time the Confederate Army surrendered, the War Between the States had left untouched no sector of American life.

Note how redundancy is eliminated by:

- Varying vocabulary (e.g., 'parts of societies' vs. 'sector of American life').
- Replacing proper nouns with more generic nouns (e.g., 'Civil War' vs. 'it'). In other cases, demonstrative adjectives, such as 'that' or 'this', can fulfil the same purpose.
- Providing new and substantive details (e.g., 'the War Between the States' is both a way of not saying 'Civil War' again and a way of telling readers that the Civil War is also known by another name).
- Not expressing the same idea more than once when this is unnecessary. ('The United States Civil War began in 1861. On 12 April 1861,

civil war broke out when battle broke out at Fort Sumter.' It is obvious from the first sentence that the 'Civil War began in 1861.' Therefore, it is not necessary to begin the second sentence with, 'On 12 April 1861, civil war broke out.' The two sentences can be combined as: 'The United States Civil War began on 12 April 1861, when battle broke out at Fort Sumter.')

Passage II

This paper will focus on the history of American literature. This paper will start by focusing on the history of American literature as it relates to the history of literature, in general. The history of literature is, generally, related to the history of humanity. The history of American literature is particularly concerned with the history of humanity because early American settlers and political leaders were highly influenced by the Age.

Words that are too close together include:

- **This paper** will focus on the history of American literature. **This paper** will start by focusing on the history of American literature as it relates to the history of literature, in general.
- This paper will start by focusing on the history of American literature as it relates to the history of literature, **in general**. The history of literature is, **generally**, related to the history of humanity.
- The history of American literature is particularly **concerned** with the history of humanity because early American settlers and political leaders were highly influenced by the Age of Enlightenment, which was highly **concerned** with humanity.
- The history of American literature is particularly concerned with the history of humanity because early American settlers and political leaders were **highly** influenced by the Age of Enlightenment, which was **highly** concerned with humanity.
- The history of American literature is particularly concerned with the history of **humanity** because early American settlers and political leaders were highly influenced by the Age of Enlightenment, which was highly concerned with **humanity**.

This paragraph would read better if written:

- This paper will focus on the history of American literature. It will start by considering the history of literature, which is, generally, related to the history of humanity. American literature has tended to be concerned with the course of human development, in part because early American settlers and political leaders were highly influenced by the Age of Enlightenment, which focused largely on understanding humanity.

PRACTICE EXERCISE Q

Choose the redundant expressions and rewrite the improved sentences:

1. Looking back in retrospect, I can't remember a summer of my childhood when I didn't spend most of the day outdoors getting into trouble.
2. Justin is a friendly and amicable guy.
3. Mr James was first introduced in the meeting.
4. The vote was completely and totally unanimous.
5. We could see some dilapidated ruins.
6. One of the identical twins says to the other, 'You are not fat.'
7. She herself has written her autobiography of her own life in just two weeks.
8. There is close proximity between the two sentences.
9. Ravi decided to live in lonely isolation.
10. Beauty products have an aromatic aroma.

PRACTICE EXERCISE R

Eliminate redundant words. Cross them out.

1. We need to cooperate together.
2. This is absolutely a phenomenal piece of equipment...
3. A liaison officer who is responsible for...
4. A total number of 14 APCs...
5. With the close proximity of...
6. Exactly the same number of soldiers...
7. New innovations will move our industry forward.
8. Let me summarize briefly...
9. We also have ATM machines inside the base.
10. There are 25 companies which have already expressed a desire to join the programme.
11. As far as I'm concerned, there is no need for further enhancement of the base.
12. The ministry is already in the process of reviewing the memorandum.

PRACTICE EXERCISE S

Remove unnecessary words and rewrite the sentences, but don't change the main idea.

1. Helen is a smart and intelligent woman.
2. Our top student is a physically ill student today.
3. I will complete my research paper in a period of a week.
4. John's stylish boots made of crocodile skin cost him an arm and a leg.
5. Susan is the teacher who teaches chemistry at her high school.
6. The student is writing a writing assignment for his English composition class.
7. The book, which is located on the table, is a grammar book.
8. Jennifer ran with the other runners in the 5,000-metre track event and finished third overall.
9. Her purse, which was manufactured in Italy, was stolen yesterday.
10. Many people admire her lectures for the fact that her ideas are expressed in a clear manner.

3.7 CLICHÉS

Cliché refers to an expression that has been overused to the extent that it loses its original meaning or novelty. A cliché may also refer to actions and events that are predictable because of some previous events. All examples of cliché are expressions that were once new and fresh. They won popularity in the public and hence have been used so extensively that such expressions now sound boring and at times irritating, due to the fact that they have lost their original colour. For instance, the phrase 'as red as a rose' must have been a fresh and innovative expression at some point in time, but today it is considered universally as a cliché, and does not make such an impact when used in everyday or formal writing.

Example 1
In describing time, the following expressions have turned into cliché:

- *in the nick of time* – to happen just in time
- *only time will tell* – to become clear over time
- *a matter of time* – to happen sooner or later
- *at the speed of light* – to do something very quickly
- *lasted an eternity* – to last for a very long time
- *lost track of time* – to stop paying attention to time

Example 2
In describing people, these expressions have turned into cliché:

- *as brave as a lion* – describes a very brave person
- *as clever as a fox* – describes a very clever person
- *as old as the hills* – describes an old person or idea
- *a diamond in the rough* – describes someone with a brilliant future
- *fit as a fiddle* – describes a person in a good shape
- *as meek as a lamb* – describes a person who is too weak and humble

Example 3
In describing various sentiments, a number of expressions have turned into cliché:

- *frightened to death* – to be too frightened
- *scared out of one's wits* – to be too frightened
- *all is fair in love and war* – to go to any extent to claim somebody's love
- *all is well that ends well* – a happy ending reduces the severity of problems that come in one's way
- *every cloud has a silver lining* – problems also have something good in them
- *the writing on the wall* – something clear and already understood
- *time heals all wounds* – pain and miseries will heal with the passage of time
- *haste makes waste* – people make mistakes when rushing

Example 4
Below is a list of some more common clichés:

- *They all lived happily ever after*
- *Read between the lines*
- *Fall head over heals*
- *Waking up on the wrong side of the bed*
- *The quiet before the storm*
- *Between the devil and the deep blue sea*

A cliché is a traditional form of human expression (in words, thoughts, emotions, gestures, acts, and the like) which—due to repetitive use in social life—has lost its original, often ingenious heuristic power. Although it thus fails positively to contribute meaning to social interactions and communication, it does function socially, since it manages to stimulate behaviour (cognition, emotion, volition, action), while it avoids reflection on meanings.

Clichés are often idioms. This makes clichés difficult to translate into other languages because their meaning won't always be understood by people from different cultures.

Idioms are either opaque or transparent:

- Opaque: When you translate an opaque idiom, it may not make sense because the literal meaning has very little to do with the intended meaning. An example of an opaque idiom is 'bag of bones' which means someone is very underweight.
- Transparent: A transparent idiom shows some similarity between the literal and the intended meaning. For example, 'playing your cards right' is an expression that actually came from card games and can be applied to other situations.

As a brief phrase that implies an idiom can become a cliché if it's used often enough, such as 'it's raining cats and dogs'. Its meaning will catch on and propel itself forward, much like any other cliché we use today. Overused expressions, roundabout metaphors and similes, and circumlocutions may be classified under cliché.

Find the list of commonly used clichés for refinement:

	Cliché	Improvement
1.	Pushed or stretched the envelope	took a risk or considered a new option
2.	Eyeballs on the screen	concentrate
3.	Wipe the slate clean	start again
4.	The ball is in your court	the decision is yours
5.	Fell on deaf ears	ignored
6.	In full swing	at a lively level
7.	Again and again	frequently
8.	In a nutshell	briefly
9.	Sell like hot cakes	in considerable demand
10.	A bolt from the blue	a complete surprise
11.	Almighty dollar	the power of wealth
12.	Anybody's guess	uncertain
13.	Sit on the fence	avoid becoming involved
14.	By/in leaps and bounds	very quickly, in large amounts
15.	Last but not least	important though last
16.	Short but sweet	pleasant but brief
17.	Square peg in a round hole	unsuitable
18.	Leave no stone unturned	try every possible option
19.	Calm before the storm	uneasy silence
20.	Iron out the problem	solve the problem

21. Give the green signal	approve, permit
22. Alpha and omega	the beginning and the end
23. Amiable qualities	lovable qualities
24. Angry passions	angry feelings, anger
25. As a matter of form	merely routine
26. In due course	eventually
27. Writing on the wall	prediction
28. Part and parcel	essential part
29. Call the shots	be in control or charge
30. Worst nightmare	disaster, strong competitor
31. At long last	ultimately
32. At one fell swoop	at one blow
33. At sixes and sevens	to be in a state of confusion
34. At the first blush	at first sight, at first glance
35. At the psychological moment	at the critical moment
36. Be that as it may	nevertheless
37. Beer and skittles	self-indulgence and amusement
38. Behind the scenes	in private
39. Better and better	increasingly good
40. Between the cup and the lip	expectation and fulfilment

3.7.1 Why Shouldn't You Use Clichés?

Clichés are generally not acceptable in academic writing, though some may be real and effective in day-to-day conversation and less formal writing.

1. **Clichés are vague:** It is always best to use the most accurate wording in order to present evidence and support arguments clearly. Specific facts and reasons make better evidence than overviews and common phrases.
2. **Clichés make writings and argument interchangeable with anybody else's:** Ensure that arguments and writing are precise and specific to the writing task.
3. **Clichés appear to be boring:** By using a cliché, you're telling your reader that you lack originality, making them want to yawn and stop reading your paper.
4. **Clichés make you seem lazy:** They are a hedge when you don't want to do creative and imaginative work.
5. **Clichés make you lose credibility:** A reader will not rely on you as a confident source, if you can't come up with a better description than a cliché.
6. **Clichés are poor substitutes for actual evidence:** Since clichés are not specific, they do not offer strong commentaries to prove a point. Ensure that meaningless phrases are eliminated of your paper.

PRACTICE EXERCISE T

The following paragraph contains a number of clichés. As you read through the paragraph, underline these tired, overworn phrases.

In this day and age, good teachers are few and far between. My deepest, darkest secret is my desire to be one of those teachers—one that is worth her weight in gold, who works her fingers to the bone, hand in hand with students to prepare them to meet the trials and tribulations of life. With an attitude like that, my first day of teaching was doomed to disappointment. I was walking on air as I arrived at my first class, until I realized I'd forgotten my key. A wave of optimism washed over me.

When I saw the classroom door open. I sauntered up to the door, when BANG, like a bolt from the blue, one of my new students—later proven rotten to the core—darted out and slammed the door right in my face. My anxiety was growing by leaps and bounds, when, as luck would have it, a custodian came by and unlocked the door for me. I could sense the undercurrent of excitement as I walked into the room and the mischievous student beat a hasty retreat to his seat. Anxious for my reaction, he breathed a sigh of relief when I decided not to make a tempest in a teapot about the incident. Cool as a cucumber, I posed the first discussion prompt, 'The writing process is neither writing nor a process. Discuss.' In their youthful glee, all the students jumped on the bandwagon to discuss. Slowly but surely, the humiliating experience became water under the bridge as I continue the uphill battle to become all that I can be as an English teacher.

PRACTICE EXERCISE U

Locate the clichés in the following paragraph and replace them with new phrases if possible.

In today's society, the vast majority of college graduates may struggle with finding a job that suits their major. Often times after graduation, students must face the music and realize that they may have to look to other fields in order to find employment. A viable alternative may be the pursuit of fame and fortune through exploring career opportunities. You may be green with envy if your friends have less difficulty finding a job; however, the bottom line is that the job market is a vicious circle. By the end of the long hot summer following your graduation, you may have a sneaking suspicion that your prospects are as cold as ice.

Possible clichés to reword: 'face the music', 'the pursuit of fame and fortune', 'green with envy', 'vicious circle', 'cold as ice', 'After graduation, students often realize they may have to look to other fields in order to find employment.'

PRACTICE EXERCISE V

Complete the phrase before you even finish reading it? If so, the phrase is probably a cliché.

1. Better late than ________.
2. Every cloud has a ________.
3. Fall head over ________.
4. Breathe a sigh of ________.
5. All is fair in love and ________.
6. When you have lemons, make ________.
7. As old as the ________.
8. Opposites ________.
9. All's well that ends ________.
10. Sent a shiver down my ________.
11. All that glitters is not ________.
12. The apple doesn't fall far from the________.
13. Ignorance is bliss________.
14. Better safe than ________.
15. Like father, like ________.

Cliché Worksheet 1

Directions: You're going to make up your own clichés! Create a different ending for 10 of the following. The funnier the better!!

1. Better to be safe than ________________________
   Better to be safe than sorry.
2. It's always darkest before ________________________
   It's always darkest before the storm. It's always darkest before dawn.
3. Never underestimate the power of ________________________
   Never underestimate the power of a woman.
4. You can lead a horse to water, but you can't ________________________
   You can lead a horse to water, but you can't make him drink.
5. Don't bite ________________________
   Don't bite the hand that feeds you.
6. No news is ________________________
   No news is good news.
7. A miss is as good as ________________________
   A miss is as good as a mile.
8. You can't teach an old dog ________________________
   You can't teach an old dog new tricks.
9. If you lie down with dogs, ________________________
   If you lie down with dogs, you'll rise up with fleas.

10. The pen is mightier than ______________________________
    The pen is mightier than the sword.

11. Where there's smoke ______________________________
    Where there's smoke there's fire.

12. A penny saved is ______________________________
    A penny saved is a penny earned.

13. Two's company, three's ______________________________
    Two's company, three's a crowd.

14. Don't put off till tomorrow ______________________________
    Don't put off till tomorrow what you can do today.

15. Children should be ______________ and not ______________
    Children should be seen and not heard.

16. If at first you don't succeed ______________________________
    If at first you don't succeed, try, try again.

17. You get out of something ______________________________
    You get out of something what you put into it.

18. Better late than ______________________________
    Better late than never.

19. Every cloud has ______________________________
    Every cloud has a silver lining.

20. The early bird ______________________________
    The early bird gets the worm.

Cliché Worksheet 2

Directions: You're going to make up your own clichés! Create a different ending for 10 of the following. The funnier the better!

1. Every rose has ______________________________
   Every rose has its thorn.

2. That's just like the pot ______________________________
   That's just like the pot calling the kettle black.

3. They're like ______________________________
   They're like two peas in a pod.

4. Behind the clouds, ______________________________
   Behind the clouds, the sun is shining.

5. Tomorrow is ______________________________
   Tomorrow is another day.

6. It has to get worse, ______________________________
   It has to get worse, before it gets better.

7. Early to bed, early to rise makes a man ______________________
   Early to bed, early to rise makes a man healthy, wealthy, and wise.
8. A penny saved is ______________________
   A penny saved is a penny earned.
9. An apple a day ______________________
   An apple a day keeps the doctor away.
10. Don't let the bedbugs ______________________
    Don't let the bedbugs bite.
11. This hurts me worse than ______________________
    This hurts me worse than it hurts you.
12. When life gives you lemons, ______________________
    When life gives you lemons, make lemonade.
13. Don't worry, ______________________
    Don't worry, be happy!
14. Absence makes ______________________
    Absence makes the heart grow fonder.
15. Have your cake and ______________________
    Have your cake and eat it too.
16. It'll all come out ______________________
    It'll all come out in the wash.
17. Separate the ______________ from the ______________
    Separate the men from the boys.
18. All good things come to ______________________
    All good things come to those who wait.
19. When the going gets tough, ______________________
    When the going gets tough, the tough get going.
20. There is nothing to fear, but ______________________
    There is nothing to fear, but fear itself.

PRACTICE EXERCISE W

Edit the following paragraphs with correct subject–verb agreement or noun–pronoun agreement:

Paragraph 1

(1) My family enjoy scuba diving, so nearly every vacation, we go on a diving trip. **(2)** We have noticed that there is three completely different kinds of divers.

(3) We call them the 'nature lovers', the 'pool guys', and the 'seals'. **(4)** The people whom we call 'nature lovers' enjoy getting in the water for a short swim to look at the rocks, seaweed, and underwater creatures, which is swimming around. **(5)** The 'pool guys', who wear the latest hi-tech equipment, comes for a short while to have a swim and test how good their equipment are. **(6)** The 'seals', who wear only their swimsuits, dive in the water and disappear for what seem like hours. **(7)** Each of the divers enjoy the ocean in a different way.

Paragraph 2

(1) My family are a combination of all three types. **(2)** All my brother wants to do are try out different kinds of equipment and see how deep he can dive. **(3)** As for my father, he is a 'seal': Swimming around and cooking his 'catch' are what he enjoy most. **(4)** My mother and I are 'nature lovers': swimming with snorkels and fins is fun, but neither of us have any interest in diving 50 feet down or reaching under a rock to find a slimy abalone. **(5)** So we all enjoy our diving trips in our own way.

Paragraph 3

(1) The 'nature lovers' are the one who enjoy snorkelling around for brief periods of time. **(2)** They always try to have a minimal impact on the environment. **(3)** For example, their trash, or garbage, are always taken away. **(4)** Taking rocks and shells are something they would never do. **(5)** They are there to see but not spoil the beauty of nature that are under water.

FURTHER READING

1. Turton, Nigel D. *ABC of Common Grammatical Errors*. New Delhi: Macmillan India, 1995 (reprinted in 1996).
2. Soundararaj, Francis. *Speaking and Writing for Effective Business Communication in English*. New Delhi: Macmillan India, 2007.
3. Parker, Edward. *Written English: A Grammar of English* (specially prepared for Indian students). Harlow: Longmans, Green & Co., 1940.
4. Wood, Fredrick T. *The Remedial English Grammar for Foreign Students*. London: Macmillan, 1965 (reprinted in 1968).
5. Soundararaj, Francis. *Basics of Communication in English*. New Delhi: Macmillan India, 2012.
6. https://www.theidioms.com/nouns/ (accessed on 20 September 2018)
7. https://www.grammar-quizzes.com/agree6b.html (accessed on 20 September 2018)

4 UNIT

Nature and Style of Sensible Writing

Every writer writes for a specific purpose—for example, a writer may want to describe or define something, classify ideas, characters, or objects with shared characteristics into specific groups or categories, and persuade people to agree with his point of view. Knowing the nature and style of various types of writing and their usages is important for any writer.

4.1 DESCRIBING

The main purpose of descriptive writing is to describe. It is a style of writing that focuses on describing a character, an event, or a place in minute detail. The best descriptive writing appeals to all five senses—smell, sight, taste, touch, and hearing. Descriptive writing is often found in fiction, though it can make an appearance in nonfiction as well (for example, memoirs, first-hand accounts of events, or travel guides). When authors write in a descriptive style, they are painting a picture in words of a person, place, or thing for their audience.

Descriptive writing includes:

- Poetry
- Journal/Diary writing
- Descriptions of Nature
- Fictional novels or plays

4.1.1 Elements of Descriptive Writing

Wide Sensory Appeal

- Hear, smell, taste, touch, see
- Don't over-rely on visual appeal
- Don't point out the obvious; subtlety

Specific Detail and Imagery

- Describes more than the facts
- Creates a mood or feeling
- Unconcerned with the relay of information

Language Choices

- Words chosen for connotation, not denotation
- Words chosen because they sound interesting
- Words chosen to create mood or tone
- Words chosen for their alliteration or assonance

Subjects for Description

- Character traits
- Environment and setting
- Objects and actions of interest

Example 1
In good descriptive writing, the author will not just say: 'The cloudy sky looks beautiful during sunset.'

He or she will change the sentence, focusing on more details and descriptions, like 'The sunset filled the entire sky with the deep colour of rubies, setting the clouds ablaze.'

Example 2
Chairman Mao, our beloved leader, smiled down at us from his place above the blackboard. The sounds and smells of the tantalizing May afternoon drifted in through the window. The sweet breeze carried the scent of new leaves and tender young grass and rippled the paper slogan below Chairman Mao's picture: STUDY HARD AND ADVANCE EVERY DAY. (*Red Scarf Girl* by Ji-li Jiang)

Let's do a recap:

- What is she looking at?—A Chairman Mao poster.
- What does she hear?—May afternoon breeze and sounds.

- What does she smell?—New leaves.
- What does she feel?—Pride.

Non-example:
The paper slogan 'STUDY HARD AND ADVANCE EVERY DAY' below Chairman Mao's picture placed above the blackboard was rippled by the breeze on May afternoon.

PRACTICE EXERCISE A

Convert the following sentences into descriptive form using your imagination:

a) There were grapes in the bowl in kitchen.
b) Samuel took his dog to the park.
c) Drew's skateboard was on the floor.
d) He went to the store on his bicycle.
e) She ran outside.

4.2 DEFINING

Its main purpose is to explain. The author focuses on defining a given topic or subject without voicing his personal opinion. It is usually in a logical order and sequence.

Example:
Many people associate the taste of pumpkins with fall. In October, companies from Starbucks to McDonalds roll out their pumpkin-flavoured lattes and desserts. Here is how to make an easy pumpkin pie using only five ingredients. First, make sure you have all of the ingredients.

This writing is expository because it is *explaining*. In this case, you can already tell that the piece will be about how to make a pumpkin pie.

Non-example:
Everyone knows that the best part about fall is all of the pumpkin-flavoured desserts. Pumpkin pie is the best fall treat because it is not only delicious but also nutritious. Pumpkin is filled with vitamin A, which is essential for a healthy immune system and good vision.

This is not expository because several opinions are stated, such as 'Pumpkin pie is the best fall treat....' Although this excerpt contains a fact about pumpkin containing vitamin A, that fact is used as evidence to support the opinion.

Example:
Kleptomania is the inability to refrain from the urge for stealing items and is usually done for reasons other than personal use or financial gain. First described in 1816, kleptomania is classified in psychiatry as an impulse control disorder. People diagnosed with kleptomania often have other types of disorders involving mood, anxiety, eating, impulse control, and drug use. They also have great levels of stress, guilt, and remorse, and privacy issues accompanying the act of stealing. The characteristics of the behaviours associated with stealing could result in other problems as well, which include social segregation and substance abuse.

Non-example:
It still shocks me when people react negatively to my stealing. I guess part of the horror/beauty of mental illness is the totally blinkered relationship you develop with risk. Getting busted doesn't even occur to me. (*My Life as a Kleptomaniac*, Patrick Marlborough)

PRACTICE EXERCISE B

Try defining the following simple items you encounter daily:

a. Chair
b. Car
c. Dog
d. Table
e. Colony

4.3 CLASSIFYING

In classification writing, things are organized, divided, sorted, or classified into groups or categories. One of the most important things in classification writing is to get the right or best groups or categories.

4.3.1 Developing a Thesis

Once you have decided on your group, purpose, and categories, develop a thesis statement that does the following three things:

- names what group of people or things you intend to classify
- describes the basis of the classification
- labels the categories you have developed

Example:
Here is a thesis statement for a classification paper written for a health and human fitness class that includes all three of the above elements, underlined:

Our last five US presidents have practised physical fitness regimens that varied from the very formal to the informal. They have been either regular private gym-goers, disciplined public joggers, or casual active sports enthusiasts.

Ordering Categories

Order is the way you arrange ideas to show how they relate to one another. For example, it is common to arrange facts and discussion pointing from the most to the least important or from the least to the most important, or from the oldest to the most recent or the longest to the shortest. The example thesis statement above is ordered from most to least formal physical fitness activities. There is no one right way; use an ordering system that seems best to suit your purpose and the type of information you are working with.

Signal Words

Signal phrases, or transitions, typically used for classification papers include the following:

- this type of ...
- several kinds of ...
- in this category ...
- can be divided into ...
- classified according to ...
- is categorized by ...

These phrases signal to the reader your intention to divide and sort things. They also contribute to the unity of the paper.

Classification requires that you invent (or discover) abstract categories, impose them on a concrete whole, and derive something new—a tall order that you can, nevertheless, manage if you resist the temptation to skip the brainstorming steps. The point of classification is to reveal and communicate something meaningful.

Examples of Classification Paragraphs

The Great Gardens of Jamaica

Each of Jamaica's four great gardens, although established along similar principles, has acquired its own distinctive aura. Hope Gardens, in the heart of Kingston, evokes postcard pictures from the 1950s of public parks, gracious and vaguely suburban and filled with familiar favourites—lantana and marigolds—as well as exotics. Bath has retained its Old World character; it is the easiest to conjure as it must have looked in Bligh's time. Cinchona of the clouds is otherworldly. And Castleton, the garden established to replace Bath, fleetingly evokes that golden age of Jamaican tourism, when visitors arrived in their own yachts—the era of Ian Fleming and Noel Coward, before commercial air travel unloaded ordinary mortals all over the island.[1]

Cybercriminals

'Cybercriminals generally fall into one of three categories,' he [Michael DeCesare, president of McAfee] says. First there are the 'Anonymous of the world' or the hacktivists—people who expose information about a company or government they morally oppose. Second is organized crime. 'They're realizing there's far more money in cybercrime than prostitution,' Mr DeCesare says. 'You can buy somebody's I.D. for less than $10 online.' Third are activities funded by states and other political groups. 'Every government has a cyber division,' he says, including the United States. But cyber dangers now stretch beyond state lines to groups such as Al-Qaeda. 'Cybercrime is a lot like that—[the country is] almost not relevant anymore', making it difficult to hold governments accountable.[2]

PRACTICE EXERCISE C

Try classifying the following into paragraphs:

a. Cheaters
b. Shoppers
c. Hobbies
d. Dancing styles
e. Reality shows on television
f. Attitudes towards money
g. Ways of quitting smoking
h. Diets
i. Study habits
j. Road trips

---

[1] Caroline Alexander, 'Captain Bligh's Cursed Breadfruit', *The Smithsonian* (September 2009).

[2] Alexandra Wolfe, 'Michael DeCesare', *The Wall Street Journal* (14–15 December 2013).

TV Interviewers

'Local TV interviewers come in two varieties. One is a bulimic blond person with a deviated septum and a severe cognitive disorder who went into broadcasting because he or she was too emotionally disturbed for telephone sales work. The other variety is suave, sagacious, grossly overqualified for the job, and too depressed to talk to you. Good local TV people are always depressed because their field is so crowded.[3]

4.4 PROVIDING EXAMPLES OR EVIDENCE

Research requires us to scrutinize information and assess its credibility. Accordingly, when we think about various phenomena, we examine empirical data and craft detailed explanations justifying our interpretations. An essential component of constructing our research narratives is providing supporting evidence and examples.

Evidence can be separated into two categories: primary and secondary sources.

4.4.1 What Are Primary Sources?

Primary sources are first-hand experiences, accounts, observations, reports, or narratives. Such sources could include diaries, letters, contemporary newspapers, or eyewitness accounts of events. Official documents (e.g., the Canadian Charter of Rights and Freedoms), data collected from surveys, and lab results are also primary sources. In the humanities, the text you are writing about is also considered your primary text. So, for example, if you are writing a paper on *Macbeth*, then the play is your primary source. In the sciences, primary sources are also the results of an experiment that have been peer-reviewed and published in an academic journal.

4.4.2 What Are Secondary Sources?

Secondary sources are critiques written by academics and scholars. These sources are considered secondary because they examine primary sources to present an

[3] P. J. O'Rourke, 'Book Tour', in *Age and Guile Beat Youth, Innocence, and a Bad Haircut* (New York: Atlantic Monthly Press, 1995).

argument or support a point of view; as such, they may be selective with their evidence or insert themselves in a debate happening among a number of scholars. In the sciences, reviews, which are surveys of articles that demonstrate an understanding of a field, are considered secondary. It is a good idea to be aware of the bias in secondary sources when employing them as evidence.

Frequently, the assignment will specify whether you need to use primary or secondary sources; however, if you are unsure about what kind of sources you need, ask your professor for clarification.

Among the forms of evidence you might draw from are:

- Graphs, charts, tables, or figures
- Statistics
- Experiments or studies done by peer-reviewed sources
- Surveys conducted by reputable sources
- Interviews
- Quotes or paraphrases from primary sources
- Quotes or paraphrases from secondary sources

4.4.3 When to Introduce Evidence and Examples

Evidence and examples create the foundation upon which your claims can stand firm. Without proof, your arguments lack credibility. You should introduce and link your arguments to evidence when you:

- state information that is not 'common knowledge';
- draw conclusions, make inferences, or suggest implications based on specific data;
- need to clarify a prior statement, and it would be more effectively done with an illustration;
- need to identify representative examples of a category;
- desire to distinguish concepts; and
- emphasize a point by highlighting a specific situation.

4.4.4 Introductory Phrases to Use and Their Contexts

To assist with effectively supporting statements, the introductory phrases are organized below according to their function.

Purpose	*Introductory Phrase*	*Example*
Stating information that is not 'common knowledge'	• [use relevant style guide's in-text citation format] • As [Author] indicated/stated/discovered • According to [Author]	✓ As Smith indicated in a 2010 study ... ✓ According to Marks and Peters ...
Drawing conclusions, making inferences, or suggesting implications based on specific data	• Suggests • as evidenced/suggested/indicated by • based on • can be seen/observed when • as seen in • which is made apparent when • is demonstrated by/through/when • hinges on	✓ The strong negative correlation suggests that ... ✓ As evidenced/suggested/indicated by their enlarged adrenal glands, patients with ... ✓ Based on self-reported survey results ... ✓ This phenomenon can be seen/observed when wind speeds exceed ... ✓ As seen in the high recurrence rates of ... ✓ The causal link between A and B, which is made apparent when B triggers ... ✓ The efficacy of chocolate as a cure for unhappiness is demonstrated by survey results highlighted in ... ✓ This conclusion hinges on ...
Clarifying a prior statement	• for example • for instance • by way of illustration • as an example • to clarify • to explain further • namely • to be specific • that is • in other words	✓ This occurrence is rare. For example, only 1 in 20 ... ✓ It is unlikely that current population growth rates are sustainable. For instance, several major coastal cities are already suffering from ... ✓ By way of illustration, less than 20 per cent of new matriculates feel prepared for ... ✓ As an example, when a country faces economic recession, polls indicate that over 80 per cent of the population supports ... ✓ To clarify, not all government-funded facilities provide ... ✓ To explain further, large doses of Agent O can trigger ... ✓ Millennials prefer flexible work conditions, namely the ability to work remotely. ✓ To be specific, bull markets can ... ✓ That is, significant and sudden drops in temperature can ... ✓ In other words, short bursts of high-intensity ultrasound can ...

Purpose	*Introductory Phrase*	*Example*
Identifying representative examples of a category	• for example/instance • such as* • e.g., • one/another example • like* • excluding • including • an example being * NOTE: 'such as' and 'like' have two different uses. 'Such as' introduces a specific example that is part of a category. 'Like' suggests the listed items are similar to, but not included in, the topic discussed.	✓ Typhoons are considered acts of God, for example/instance. ✓ The island is home to many native carnivorous plants, such as Venus flytraps. ✓ The only known bioluminescent vertebrates are fish (e.g., the anglerfish and lantern fish). ✓ One/Another example of this exception is ... ✓ I prefer outdoor sports like mountain climbing because they allow me to enjoy nature while exercising. ✓ All mammals, excluding humans, stop drinking milk at a young age. ✓ All stars, including our sun, ... ✓ Hawks feast on rodents, an example being ...
Distinguishing concepts	• in a similar case • unlike the case of • in the same way • as a case in point • in a typical situation • in a normal scenario	✓ In a similar case, a male patient with arthritis ... ✓ Unlike a single-blind study, a double-blind study reduces the risk of observer bias. ✓ Redundancy and wordiness can be reduced in the same way: through careful editing. ✓ As a case in point, let's look at the situation in which ... ✓ In a typical situation, marsupials would ... ✓ In a normal scenario, cortisol suppressant effects ...
Emphasizing a point by highlighting a specific situation	• for example • indeed • in fact • notably • markedly • as a case in point	✓ Nocturnal marsupials, for example, have ... ✓ Indeed, since the World Health Organization declared an end to the Ebola outbreak in the Democratic Republic of the Congo ... ✓ Ice-free habitats around Antarctica, in fact, have ... ✓ High-carbon steel alloys, notably, undergo a transformation when ... ✓ Markedly, the deserts irregular rainfall levels have ... ✓ As a case in point, the last known male northern white rhinoceros ...

4.4.5 How to Use Evidence?

Standards for Evidence

Each discipline and each genre of writing will have standards against which it will gauge the academic merit and use of evidence. But some general rules apply (a detailed explanation of each rule follows this list):

- Make sure your evidence is appropriate to the paper you are writing.
- Make sure the evidence does, in fact, support your argument or your claims.
- Tell your reader why this evidence supports your argument/claims.
- Make sure you have an appropriate amount of evidence.
- Make sure to appropriately cite your evidence.

NOTE: Though not a general rule, your paper will be strengthened by acknowledging competing evidence—evidence that challenges your argument. This demonstrates that you have fully researched your topic and can counter claims against your argument.

4.4.6 Selecting Evidence

Much of how to use evidence is about finding a clear and logical relation between the evidence you use and your claim. For example, if you are asked to write a paper on the effects of pollution on watersheds, you would not use a story your grandfather told you about the river he used to swim in that is now polluted. You would look for peer-reviewed journal articles by experts on the subject.

Once you have found the appropriate type of evidence, it is important to select the evidence that supports your specific claim. For example, if you are writing a psychology paper on the role of emotions in decision-making, you would look for psychology journal articles that connect these two elements.

Example:
Emotions play a larger role in rational decision-making than most of us think (Claim). Subjects deciding to wear a seat belt demonstrated an activity in the ventromedial frontal lobe—the part of the brain that governs emotion (Shibata 2001; Evidence).[4] Or, if you are asked to write a paper on the Gothic elements of *Dr Jekyll and Mr Hyde*, you might use as evidence a quote or two from the text itself.

Example:
The physical descriptions of the laboratory and the main house in Dr Jekyll and Mr Hyde metaphorically point to the Gothic elements in the novel. (Claim)

[4] Shibata presented his study findings Monday at the 87th Scientific Assembly and Annual Meeting of the Radiological Society of North America in Chicago.

The main house had 'a great air of wealth and comfort' (13) while the laboratory door 'which was equipped with neither bell nor knocker, was blistered and distained'. (3) (Evidence)

By referencing the study in the first example and supplying textual evidence in the second, the initial statement in the paragraph moves from opinion to supported argument; however, you must still analyse your evidence.

Incorporating Evidence

There are three standard ways to incorporate evidence into your paper: paraphrasing, summarizing, and quoting.

Paraphrasing and Summarizing

Paraphrasing is communicating the ideas of a source in your own words. Summarizing is communicating the essential or distilled argument of a source in your own words, without changing the meaning or intent of the original source. Paraphrasing and summarizing allow you to interrogate, criticize, analyse, or build on someone else's argument.

When paraphrasing or summarizing, you must make it absolutely clear that the ideas being presented are not your own, even if the words you are using to communicate them are yours.

Example:
If you are writing a philosophy paper that asks you to argue for an effective form of governance, you might choose to summarize Rousseau's ideas of participatory democracy and Hobbes' ideas on absolute monarchy; you could use phrases like 'Hobbes argues ...' or 'Rousseau insists ...' to highlight that what follows is not your original idea. You would then insert a citation at the end of the paraphrased or summarized evidence. You could then use this summary to compare the ideas, forming your own analysis.

Quotations

Quotations are rarely used in scientific writing. Even in other disciplines, they should be used selectively; you want to make sure that the focus of your essay is on your own understanding of the topic and your own voice. However, quoting is useful when the source's exact words are special or distinctive, or when you want to preserve the full impact of the original source.

Depending on the assignment, you may also want to use quotations when the source itself is written by an authority on the topic.

Example:
If you are writing a paper on the history of multiculturalism in Canada, you may want to quote Pierre Trudeau as the first Prime Minister to create an official policy on multiculturalism in Canada.

There are two types of quotations: short and long. Generally, shorter quotations are more effective. Shorter quotations enable you to maintain your own critical voice while using evidence to support your own analysis. When we make decisions about what to include in a shorter quotation, a central question must be asked: Does the choice of words matter? If the specific words used do add to your argument, then quote. However, if there is nothing remarkable about the words used, paraphrase or summarize the argument.

So to review what has been said so far, when you are wondering whether to quote, ask yourself: Why did I choose this particular quote? Why does this evidence matter to my argument? Why does the particular language of the quote matter?

It is important to remember that evidence does lend your claims credibility; without evidence, your claims will register only as opinion. It is also very important to remember that to use evidence effectively means to incorporate it well and to analyse it in a way that makes its connection to your argument clear and logical.

4.5 WRITING INTRODUCTION AND CONCLUSION

Introductions and conclusions play a special role in an academic essay, and they frequently demand much of your attention as a writer. A good introduction should identify your topic, provide essential context, and indicate your particular focus in the essay. It also needs to engage your readers' interest. A strong conclusion will provide a sense of closure to the essay while again placing your concepts in a somewhat wider context. It will also, in some instances, add a stimulus to further thought.

4.5.1 How to Write an Interesting, Effective Introduction?

1. Find a startling statistic that illustrates the seriousness of the problem you will address.
2. Quote an expert (but be sure to introduce him or her first).
3. Mention a common misperception that your thesis will argue *against*.
4. Give some background information necessary for understanding the essay.
5. Use a brief narrative or anecdote that exemplifies your reason for choosing the topic. In an assignment that encourages personal reflection, you may draw on your own experiences; in a research essay, the narrative may illustrate a common real-world scenario.
6. In a science paper, explain key scientific concepts and refer to relevant literature. Lead up to your own contribution or intervention.
7. In a more technical paper, define a term that is possibly unfamiliar to your audience but is central to understanding the essay.

4.5.2 Avoid Some Common Pitfalls in Introduction

1. Don't provide dictionary definitions, especially of words your audience already knows.
2. Don't repeat the assignment specifications using the professor's wording.
3. Don't give details and in-depth explanations that really belong in your body paragraphs. You can usually postpone background material to the body of the essay.

4.5.3 How to Write an Interesting and Effective Conclusion?

1. If your essay deals with a contemporary problem, warn readers of the possible consequences of not attending to the problem.
2. Recommend a specific course of action.
3. Use an apt quotation or expert opinion to lend authority to the conclusion you have reached.
4. Give a startling statistic, fact, or visual image to drive home the ultimate point of your paper.
5. If your discipline encourages personal reflection, illustrate your concluding point with a relevant narrative drawn from your own life experiences.
6. Return to an anecdote, example, or quotation that you introduced in your introduction, but add further insight that derives from the body of your essay.
7. In a science or social science paper, mention worthwhile avenues for future research on your topic.

Example 1
Model essays show how introductory paragraphs are developed.

Model Essay 1

Introductory Paragraph

Keys to a Successful Essay

Many students find essay writing difficult and frustrating.[1] They know what they want to say, but when it comes to expressing themselves through the essay medium, they encounter problems.[2] Not only do they have to address the complexities of their topic, but they also have to follow the conventions of the formal academic essay.[3] The task seems daunting.[4] Broken down into its basic components, however, essay writing is not so difficult.[5] In fact, by addressing three key elements, every student can write an effective essay.[6] These three key elements are focus, organization, and clarity.[7]

Analysis

The **first six sentences** in this introductory paragraph prepare the reader for the thesis statement in Sentence 7 that the three key elements of a successful essay are '*focus, organization,* and *clarity*'.

1. **Sentence 1** makes the generalization that students 'find essay writing difficult and frustrating'.
2. **Sentences 2** and **3** expand on this generalization.
3. **Sentence 4** reinforces the idea of difficulty.
4. **Sentence 5** turns the paragraph away from the difficulties of essay writing towards a way of addressing the difficulties by breaking the essay into components. (The word 'however' signals this change of direction.)
5. **Sentence 6** suggests that there are three of these components, preparing the way for the thesis statement—that 'focus, organization, and clarity' are these components.

Example 1
Model essays show how concluding paragraphs are developed.

Model Essay 1

Concluding Paragraph

Clearly then, focus, organization, and clarity are the three key elements of a successful essay.[1] Of course, the content must also be sound and the essay must appropriately meet the requirements of the assignment brief, but this is not enough to gain the highest grades.[2] Student essay writers must therefore work at developing strong thesis statements, planning the structure of their essays, and writing clearly and concisely.[3] Essay writing is never easy, but by addressing the three key elements of focus, organization, and clarity, every student can succeed.[4]

Analysis

1. **Sentence 1** restates the thesis that focus, organization, and clarity are the key elements of a successful essay. The phrase 'clearly then' implies that, having read the case for focus, organization, and clarity being identified as the 'key elements', the reader agrees with the thesis.
2. **Sentence 2** acknowledges the importance of the essay's content but asserts that sound content isn't enough for success.
3. **Sentence 3** sums up the points made in the middle three paragraphs.

4. **Sentence 4** restates the generalization the essay started with—that students find essay writing difficult—but then ends on a high note with the prediction that addressing the key elements discussed in the middle paragraphs will ensure success.

Example 2
Introductory Paragraph

Model Essay 2

Introductory Paragraph

The Relevance of Essay Writing

Although the essay as a genre of writing has a history going back over several hundred years, essay writing is still a common assessment task in most university courses.[1] The modern academic essay is very different from the earliest essays, but it shares with them important characteristics.[2] Essays are still short pieces of prose presenting the writer's perspective on a topic, and supporting this perspective with sound evidence and logical argument.[3] In an academic environment essay writing requires from students a high investment of time, effort, and intellectual engagement but the learning dividends are also high.[4] The essay continues to be a valuable learning and assessment medium.[5]

Analysis
The **first four sentences** in this introductory paragraph prepare the reader for the thesis statement in **Sentence 5** that the essay 'continues to be a valuable learning and assessment medium'.

1. **Sentence 1** makes the generalization that despite the age of the genre, essays are still set as assessment tasks.
2. **Sentence 2** notes that the genre has changed but some characteristics remain.
3. **Sentence 3** lists some of these characteristics.
4. **Sentence 4** asserts essay writing is demanding, but the 'learning dividends are high', and thereby leads into the thesis statement.

Example 2
Concluding Paragraph

Model Essay 2

Concluding Paragraph

Bringing together such a wide range of learning experiences, the essay remains an excellent medium of learning as well as of assessment.[1] It encourages students to undertake deep rather than surface learning and gives lecturers an opportunity to provide insightful feedback.[2] It also develops the transferable skills graduates need in the professional workplace, and, most importantly, it presents students with an intellectual challenge that can be met only by developing sophisticated ways of thinking and communicating.[3] The essay may have a long history, but its relevance to the university learning experience continues.[4]

Analysis

1. **Sentence 1** restates the thesis that the essay continues to be a valuable learning and assessment medium.
2. **Sentences 2** and **3** summarize the main points of the middle three paragraphs.
3. **Sentence 4** picks up the reference to the age of the essay genre, with which the essay begins, but then affirms the essay's continuing relevance.

PRACTICE EXERCISE D

1. Put these sentences in the correct order for the introduction to an essay with this title: **Compare two methods of teaching prepositions and explain which one is more successful.**
   a. Such language differences make teaching of this area very difficult.
   b. Another method takes a cognitive linguistics approach, in which prepositions are studied in relation to spatial relationships.
   c. Using prepositions correctly in English is very difficult if English is not a person's first language.
   d. The essay which follows gives a brief history of prepositional theory and compares the traditional and cognitive linguistics approaches, arguing that a cognitive linguistics approach helps students to understand the concepts underlying prepositions and so is more effective in helping students to use prepositions correctly.
   e. Prepositions are small connecting words that do not necessarily exist in other languages, or may not have exactly the same meanings.
   f. One popular teaching method relies on students' learning combinations of nouns and prepositions.

2. Put these sentences in the correct order for the conclusion to an essay with this title: **Compare two methods of teaching prepositions and explain which one is more successful.**
   a. Spatial relationships, however, may differ from one language to another, and so this method is not completely effective.
   b. By studying spatial relationships, students appear to remember prepositions more accurately than they do using the traditional memorization method.
   c. Nevertheless, the cognitive linguistic approach appears to be useful for many students, and it is recommended that researchers study this approach further to see whether it is applicable for students with different language backgrounds and at different levels of language study.
   d. This essay has argued that a cognitive linguistics perspective is more effective than simple memorization in helping students to remember noun and preposition combinations.

FURTHER READING

1. Shmoop Editorial Team. 'Red Scarf Girl Writing Style'. Shmoop. Shmoop University. 11 November 2008. Web, 12 June 2018.
2. https://openoregon.pressbooks.pub/aboutwriting/chapter/types-of-writing-styles/ (accessed on 21 September 2018)
3. https://www.grossmont.edu/people/karl.../xrcs-narrative-descriptive-writing.aspx (accessed on 5 April 2017)
4. mysite.du.edu/~bkiteley/exercises.html (accessed on 21 September 2018)
5. www.butte.edu/departments/cas/tipsheets/style_purpose.../classification_paper.html (accessed on 5 April 2017)
6. O'Rourke, P. J. 'Book Tour'. *Age and Guile Beat Youth, Innocence, and a Bad Haircut.* New York: Atlantic Monthly Press, 1995.
7. Wolfe, Alexandra. 'Michael DeCesare'. *The Wall Street Journal* (14–15 December 2013).
8. Alexander, Caroline. 'Captain Bligh's Cursed Breadfruit'. *The Smithsonian* (September 2009)
9. https://www.lib.uoguelph.ca/get-assistance/writing/writing.../using-evidence-effectively... (accessed on 5 April 2017)
10. advice.writing.utoronto.ca › Planning and Organizing (accessed on 21 September 2018)
11. studyskills.curtin.edu.au/essays/step-6-write-introduction-and-conclusion/ (accessed on 21 September 2018)
12. Miller, Julia, and Richard Warner. 'Essay Writing Exercises'. English for Uni. www.adelaide.edu.au/english-for-uni (accessed on 21 September 2018)
13. https://www.thoughtco.com › ... › English Grammar › Glossary of Key Terms (accessed on 21 September 2018)

5

UNIT

Writing Practices

5.1 COMPREHENSION

5.1.1 What Is Comprehension?

A comprehension exercise has a passage upon which questions are set to test a reader's understanding of the contents of the given text and his ability to reproduce it. Thus, comprehension is a two-fold process; it requires understanding of what is presented and reproducing it. Comprehension is the understanding and interpretation of what is read. To be able to accurately understand written material, readers should be able to:

1. Decode what they read.
2. Make connections between what they read and what they already know.
3. Think deeply about what they have read.

One big part of comprehension is having a sufficient vocabulary, or knowing the meanings of enough words. Readers who have strong comprehension are able to draw conclusions about what they read—what is important, what is a fact, what caused an event to happen, which characters are funny, and so on. Thus comprehension involves combining reading with thinking and reasoning.

5.1.2 Process of Comprehension

The process of comprehension involves speedy reading, quick understanding, and precise reproduction. There is a large demand of this skill in practical life, and it can be developed with intelligent effort like any other skill.

1. Read the passage to get its general meaning. Here the objective is only to get a rough idea of what the passage is about.
2. Don't spend too much time on a passage, but don't rush through it either. Make sure that you understand the gist of the passage and can remember the important details. A good reader is one who, keeping his purpose in mind, can quickly attain the required speed.
3. You may come across words whose meanings you do not know. Try to make a guess; very often the context will help you arrive at the meaning. Remember that words have no intrinsic value; they are arbitrary symbols of things, ideas, thoughts, actions, feelings, and so on. They only serve as a medium to convey the message.
4. Now take each question in turn and look for the answers one by one. Your answers should be, as far as possible, in your own words. Use complete sentences to answer the questions. Be precise in answering the questions. There is no virtue in giving more than the required information.
5. While answering comprehension passages, remember that your opinion does not matter at all. The passage contains the opinion of the author and you are asked to answer questions on the basis of author's opinion.
6. Check carefully the grammar, spelling, and punctuation of what you write.

5.1.3 Passages for Practice

Reading Suggestion 1
Summary for this article:
The author talks about the annual study of the state budgets done by the RBI. The outcome of this study has put forth three important factors that will shape up the state finances in the mid-term future. First, GST bill; second, delegation of power from centre to states; and third, adherence to rule-based fiscal policy.

The study shows that the states' fiscal position has deteriorated in the last five years as compared to the previous quinquennium (period of 5 years). This has happened partly because of increase in loans and borrowings under Ujjwal Discoms Assurance Yojana, a scheme to uplift power distribution companies (discoms) in the states by lending them necessary finances.

The solution to this problem as per the author lies in the effectiveness of GST and voluntary compliance. The states should make necessary efforts to enhance their tax and non-tax revenues. Along with that, efficient delivery of services and commercial principle pricing of commercial goods also assume critical importance.

Words to learn from this article:
Quinquennium: period of five years
Fiscal deficit: A fiscal deficit occurs when a government's total expenditures exceed the revenue that it generates, excluding money from borrowings.
Perusal: to read through something specially to find the part you are most interested in
(Article Name: 'We Must Worry about State Finances'
Authors Names: R. K. Pattnaik/Jagdish Rattanani
Source: *The Hindu*
Category: Business Line)[1]

Reading Suggestion 2
Summary for this article:
India being a diverse nation has diverse languages being spoken by people belonging to different cultures and hence the language policy argument is never a surprise.

In this article the writer stresses on the importance of having a clear language policy by relooking at its language policy under Part XVII of the Indian Constitution which states the replacement of English to Hindi language at the national level and with other languages in the Eighth Schedule in their respective states.

He further ends up giving his opinion on the matter. The nation must adopt mother tongue plus English, with Hindi accorded a place of pride for ceremonial occasions at national and international levels.

Words to learn from this article:
Dispensation: exemption from something
Efficacy: the capability to produce an intended result
Muddle: in a confused state
Reinvent the wheel: wasting one's time in order to invent or create something that already exists
(Article Name: 'Beyond the Language Conflict: The Need for a Clear Language Policy'
Author Name: D. Shyam Babu
Source: *The Hindu*
Category: Politics)[2]

---

[1] https://wordpandit.com/practice-reading-comprehension/ (accessed on 21 September 2018)
[2] Ibid.

Reading Suggestion 3
Summary for this article:
The Major Gogoi incident that saw arguments and debates across all the news channels witnessing a lot of noise across the nation is the very subject of this article.

The writer questions the ethical nature of the entire incident. The honouring of Major Gogoi at a time when the case hearing still needs to be done makes it clear where our Army stands.

The entire article while focusing on this major issue of using a human shield to save lives by Major Gogoi also expresses the author's take on the incident.

Words to learn from this article:
Archetypal: something original
Perpetrated: to commit some harmful or immoral action
Jingoism: extreme patriotism
Hagiography: biography of saints
Proscription: forbidding something; banning
(Article Name: 'On Human Shields and Questions That Won't Go Away'
Author Name: Shiv Vishwanathan
Source: *The Hindu*
Category: Ethics and Politics)[3]

Passages for Practice (TOEFL, GMAT, TEFL model)
Read the passages carefully and answer the questions that follow in your own words as far as possible:

Passage 1
Research suggests that there are creatures that do not know what light means at the bottom of the sea. They don't have either eyes or ears; they can only feel. There is no day or night for them. There are no winters, no summers, no sun, no moon, and no stars. It is as if a child spent its life in darkness in bed, with nothing to see or hear. How different our own life is! Sight shows us the ground beneath our feet and the heavens above us—the sun, moon, and stars, shooting stars, lightning, and the sunset. It shows us day and night. We are able to hear voices, the sound of the sea, and music. We feel, we taste, and we smell. How fortunate we are![4]

1. **Judging from the passage, we can say that this story is mainly about**
   - ❍ A. life of sea creatures at the bottom of the sea.
   - ❍ B. how changes in the seasons are perceived by the deep-sea creatures.

[3] Ibid.
[4] http://www.testyourenglish.net/index.htm (accessed on 21 September 2018)

- ❍ C. how wonderful our lives were and will be.
- ❍ D. the differences among creatures of the earth and those of the sea.
- ❍ E. the superiority of human beings over some creatures in terms of senses.

2. **We discover that the sea creatures in the story**
   - ❍ A. have the same senses that we do.
   - ❍ B. have no sense of hearing as well as sight.
   - ❍ C. hear the sounds of the ocean.
   - ❍ D. live in darkness because no light reaches to the bottom.
   - ❍ E. do not hear the sound of sea as they are accustomed to it.
3. **In the passage a child in darkness is likened to**
   - ❍ A. someone who lives where there are no seasons.
   - ❍ B. an animal without the sense of touch.
   - ❍ C. a sea creature with no seeing or hearing ability.
   - ❍ D. a deaf child unaffected by the environment.
   - ❍ E. a perfect sleeper, for there is no sound around to hear.

Passage 2

Erosion is regarded not merely as the physical removal of soil by water and wind, but rather as the deterioration of all the component parts of the habitat in which man and his crops and livestock have to exist. Since there is no conclusive evidence for any major climatic change in historic times to explain this deterioration, we must conclude that the eroding of the total environment has been primarily due to thoughtless destruction of the vegetative cover. This has led to deterioration of the microclimate above and below the surface, generally in the direction of an overall drying out of the soil which has exposed it to erosive action of wind and rainfall of high intensity or frequency, and to the loss of organic matter in the soil, thus reducing its capacity to resist erosion by conserving the water that falls on the surface. If everything possible is done within the total ambit of the environment to conserve the naturally planted or cultivated vegetation, this will also ensure optimal conservation of soil and water.[5]

1. **It is argued in the passage that the impoverishment of the world's habitat**
   - ❍ A. is first and foremost due to man's irresponsible abuse of the vegetable cover of the earth.
   - ❍ B. is largely due to gradual changes in climate over long years.
   - ❍ C. became inevitable as soon as agricultural and animal husbandry developed.
   - ❍ D. cannot be remedied.
   - ❍ E. has been needlessly exaggerated.

---

[5] Ibid.

2. **The definition of erosion given in this passage**
   - ❍ A. is a strictly regional one.
   - ❍ B. disregards man's role in it.
   - ❍ C. concentrates on flooding.
   - ❍ D. assumes that the process is inevitable.
   - ❍ E. is a broad one.
3. **It is pointed out in the passage that the loss of organic matter in the soil**
   - ❍ A. led to the destruction of the world's vegetative cover.
   - ❍ B. is a direct result of insufficient rain.
   - ❍ C. is an irreversible process.
   - ❍ D. has made the soil more susceptible to erosion.
   - ❍ E. came about through overplanting which robbed the soil of nutrients.

Passage 3

Have you ever wondered whether fish drink or not? All living things must drink, and they require a fresh supply of water. A person can go without food for many days, but he or she cannot go for long without water. Fish drink, and fish that live in salt water must drink salt water. However, when we watch them in an aquarium and see them opening and closing their mouths, we must not assume that they are drinking. Fish need water for their oxygen. The water that they seem to be gulping gives them oxygen, which is present in the water. On the other hand, when a fish drinks, it swallows water, just the way we do.[6]

1. **It is stated in the passage that a fish opens and closes its mouth**
   - ❍ A. in order to get oxygen.
   - ❍ B. so as to gulp.
   - ❍ C. to drink to stay alive
   - ❍ D. to swim in an aquarium.
   - ❍ E. so that they can obtain salt.
2. **We are informed by the passage that a person**
   - ❍ A. can live for a long time without water.
   - ❍ B. can live for a long time without food.
   - ❍ C. has no need for food and water.
   - ❍ D. has no need for a fresh supply of water.
   - ❍ E. does need water to get oxygen.
3. **When a fish drinks water,**
   - ❍ A. it requires fresh water.
   - ❍ B. it swallows water just like us.
   - ❍ C. it requires salt water.
   - ❍ D. it does so for its oxygen.
   - ❍ E. it stays motionless for a while to swallow.

[6] Ibid.

Passage 4

There was a man who lived before the time of Christopher Columbus, who was the world's first great traveller. His name was Marco Polo. With his father and his uncle, he travelled from Italy to China, crossing mountains and deserts to get there. In China a king called Kublai Khan was pleased to see the Polos and had them live near to him. They stayed for 23 years. Kublai Khan sent Marco to other countries to do business for him. When Marco finally returned to Italy, he wrote all about his adventures in a book, which was read by Columbus and many other people, who also became interested in travelling to strange countries.[7]

1. **This story is mainly about**
   - ❍ A. the world's first great traveller.
   - ❍ B. travelling from Italy to China.
   - ❍ C. why Polo went to the Far East.
   - ❍ D. Marco Polo and Kublai Khan.
   - ❍ E. in what ways Columbus affected Polo.
2. **The reason that Marco Polo is called great is not that**
   - ❍ A. he travelled very far to reach China for a new world.
   - ❍ B. he wrote about his adventures in a book, which many people read.
   - ❍ C. he was so well liked by the king of China.
   - ❍ D. he crossed mountains and deserts to reach China.
   - ❍ E. he achieved fame, thanks to his good reasoning.
3. **We know from the story that after he turned back,**
   - ❍ A. Marco brought out a book inspiring new voyages.
   - ❍ B. Marco stayed in Italy for 23 years.
   - ❍ C. Kublai Khan knew that Marco had crossed mountains and deserts.
   - ❍ D. Kublai Khan sent Columbus to other countries for business.
   - ❍ E. Marco set out for a new adventure.

PRACTICE EXERCISE A

Read the passages carefully and answer the questions that follow in your own words as far as possible:

[7] Ibid.

Exercise 1

Joti, a gardener's son, was once invited to attend the marriage ceremony of a Brahmin friend. As he loved his friend dearly, he attended the function. The bridegroom was being led in a procession to the bride's house. The procession consisted of men, women, and children, and most of them were Brahmins. Joti was also walking along with the procession.

One orthodox Brahmin recognized him and was annoyed at the sight of a low-caste boy walking with the Brahmins in the marriage procession. Unable to control himself, he shouted, 'How dare you walk along with us? You are not our equal. Get behind! Otherwise, go away.' Joti felt insulted. He left the procession and returned home. He narrated the whole incident to his father with anger in his eyes. However, his father advised him to observe old customs. That night Joti could not sleep. What could he do for the equality of human beings? Caste system was deep-rooted. As the lower caste people were not educated, they had accepted the mental slavery for ages. Joti, therefore, resolved to revolt against this mental slavery and educate the lower caste people. He became the first Indian to start a school for the untouchables as well as a girls' school in Maharashtra. We recognize him today as Mahatma Phule.

Q1. According to the passage, what has made low-caste people accept mental slavery?
Q2. What kind of a man was Joti's father?
Q3. What did Joti do after his insult?
Q4. Why did Joti attend the marriage?
Q5. Why could Joti not sleep that night?
Q6. Why was the Brahmin annoyed with Joti?
Q7. According to the passage, why did Joti quit the marriage procession?
Q8. What does the author highlight in this passage?

Exercise 2

The best way of understanding our own civilization is to take an ordinary sort of day in the life of an ordinary sort of man, myself for instance, and to see what he does. My home is in London. I get up in the morning when the alarm clock rings on the table by my bed. It is quite a complicated machine and works perfectly. I get into a bath, the water for which has been heated by gas. The gas is supplied by the Gas Board for the area in which I live; it is part of a national system. The water is supplied by the City Water Board. After bathing, I shave. The water for my shave comes from a kettle which has been heated by electricity. As far as I am concerned, what happens is very simple: I put a plug in the wall and put on the switch and the electricity does the rest. I use a safety razor, the blade of which, made of finely tempered steel, has been cut, together with millions of other blades, by machines. The clothes which l put on have also been spun and woven largely by steam or electrically driven machines.

Q1. What does the 'I' in this passage represent?
Q2. What is the ideal way of understanding a civilization?
Q3. What does the 'complicated machine' in the passage refer to?

Q4. The gas being 'supplied by a national system' means that
- A. it is supplied by a nationalist government.
- B. it is supplied only nationally and not internationally.
- C. it is supplied all over the country by a central agency.
- D. it is supplied to only those who believe in a national system.

Q5. What does the kind of life experienced by the writer represent?

Exercise 3

Our body is a wondrous mechanism and when subjected to unusual stress over a period of time, it adapts itself to deal more effectively with that stress. Therefore, when you exert your muscles against resistance, they are forced to adapt and deal with this extraordinary work load. This is the principle of weight training. Strands of muscle fibres become thicker and stronger in response to the demands placed on them.

One of the great merits of weight training is the strength of the heart. During weight training, your heart is forced to beat faster and stronger in order to pump sufficient blood to the muscles being worked. In time, the heart, like your body, will adapt to this extra workload by becoming stronger and more efficient. Since your body needs a given amount of blood to perform its routine tasks, your heart will now need fewer beats to pump the same quantity of blood. Sounds good? There's more. Your entire circulatory system is given a thorough workout every time you exercise, which increases its overall efficiency. Even the neural paths from the brain's command centres to each individual muscle become more effective, enabling easier recruitment of muscle fibres for carrying out physical tasks. On the whole, your body becomes a well-oiled and finely tuned piece of machinery, whirring along without any breakdown. In today's stress-filled world, you need all help you can get.

Q1. What is the principal training of weightlifting?
Q2. What affects the nature of muscle fibres?
Q3. How does the heart become stronger owing to physical exercise?
Q4. How much blood does the heart pump at the same number of heartbeats when exposed to excessive stress?
Q5. What happens to our body due to physical exercise?
Q6. What does the term 'well-oiled' in the passage denote?
Q7. What can be the most appropriate title for the passage?
Q8. What is the importance of physical exercise in the present world?
Q9. What, according to the passage, is the function of the heart?
Q10. What does the above passage suggest?

Exercise 4

The first thing the children wanted to do at the zoo was to ride the elephant. They were frightened as they climbed the ladder to take their seats on the swaying back of the huge beast. Elephants seem awkward creatures as they move along heavily, their legs covered with loose folds of tough skin and their trunks swinging from side to side in search of food or water. An elephant has great strength in its trunk, and can drag heavy loads with ropes, but it can also use its trunk to pick up small articles such as coins or nuts from the ground. After their ride on the elephant, the children went to see the lions and tigers. Crowds of people stood watching, protected from the cruel beasts by the strong metal bars of the cages.

From there, they went to see the monkeys. Those merry creatures were jumping about the rocks, swinging on the wires of their cages, or begging for nuts from the passers-by. If anyone annoyed them, they would reproach him angrily and beat their chests with the hands.

In the end, they saw some curious creatures such as the giraffe with its long neck and the camel with its short beard.

Q1. What is the reaction of monkeys when they get irritated?
Q2. Why are the cages of lions made of strong metal bars?
Q3. What is the chief function of the trunk of elephants?
Q4. Why were the children afraid of riding on the elephant?
Q5. Which is a ferocious animal?
Q6. What makes the elephant awkward in appearance?
Q7. What is typical of the giraffe?

Exercise 5

We develop the vital bond of attachment between a mother and her child through a smiling response. As a visual stimulus, the smile has attained its unique configuration principally by the simple act of turning up the corners of the mouth. The mouth is opened to an extent and the lips pulled back, as in the expression of fear, but with the curling up of the corners, the character of the expression is radically changed. This development has in turn led to the possibility of another and contrasting facial posture—that of the down-turned mouth. By adopting a mouth line that is the complete opposite of the smile, it is possible to signal an anti-smile. Just as laughing, so also the unfriendly face has evolved by a pendulum swing from the friendly face.

But there is more to smiling than a line of the mouth. As adults, we may be able to convey our mood by a mere twist of the lips, but an infant throws much more into the battle. When smiling at full intensity, it also kicks and waves its arms about, stretches its hands out towards the stimulus and moves them about, produces babbling sounds, tilts back its head and projects its chin, leans its trunk forward or rolls it to one side, and exaggerates its breathing. Its eyes become brighter and may close slightly; wrinkles appear underneath the eye and sometimes also on the bridge of the nose; the fold of the skin between the sides of the nose and the side of the mouth becomes more accentuated, and the tongue may be slightly protruded. The body movements seem to indicate a struggle on the infant's part to get in touch with the mother. With its clumsy physique, the baby is probably showing us all that remains of the ancestral private clinging response.

Q1. How do we recognize a smile?
Q2. How does an adult convey his smile?
Q3. Which statement is true?
   A. A baby's smile is more vigorous than that of an adult.
   B. When compared to adults, a baby smiles more quietly.
   C. It is not possible to speak when one is smiling, especially when the person is a baby.

D. Babies make babbling noises, tilt their heads back, and protrude their chin before they can smile.

Q4. What does a child struggle to show when it smiles?

Exercise 6

A vexed problem facing us is the clamour to open more colleges and to reserve more seats for backward classes. But it will be a sheer folly to expand such facilities recklessly without giving any thought to the quality of education imparted. If admissions are made far more selective, it will automatically reduce the number of entrants. This should apply particularly to new colleges, many of them are little more than degree factories. Only then can the authorities hope to bring down the teacher–student ratio to manageable proportion. What is more, teachers should be given refresher courses and trainings every summer to brush up their knowledge. Besides, if college managements increase the library budget it will help both the staff and the students a great deal.

At the same time, however, it will be unfair to deny college education to thousands of young people, unless employers stop insisting on degrees even for clerical jobs. For a start, why cannot the government disqualify graduates from securing certain jobs, say Classes III and IV posts? Once the link between degrees and jobs is severed, at least in some important departments, it will make young people think twice before joining college.

Q1. What can automatically help to reduce admissions?

Q2. How can the standards of education be raised?

Q3. How can teachers be helped to brush up their knowledge?

Q4. The author is not in favour of restricting admissions

A. unless degree are delinked from jobs.

B. unless alternative opportunities are provided.

C. unless other incentives are offered.

D. unless the teacher–student ratio is changed.

Q5. What does the phrase 'vexed problem' mean?

Exercise 7

The very shape of man's body is such that it makes him a restless creature. He cannot do without work. It is truly said 'An idle man's brain is a devil's workshop.'

The whole civilization of man has evolved itself only through hard work. All the inventions and discoveries of science are the result of human labour. Constant work improving upon its own findings progressively has enabled mankind to tread on the moon.

Even in our daily life we see that hard work pays dividends. A student who works regularly and systematically shows better results than the one who does not do so. Similarly, a player who practises regularly on the field is much better than the one who does not. Work not only leads to better results in the long run but also increases our self-confidence. Work may be physical or intellectual. It is important in all its forms. But it should be constructive too. Great nations of the world such as Japan, Germany, and China emerged strong only through hard work put in individually and collectively.

In India, we worship Lord Vishwakarma, the great god of the workers, but unfortunately we are a nation of shirkers. We work little and we work even less for our country. One can work better and more effectively if one is dedicated to some cause.

Let us all be dedicated to the cause of our country. Only then we can see our country great and strong, and we ourselves can be great and strong only if our country is so. There is no shortcut, no escape route. Hard work is the only way out. In whatever area we are, we must do our duty with utmost devotion and meticulousness.

Q1. What message does the author want to convey through the passage?
Q2. What, according to the passage, is necessary for the effective work output?
Q3. Which of the following group of words is similar in meaning of the word 'dividend' as used in the passage?
  A. produce an advantage
  B. useful in the past
  C. produce indolents
  D. hard work
  E. bring devotion and conscientiousness
Q4. What, according to the passage, is important with regard to the work that we get involved in?
Q5. How, according to the passage, the great nations have become stronger?

Exercise 8

The idea of evolution (which is a gradual change) was not a new one. The Greeks had thought of it. So had Erasmus Darwin, the grandfather of Charles Darwin, and also the Frenchman, Lamarck. It is one thing to have an idea; we can all guess and sometimes make a lucky guess. It is quite another thing to produce a proof of the correctness of that idea. Darwin thought he had that proof in his notebook. He saw that all animals had to struggle to survive. Those which were best at surviving their environment passed on the good qualities which helped them to their descendants. This was called 'the survival of the fittest'. For example, in a cold climate, those who have the warmest fur live. Darwin believed that this necessity for an animal to deal with its environment explained the immense variety of creatures.

Q1. At the time that Darwin arrived on the scene, the idea of evolution
  A. was an idea unheard of.
  B. had already been proved beyond doubt.
  C. had been thought of but not proved.
  D. was not thought fit for exploration.
Q2. According to Darwinian thought, the world of animals is marked by
  A. peaceful coexistence.
  B. a struggle for survival.
  C. indifference towards each other.
  D. love and friendship.
Q3. The expression 'the survival of the fittest' means that
  A. the strong will survive while the weak will perish.

B. the strong and the weak will live peacefully.
C. the strong will help the weak survive.
D. both the strong and the weak will survive.

Q4. In colder climates
A. all animals can survive.
B. no animal can survive.
C. only animals with fur can survive.
D. animals are hard to come by.

Q5. Darwin thought that the environment
A. has no effect on animals.
B. has a lot of effect on animals.
C. has a marginal effect on animals.
D. has an effect on man but not on animals.

Exercise 9

It is true that the smokers cause some nuisance to the non-smokers, but this nuisance is physical while the nuisance that the non-smokers cause the smokers is spiritual. There are, of course, a lot of non-smokers who don't try to interfere with the smokers. It is sometimes assumed that the non-smokers are morally superior, not realizing that they have missed one of the greatest pleasures of mankind. I am willing to allow that smoking is a moral weakness, but on the other hand, we must beware of a man without weakness. He is not to be trusted. He is apt to be always sober and he cannot make a single mistake. His habits are too regular, his existence too mechanical and his head always maintains its supremacy over his heart. Much as I like reasonable persons, I hate completely rational beings. For that reason, I am always scared and ill at ease when I enter a house in which there are no ash-trays. The room is apt to be too clean and orderly, and the people are apt to be correct and unemotional. Now, the moral and spiritual benefits of smoking have never been appreciated by these correct, righteous, unemotional, and unpoetic souls. In my opinion the smokers' morality is, on the whole, higher than that of the non-smokers. The man with a pipe in his mouth is the man after my heart. He is more genial, more open-hearted, and often brilliant in conversation. As Thackeray observes, 'The pipe draws wisdom from the lips of the philosopher and shuts up the mouth of the foolish; it generates a style of conversation that is contemplative, thoughtful, benevolent and unaffected.'

Q1. What kind of hardship do a smoker and a non-smoker cause to each other?
Q2. Why is it wrong to think that a non-smoker is morally superior to a smoker?
Q3. Why is a man without any moral weakness untrustworthy?
Q4. What pleasure of life is missed by a non-smoker?
Q5. What does Thackeray mean to say?

Exercise 10

First, let us examine our attitude towards peace itself. Too many of us think it is impossible. Too many think it unreal. But that is a dangerous, defeatist belief. It leads to the conclusion that war is inevitable, that mankind is doomed, that we are gripped by forces we cannot control.

We need not accept that view. Our problems are man-made; therefore, they can be solved by man. And man can be as big as he wants. No problem of human destiny is beyond human beings. Man's reason and spirit have often solved the seemingly unsolvable, and we believe they can do it again.

I am not referring to the absolute, infinite concept of universal peace and goodwill of which some fantasts and fanatics dream. I do not deny the value of hopes and dreams, but we merely invite discouragement and incredulity by making them our only and immediate goal.

Let us focus instead on a more practical, more attainable peace, based not on a sudden revolution in human nature but on a gradual evolution in human institutions, on a series of concrete actions and effective agreements which are in the interest of all concerned. Genuine peace must be the product of all nations, the sum of many acts. It must be dynamic, not static, changing to meet the challenge of each new generation. For peace is a process, a way of solving problems.
[*Source:* From Asst. Grade (Main) Exam (1996)]

Q1. What is our attitude to peace?
Q2. Why does man think peace is impossible to attain?
Q3. Identify the difference between peace as a concept and an attainable reality.
Q4. Explain why 'peace' is a process.
Q5. Give the meaning of the following words and use in sentences of your own:
   A. incredulity
   B. dynamic
   C. revolution
   D. evolution
Q6. Give a suitable title.

Exercise 11

A close study of the lives and works of great teachers and high educational dignitaries such as Radhakrishnan, Zakir Hussain, and Saiyadain indicates that these luminaries from the very beginning were committed to high ideals and superior academic norms, which placed the stamp of excellence on their achievements in the field of education. Many of them made noble efforts for strengthening and enriching the educational curricula and programmes and the teacher education courses, and in imbuing education with a distinct personality of its own. They, in fact, were the cultivated minds and integrated personalities, inspired by and infused with the high ideals of our great and ancient heritage, willing and ready to work in the service of the nation. If all teachers follow the path shown by such educational authorities, education is bound to achieve its goal of all-round development.

Education, of which teachers are the purveyors, is the sacred instrument for building the nation. Teacher's is the most crucial job of moulding the character of individuals and thereby of shaping the society itself. Education is a medium through which the teacher will direct human energies and human capacities to the advancement of human weal. Upon the nature and character of education imparted by him depends the future of the nation.

It need not be overemphasized that there is a causal relationship between education, on the one hand, and economic growth and social progress, on the other. As teachers alone have to administer this education, one can imagine the colossal responsibility they have of performing this stupendous task. While they perform this task, they should keep in mind that education is not learning what to do, but becoming the kind of person who knows what to do. Child is not just a learner of history or science. His interests, his aptitude, his habits, and everything else which goes into the make-up of his personality come within the teachers' purview. Teachers have to produce mentally healthy individuals who have wholesome personalities.

Teachers represent the ideals and aspirations of the nation and owe to it the moral and mental accountability of equipping the youth for active participation in the high enterprise of creating a social order which shall dispense equal justice to all and sundry. As ideal teachers, they have to strive, along with their wards, to build up the nation in conformity with the lofty ideals laid down in our Constitution. This great aim can be realized by effective, brilliant teachers, teachers who are equipped with the training that has a direct bearing on the quality of life in the community, and that will serve as the chief means for the transformation of society. Such teachers can make their contribution to the building up of a new India—India that is both holding fast to the traditional culture of the past and is forward looking and future-oriented. It is these teachers alone who can provide, through rich and dynamic education, all that the country needs for its prosperity. [*Source:* Adapted from S. B. Kakkar, *Changing Perspectives in Education*]

Q1. List four qualities of Tagore, Radhakrishnan, Zakir Hussain, and Saiyadain which made them great teachers.

Q2. Why Tagore, Radhakrishnan, Zakir Hussain, and the like are known as great teachers and educationists?

Q3. Why Tagore, Radhakrishnan, Zakir Hussain, and such others are called cultivated minds? These personalities were the cultivated minds because ....

Q4. How education can be used?

Q5. Teachers have a great responsibility. Why?

Q6. 'This great aim can be realized by effective, brilliant teachers....' What is the aim?

Q7. Find words in the passage which mean the opposite of each of the following:

A. inferior
B. ignoble
C. desecrated
D. immoral
E. backward-looking

Exercise 12

Ever since man came on this earth he has been hunting wild animals either for food or self-protection or, in more recent times, for sport. Some 40 years ago, I began to realize that shooting wild animals no longer gave me pleasure; it was simply a one-sided game because the animals had little chance before the modern weapons. I wanted to hunt the wild animals in their natural wild state, in all their natural beauty. I also wanted to bring home some proof of what I had seen. So hunting with a camera was my weapon. It would shoot without hurting, certainly without killing, and yet give me the trophies of the chase.

At first when I tried what was then the new sport I became almost discouraged, the cameras would not do the work. They would go wrong at the right time. At first I contented myself with photographing wild birds, mostly on or near their nests. From birds I gradually took up animals as my subjects and I was, I think, one of the very first in getting really clear photographs of wild beasts. In 1908, I went on a big trip to East Africa (now Kenya). I was anxious to take a photo of a rhinoceros charging. But I had no thought how risky it would be. A few days later, we camped near Kilimanjaro and could see it in the distance.

The first day we met our first rhino. I had the fright of my life. The pair had got our scent before we spotted them, and being bad-tempered beasts, they rushed at us. I could not take the photograph. But the next day, I saw one standing on a low hill. While we were preparing to shoot, he lay down and went to sleep. Clark and I stood up, he with his rifle ready in case of trouble and I with my big camera.

When I shouted at it, he jumped with a remarkable speed, gave us a horrid snort and came at full tilt straight at us. He looked as big as a house. When the charging mass of bad temper was 15 yards away I pressed the shutter release and took the first photograph of the kind ever made. Clark fired a shot to make him turn. The bullet grazed his shoulder and he rushed past us scarcely five yards away.

This all made me give up rhino hunting for a while. But fortune smiled on me again when I desired to shoot a lion. After countless nights of waiting, I saw the great cat only 12 yards away standing still and looking straight into my eyes. It was a thrilling moment when my electric torch revealed the sight. I pressed the flash-light connection and off went the light with a loud explosion and dazzling glare. We were blinded for a few moments—and what moments those were! Who could tell what the lioness was doing or had she bolted? It was, in fact, the first successful photo of wild lion ever made.

Now, though hunting dangerous wild animals with a camera is the most intensely exciting form of sport that I know of, it must not be thought that hunting the more inoffensive ones—deer, zebra, antelope, giraffe, and others—is devoid of thrills. I also had the good luck to get a herd of giraffe to come within easy range of my camera. I was able to secure a splendid film of these graceful, shy creatures literally posing for me in all sorts of positions.

Hunting with a camera is one of the finest sports and one of the greatest things in its favour is that it involves no killing or cruelty. It gives trophies that are far more beautiful than any obtained with the rifle.

[*Source:* Adapted from Major Radclyffe Dugmora.]

Q1. List four solid reasons that made the author opt for hunting wild animals with a camera.

Q2. The author states that man hunted wild animals for food and self-protection in the past. But he got more pleasure in this hunting than other kinds of hunting. Why?

Q3. 'But I had no thought how risky it would be!' What was the risky thing?

Q4. When the author shouted at the rhinoceros, it did two things in reaction. What were those?

Q5. 'I could not take the photograph.' Why?

Q6. Find words in the passage which mean the opposite of each of the following:

A. going after food or sport
B. right
C. safe
D. misfortune
E. boring

Exercise 13

One of the most prolific authors of all time, Isaac Asimov was influential both in science fiction and in the popularization of science during the twentieth century, but he is also justly famous for the scope of his interests. Although the common claim that Asimov is the only author to have written a book in every category of the Dewey decimal system is untrue, its spirit provides an accurate picture of the man: a dedicated humanist who lauded the far-reaching power of reason. His most famous work, the *Foundation* trilogy, can be read as an illustration of Asimov's belief in reason and science, but even while he expressed that belief, science itself was calling it into question.

Foundation describes a time in which a vast Empire spanning the galaxy is on the verge of collapse. Its inevitable doom is a consequence not of its size, but of the shortsightedness of its leaders. In this environment, a scientist named Hari Seldon devises an all-encompassing plan to help human civilization recover from the trauma of the Empire's coming collapse. Using mathematics, Seldon is able to predict the future course of history for thousands of years, and he takes steps that are geared towards guiding that future in a beneficial direction. The trope of the benevolent and paternalistic scientist shaping existence from behind the scenes, present in much of Asimov's fiction, is never more explicit than in the *Foundation* series, which describes with an epic sweep the course and progress of the Seldon Plan.

As naive and, perhaps, self-serving as the conceit of *Foundation* may seem to contemporary readers, it retains to some degree its ability of comfort by offering an antidote to the complex and unpredictable nature of experience. Science in Asimov's time was, in popular conceptions, engaged in just this pursuit: discerning immutable laws that operate beneath a surface appearance of contingency, inexplicability, and change. But even while Asimov wrote, science itself was changing. In physics, the study of matter at the subatomic level showed that indeterminacy was not a transitory difficulty to be overcome, but an essential physical principle. In biology, the sense of evolution as a steady progress towards better adapted forms was being disturbed by proof of a past large-scale evolution taking place in brief explosions of frantic change. At the time of Asimov's death, even mathematics was gaining popular notice for its interest in chaos and inexplicability. Usually summarized in terms of the so-called 'butterfly effect', chaos theory showed that perfect prediction could take place only on the basis of perfect information, which was by nature impossible to obtain. Science had dispensed with the very assumptions that motivated Asimov's idealization of it in the Seldon Plan. Indeed it was possible to see chaos at work in *Foundation* itself: As sequels multiplied and began to be tied into narrative threads from Asimov's other novels, the urge to weave one grand narrative spawned myriad internal inconsistencies that were never resolved.

Q1. Which one of the following most accurately expresses the main point of the passage?
   A. Isaac Asimov's greatest work, the *Foundation* trilogy, is an expression of the common trope of the benevolent and paternalistic scientist.
   B. Popularizations of science are always to some degree dependent idealizations and simplifications of that science as Isaac Asimov's work demonstrates.
   C. The impossibility of the conceit on which Isaac Asimov's *Foundation* trilogy is based demonstrates that Asimov's fiction was based on imperfect understandings of science.
   D. Isaac Asimov's idealization of science as revealed in his *Foundation* series was called into question by the science of his time, which was increasingly focused on chaos and indeterminacy.

Q2. Which one of the following statements most accurately expresses the purpose of the final paragraph?
   A. The ultimate failure of the *Foundation* series as a coherent scientific narrative is discussed.
   B. A claim is made about the purpose of Asimov's writing and then is finally rejected.
   C. A key theme of Asimov's *Foundation* series is described and discoveries in science that seem contrary to that theme are outlined.
   D. The history of science is used to demonstrate the falsity of a widely believed claim about the power of human reason.

Q3. The author's reference to a common claim made about Isaac Asimov serves to
   A. demonstrate that many untrue beliefs are held about him.
   B. illustrate the broad scope of his interests and writings.
   C. undermine the claim that he was a prolific writer.
   D. substantiate his belief in the power of human reason.

Q4. With respect of the Seldon Plan, the author's attitude can most properly be described as
   A. amused at the naive conception of history it implies.
   B. uncertain of the practical impossibility of its application.
   C. ambivalent because of the reliance on human reason it requires.
   D. convinced that it illustrates Asimov's attitude towards science.

Q5. Which one of the following statements best illustrates the 'butterfly effect' as it is described in the passage's third paragraph?
   A. A system implemented to predict the weather worldwide for the next century is soon found to be inaccurate because it was supplied with incomplete data.
   B. Efforts to predict the result of a nuclear reaction fail because of indeterminacy inherent in the behaviour of subatomic particles.
   C. The fossil record indicates that certain adaptations found in many organisms appeared soon after a past catastrophic event.
   D. Scientific predictions about the future course of human history are found to be reasonably accurate once existing social theories are reconciled.

TOEFL Reading Question Types

TOEFL reading questions cover Basic Information skills, Inferencing skills, and Reading to Learn skills.

There are 10 question types, which are as follows:

1. **Factual Information Questions**
   These questions ask you to identify factual information that is explicitly stated in the passage. These questions focus on facts, details, definitions, or other information presented by the author. The relevant information is in one or two sentences.

2. **Negative Factual Information Questions**
   These questions ask you to identify what information is true and what information is not true or not included in the passage. The correct answer is the one that is not true.

3. **Inference Questions**
   These questions measure your ability to comprehend an argument or an idea that is strongly implied but not explicitly stated in the text. These questions ask for the cause or basis of the comparison. You have to think for the logical implications of the words.

4. **Rhetorical Purpose Questions**
   Rhetoric is the art of speaking or writing effectively. In these questions you are asked why the author has presented a particular piece of information in a particular place or manner.

5. **Vocabulary Questions**
   These questions ask you to identify the meanings of individual words and phrases as they are used in the reading passage.

6. **Reference Questions**
   These questions ask you to identify referential relationships between the words in the passage. Often the relationship is between a pronoun and its antecedent (the word to which the pronoun refers). Sometimes other kinds of grammatical references are tested.

7. **Sentence Simplification Questions**
   In these questions you are asked to choose a sentence that has the same essential meaning as a sentence that occurs in the passage.

8. **Insert Text Questions**
   In these questions you are given a new sentence and are asked where in the passage it would best fit. You need to understand the logic of the passage as well as the grammatical connections between sentences.

9. **Reading to Learn Questions**
These questions will require you to demonstrate an understanding of the passage as a whole, not just specific information within it.

10. **Prose Summary Questions**
These questions ask you to show an understanding of the different parts of the passage; hence it is necessary to read the entire passage. It measures your ability to understand and recognize the major ideas and the relative importance of information.

PRACTICE EXERCISE B

Desert Formation

Paragraph 1

The deserts which already occupy approximately one-fourth of the earth's land surface have in recent decades been increasing at an alarming pace. The expansion of desert-like conditions into areas where they did not previously exist is called desertification. It has been estimated that an additional one-fourth of the earth's land surface is threatened by this process.

1. **The word 'threatened' in the passage is closest in meaning to**
   - restricted
   - endangered
   - prevented
   - rejected

Ans. This is a vocabulary question. To threaten means to speak or act as if you will cause harm to someone or something. The object of threat is in danger of being hurt, so the correct answer is *endangered.*

Paragraph 2

Even in the areas that retain a soil cover, the reduction of vegetation typically results in the loss of the soil's ability to absorb substantial quantities of water. The impact of raindrops on the loose soil tends to transfer fine clay particles into the tiniest soil spaces, sealing them and producing a surface that allows very little water penetration. Water absorption is greatly reduced; consequently run-off is increased, resulting in accelerated erosion rates. The gradual drying of the soil caused by its diminished ability to absorb water results in the further loss of vegetation, so that a cycle of progressive surface deterioration is established.

2. **The loss of natural vegetation has which of the following consequences for soil?**
   - Increased stony content
   - Reduced water absorption

- Increased numbers of spaces in the soil
- Reduced water run-off

Ans. This is a factual information question. The correct answer is *reduced water absorption*. The reduction of vegetation greatly reduces water absorption.

Paragraph 3

There is little doubt, however, that desertification in most areas results primarily from human activities rather than natural processes. The semi-arid lands bordering the deserts exist in a delicate ecological balance and are limited in their potential to adjust to increased environmental pressures. Expanding populations are subjecting the land to increasing pressures to provide them with food and fuel. In wet periods, the land may be able to respond to these stresses. During the dry periods that are common phenomena along the desert margins, though, the pressure on the land is often far in excess of its diminished capacity and desertification results.

3. **The word delicate in the passage is closest in meaning to**
   - fragile
   - predictable
   - complex
   - valuable

Ans. This is vocabulary question. The correct answer is *fragile* meaning easily broken. Delicate has the same meaning as fragile.

4. **In dry periods, border areas have difficulty**
   - adjusting to stresses created by settlement.
   - retaining their fertility after desertification.
   - providing water for irrigating crops.
   - attracting populations in search of food and fuel.

Ans. This is factual information question. The correct answer is *adjusting to stresses created by settlement*. The paragraph says expanding populations or settlement, subject border areas to pressures or stress that the land may not be able to respond to.

Paragraph 4

Four specific activities have been identified as major contributors to the desertification processes: over cultivation, overgrazing, firewood gathering, and over irrigation. The cultivation of crops has expanded into progressively drier regions as population densities have grown. These regions are especially likely to have periods of severe dryness, so that crop failures are common. Since the raising of most crops necessitates the prior removal of the natural vegetation, crop failures leave extensive tracts of land devoid of a plant cover and susceptible to wind and water erosion.

5. **The word progressively in the passage is closest to**
   - Openly
   - Impressively
   - Objectively
   - increasingly

Ans. This is vocabulary question. The correct answer is *increasingly.* Progressively used here means more and more of something that it is increasing.

6. **Which of the following is often associated with raising crops?**
   - Lack of proper irrigation techniques
   - Failure to plant crops suited to particular area
   - Removal of the original vegetation
   - Excessive use of dried animal waste

Ans. This is a factual information question. The correct answer is *removal of the original vegetation.*

7. **The phrase 'devoid of' in the passage is closest in meaning to**
   - consisting of
   - hidden by
   - except for
   - lacking in

Ans. This is vocabulary question. The correct answer is *lacking in.*

Paragraph 5

The final major human cause of desertification is soil salinization resulting from over-irrigation. Excess water from irrigation sinks down into the water table. If no drainage system exists, the water table rises, bringing dissolved salts to the surface. The water evaporates and the salts are left behind, creating a white crustal layer that prevents air and water from reaching the underlying soil.

8. **The ground's absorption of excess water is a factor in desertification because it can**
   - interfere with the irrigation of land
   - limit the evaporation of water
   - require more absorption of air by the soil
   - bring salts to the surface

Ans. This is factual information question. The correct answer is *bring salts to the surface.* It means that the final human cause of desertification is salinization resulting from over-irrigation.

5.2 PRECIS WRITING

The word 'precis' means exact or terse. A precis is actually a summary, 'a miniature portrait of a passage'. It teaches how to express one's thoughts concisely and effectively. Precis writing requires intensive brainwork.

How to write a precis?

The various steps of precis writing are suggested below:

Step 1
Read the passage thoroughly. Ask yourself what the author wants to say in the passage. That will help you in getting the general idea of the passage.

Step 2
Try to write down the general idea of the passage and sum it up in a suitable heading.

Step 3
Re-read the passage. Detailed study of this kind is necessary because by missing a single sentence, a phrase, or even a single word, one can miss the whole point.

Step 4
Separate the essential parts of the passage from comparatively unimportant parts. This can be done by underlining the important ideas.

Step 5
Take brief notes in your own language. With the help of these notes put down the sum and substance of the passage in a well-connected readable paragraph. It is not likely that this will be a complete success. The draft may probably be too long.

Step 6
Count the words in the rough draft. A precis should be about one-third of the length of the original passage. Now make necessary changes in the rough draft to get the required length.

Step 7
After writing the precis, mention the total number of words of the precis.

5.2.1 Points to Be Remembered

i. The precis should be written in one's own language. The phrases, idioms, examples, quotations, and so on used by the author shouldn't be used in the precis.
ii. It should also be noted that one has to reproduce the original passage without giving one's own comments about the passage. The originality of the passage should remain intact without subjective interpretations.
iii. A precis should be a self-contained unit. It should not appear as if it is something dependent upon the passage. It should be fairly intelligible even to a person who has not gone through the passage. At the end of the day, the précis should make sense and be logical in its presentation.

5.2.2 How to Abridge Sentences

1. Try to replace a sentence or a clause by a phrase and a phrase by a word; for example,

i.	When the officer had inquired into the matter he found the worker was innocent.	On inquiry the officer found the worker innocent.
ii.	There came to his recollection.	He remembered.
iii.	The clerk who is now on his employ.	The present clerk.
iv.	He behaved in such an outlandish manner that we were greatly alarmed and wondered whether he had taken leave of his senses.	His outlandish behaviour made us doubtful of his sanity.
v.	Our country has launched a campaign to reduce the number of those who can neither read nor write.	Our country has launched a campaign against illiteracy.

2. By removing superfluous or ornamental words; for example,

i.	The word 'phone' is a shortened form of 'telephone' which has been abbreviated of 'telephone' by dropping the initial four letters.	The word 'phone' is an abbreviation.
ii.	The rain continued without intermission throughout the night and didn't cease for a moment until after the day had dawned.	The rain continued till dawn.
iii.	He was hard up for money and was being pressed by his creditor.	He was in financial difficulty.
iv.	John fell into the river and, before help could reach him, he sank.	John drowned in the river.

3. Linking of various sentences is very useful; for example,

There were many fishermen's cottages. They extended along the harbour wall. At night their lights were reflected in the water.	Lights from the fisherman's cottages extending along the harbour were reflected in the water at night.

4. Examples and comparisons should be avoided; for example,

A school boy may daydream of becoming Amitabh Bachchan, a young dancer of applauding crowds,	Brown was always thinking of rockets.

a businessman of government contracts. Brown's day dream, however, was different. He thought only of rocket.

PRACTICE EXERCISE C

Example 1

Students' participation in politics is a highly debatable issue. Strong arguments can be put forward both in favour of and against the issue. It may be said that early initiation of the youth when they are passing through a sensitive phase of their life may prove to be harmful. On the other hand, it may be argued that the current political atmosphere is so vitiated and the present lots of politicians are, generally speaking, so corrupt that unless they are completely ousted and the youth take charge of the situation, there appears to be no hope for the country. Both the arguments carry weight. However, anything attempted prematurely does not bring very happy results. If the youth are not strong enough to fight infection, they might catch the infection themselves. Both sides having been carefully considered, perhaps it is better for the students to shun politics, at least in the early stages of their student life.

Students should only be the spectators of political happenings around them. They should observe and absorb the various movements with the help of their teachers and parents. They may show a keen interest but in a peaceful manner. They will thus be better prepared for life when they complete their studies. So passive participation in politics by students is the best solution to the problem.

(221 words)

Precis

Students and Politics

Students' participation in politics has its own pros and cons. On one hand, politics can corrupt a student. On the other hand, only a student can ameliorate the present corrupt political atmosphere. But the negative aspects of participation in politics at this early stage of life outnumber the positive ones. A student should take part in politics in a different way. Instead of pursuing politics as his profession, he should cultivate political awareness. This will help him in facing life in a better way.

(85 words)

Example 2

Speech is a great blessing, but it can also be a great curse, for while it helps us to make our intentions and desires known to our fellows, it can also, if we use it carelessly, make our attitude completely misunderstood. A slip of the tongue, the use of an unusual word, or of an ambiguous word, and so on, may create an enemy where we hoped to win a friend. Again, different classes of people use different vocabularies, and the ordinary speech of an educated man may strike to an uneducated listener as showing pride, unwittingly we may use a word, which bears a different meaning to our listener from what it does to men of our own class. Thus speech is not a gift to use lightly without thought, but one which demands careful handling; only a fool will express himself alike to all kinds and conditions of men.

(151 words)

Precis

Speech: A Boon or a Bane

Speech is a valuable gift, but if we are to make ourselves understood, it should be used carefully, since we may distort our meaning not only by a careless use of words, but by ignoring the fact that words do not always mean the same thing to all people.

(49 words)

Example 3

There are two kinds of popularity which I will call intimate and long-distance popularity, and the first is far more real than the second. A man who is intimately popular is liked by those who know him, a man who is popular at long distance has, by some means, succeeded in propagating a favourable notion of himself among those who do not know him. The two kinds of popularity may go together, but often they are separate, and the man who enjoys long-distance popularity is disliked at close quarters.

Intimate popularity is always a proof of some virtue. If a man is liked by those who meet him, he may have many defects and even vices, but still he is liked for a cause, even though it be unknown to those who like him. His society gives pleasure, and it does so because he himself takes pleasure in the society of others, which means that he is disposed to like rather than to dislike them. It is to him a pleasure to meet those he has never met before, he expects to find them good company, and is, therefore, good company himself. He is ready to take risks in social intercourse, and will not wait to discover whether you are a bore before he opens out to you. He is, in fact, sanguine about human nature, and we like those who are sanguine, especially about ourselves, more than those who despond; they fill us with their own vitality and make us sharers in all their own enjoyment.

(257 words)

Precis

Intimate Popularity vs. Long-Distance Popularity

Popularity is of two kinds—intimate and long-distance. Intimate popularity is better than the long-distance popularity. One who is intimately popular is amiable, sociable, and cheerful. He exudes exuberance and gaiety which enwrap the people in his contact and dispel their gloom. These virtues overpower any vices he might possess and people adore him in spite of his vices. But long-distance popularity is often tact or a myth, and those who enjoy such popularity are usually disliked in their intimate circles.

(81 words)

Example 4

In this world of human affairs there is no worse nuisance than a boy at the age of 14. He is neither ornamental nor useful. It is impossible to shower affection on him as on a little boy; and he is always getting in the way. If he talks with childish lisp he is called a baby, and if he answers in a grown-up way he is called impertinent. In fact, any talk at all from him is resented. Then he is at the unattractive growing age. He grows out of his clothes with indecent haste; his voice grows hoarse, and breaks and quivers; his face grows suddenly angular and unsightly! It is easy to excuse the shortcomings of early childhood; but it is hard to tolerate even unavoidable lapses in a boy of 14. The lad himself becomes painfully self-conscious. When he talks with elderly people he is either unduly forward or else so unduly shy that he appears ashamed of his very existence.

Yet it is at this very age that in his heart of hearts a young lad most craves for recognition and love; and he becomes the devoted slave of anyone who shows him consideration. But none dares openly love him, for that would be regarded as undue indulgence and therefore bad for the boy. So with scolding and chiding he becomes very much like a stray dog that has lost its master.

(214 words)

Precis

A Boy of Fourteen

A boy of 14 is a source of annoyance. His behaviour is awkward. He is either too forward or too shy. The physical changes in his voice, face, and body are so fast that these make him unattractive. He becomes conscious of these changes. But he yearns for love and recognition, which are denied to him. He becomes disgusted and has nobody to patronize him.

(68 words)

Example 5

It is very important to remember, especially now when we have regained our freedom from British rule, that it was contact with Western ideas that made our own people wake up and work for a new India. Many great men and women have worked for the making of the new India in many different ways. They had different idea of what India should be. Some wanted to reform the Hindu religion, by getting rid of idol-worship, caste, and other ideas which were not in the Hindu religion of ancient times. Swami Dayanand, who founded the Arya Samaj, had this aim. Others wanted to get rid of old ideas completely and make India a modern country, with the help of scientific knowledge gained from the West. Some wanted to bring about changes more slowly, by spreading education through newspapers and schools. But all these people got their ideas through hearing or reading about the changes, which had been taking place in Europe and America. They got to know about these changes from people who came to India from the West, first to trade with them, and then to rule over them. They did not like being ruled over by foreigners, but they could not help seeing that unless they got the new knowledge which the foreigners had, they would not be able to make a new India and rule it themselves.

(220 words)

Precis

Western Ideas and Indian Freedom

Association with the West led to political awakening in India. It stirred Indian leaders to strive for their freedom. They had different methods to achieve this end. Some desired to reform the Hindu religion by abolishing the evils that had crept in it. Others wanted to root out old ideas and acquire scientific knowledge to make India a prosperous country. Some wanted to spread education but favoured slow progress but all wanted to free India from foreign yoke.

(76 words)

Example 6

The students should devote the whole of their vacation to village service. To this end, instead of taking their walks along beaten paths they should walk to the villages within easy reach of their institutions, and study the conditions of the village folk and befriend them. This habit will bring them in contact with the villagers who, when the students actually go to stay in their midst, will, by reason of the previous occasional contact, receive them as friends rather than as strangers to be looked upon with suspicion. During the long vacation they can stay in the villages, can conduct classes for adults, can teach the rules of sanitation to the villagers, and can attend to the ordinary cases of illness. They will also introduce the spinning wheel amongst them and teach them the use of every spare minute. In order that this may be done, students and teachers will have to revise their ideas of the use of vacation. Often do thoughtless teachers prescribe lessons to be done during the vacation. This, in my opinion, is in any case a vicious habit. Vacation is just the period when student's mind should be free from the routine work and be left free for self-help and original development. The village work, I have mentioned, is easily the best form of preparation for dedication to exclusive village service after finishing studies.

(228 words)

Precis

Students and Vacation

Students should go to villages in their vacation, they should live among masses, try to understand their problems, and win their confidence. They may teach the adults and tell the villagers importance of sanitation and *charkha*. Those teachers who assign homework are thoughtless. In vacation the students should be free so that they may develop good qualities. Village work will provide them recreation and will also be instructive. It will enable them to settle in villages after their studies.

(81 words)

Example 7

Raillery is the finest part of conversation; but, as it is our usual custom to counterfeit and adulterate whatever is too dear for us, so we have done with this and turned it all into what is generally called repartee, or being smart; just as when an expensive fashion comes up, those who are not able to reach it content themselves with some paltry imitation. It now passes for raillery to run a man down in discourse, to put him out of countenance, and make him ridiculous; sometimes to expose the defects of his person or understanding; on all which occasions, he is obliged not to be angry, to avoid the imputation of not being able to take a jest. It is admirable to observe one who is dexterous at this art, singling out a weak adversary, getting the laugh on his side, and then carrying all before him.

(157 words)

Precis

Raillery and Art of Conversation

Playful satire enriches conversation. But in man's enthusiasm for good humour he tries to show off. This converts raillery into repartee. The art of conversation lies in accepting a joke cheerfully and replying it with a clever reference to the weakness of his opponent and thus entertaining the whole company.

(47 words)

Example 8

On the other hand, I want to oppose the idea that the school has to teach directly that special knowledge and those accomplishments that one has to use later directly in life. The demands of life are much too manifold to let such a specialized training in school appear possible. Apart from that, moreover, it seems to me objectionable to treat the individual like a dead tool. The school should always have as its aim that the young man leaves it as a harmonious personality, not as a specialist. This in my opinion is true in a certain sense even for technical schools, whose students will devote themselves to a quite definite profession. The development of general ability for independent thinking and judgment should always be placed foremost, not the acquisition of special knowledge. If a person masters the fundamentals of his subject and has learned to think and work independently, he will surely find his way, and besides will be better able to adapt himself to progress and changes than the person whose training principally consists in the acquiring of detailed knowledge.

(174 words)

Precis

The Aim of School Education

The acquisition of specialized knowledge closely related to the future life should not be the sole aim of school education. It should aim at the mastery of the basic principles and development of the ability for independent thinking and judgment. This will better equip the pupil to adjust himself to changes and progress in life.

(55 words)

PRACTICE EXERCISE D

Make the summary of the passages given below. Give suitable title also.

1. Our civilization has many good parts. First, it has given us order and safety. Today, we do not get beaten up by another man only because he is stronger than us. We can go to law and the law will protect us. The law also protects us from robbery and violence. We may not realize the importance of this order and safety, but if there were no order and safety, civilization could not develop. The inventor could not invent, the scientist could not make any discovery and the artist could not make beautiful things. In fact order and safety are as important for us as the air. Second, modern civilization has freed man from the fear of pain. Today, men are ill much less often. Also, illness is no longer as painful as it used to be. Without good health, a man cannot enjoy anything or achieve anything. It is true that many men did great things in life in spite of their bad health, but they would have done better if they had enjoyed better health. Today, men and women enjoy better health. Therefore, they enjoy life better. Third, our civilization is more secure than any of the previous civilizations. Previous civilizations were limited. They were surrounded by uncivilized people. These people attacked them again and again and destroyed them. But modern civilization is free from that danger. It is so widespread that there are hardly any savages left who could destroy it. Fourth, modern civilization has made the world a single whole. Every country of the world has become dependent on the other country for its needs. The food that we eat comes from all over the world. Many other things we use are imported from other countries. In the same way, for many things, other countries depend on us. (303 words)
   [*Source:* K. U., BTech (1998).]
2. Still another force that went into the making of the Renaissance movement was the rise of the scientific spirit during the sixteenth century. Although the full impact of the scientific spirit was felt on the literature of the seventeenth century, it made its early, and not altogether insignificant, impact on the literature of the Renaissance also. The beginning of the scientific spirit can be dated with the birth of Nicolaus Copernicus, a German astronomer, in 1473, whose *De Revolutionibus Orbium Coelestum*, published when he was dying in 1543, gave to the world tables of the motions of the planets and proved by the application of these tables that the earth was a planet and moved around the sun. The Copernicus theory was later expounded by Giordano Bruno, an Italian philosopher, and Galilio Galilei, an Italian astronomer. In England the spirit of scientific enquiry was signalled by Francis Bacon in the sixteenth century, who was a happy combination of a scientist and a creative writer, a scientist and a humanist, and a scientist and a moral philosopher. It was he who proclaimed the necessity of experiment and investigation for discovering truth. His *Novum Organum* and *Advancement of Learning* remain the hallmark of the English Renaissance. The conflict between modern science and medieval faith, that is, between the spirit of enquiry and the

orthodox outlook, can be seen in the plays of Marlowe and Shakespeare. Besides Bacon, there were several other Englishmen who contributed to the cause of empirical or experimental science and helped promote the spirit of scientific enquiry. William Gilbert's work on magnetism and William Harvey's on the circulation of blood opened new vistas of enquiry into facts about nature and man. The spirit of enlightenment was thus initiated during the neoclassical period. The impact of science on the Renaissance movement can be described as marginal, but the first rays of the rising modern science certainly fell on the creation of the Renaissance. Thus, the scientific spirit in the Renaissance movement was mixed like the metal in ore. (356 words)

3. With the development of machinery and the speeding up of the manufacturing of all classes of goods, the hours of work have decreased. They are likely to decrease further in future. Machines have in fact become the slaves of modern life. Think for a moment of the extent to which machines do work for you. You wake, perhaps at the hoot of a siren, emitted by a machine in a neighbouring factory. You glance at a machine by your bedside to make sure that the factory machine has the right time. You wash in water brought to you by the aid of machinery, heated by machinery, and placed for your convenience in basins made by machinery. You eat your breakfast quickly cooked for you by up-to-date machinery; go to school in machines made for saving leg labour, after crossing at the cross-roads, till a machine tells you when it is safe to go on; and, if you are lucky enough to be in a very modern school, spend a part of your day in the school cinema, where a machine teaches you by one of the most pleasant methods, or listen to lessons broadcast by one of the most wonderful machines invented in modern times. (224 words)
4. The task of the sociologist in modern society is to study human relationships as social. No other student does this; not the economist, who deals with the segments of wealth getting, distributing, and consuming relations; not the political scientist, who analyses governmental and power relations; not the historian nor the anthropologist nor the psychologist, nor even the engineer—all of whom are focused more or less exclusively on some narrower aspect of man and his life in a social and physical environment or are to be distinguished by some other characteristic of subject or method. Whatever their methods, whatever their interests, however, social scientists are, as are philosophers, generally agreed that the goal of their work is knowledge of man. Man, they agree, as the ancients were the first to realize, can be understood only in the context of his social and political life. Man has his very being in his social relationships. And the study of social human relationships is the study of a process associated with a structure, just as the study of a biological organism includes analysis of both its physical structure and the process associated with it. (190 words)
5. We think of the moon as only a stone, a stone gone cold. An airless, waterless stone and the prophetic image of our own earth when, some few millions years from now, the senescent sun shall have lost its present fostering power and so on. This passage could easily be prolonged—A Study in Purple. But I forbear. Let every reader lay on as much of the royal rhetorical

colour as he finds to his taste. Anyhow, purple or no purple, there the stone is—stony. You cannot think about it for long without finding yourself invaded by one or other of several sentiments. These sentiments belong to one or the other of two contrasted and complimentary groups. The name of the first family is Sentiments of Human Insignificance, of the second, Sentiments of Human Greatness. Meditating on that derelict stone afloat there in the abyss, you may feel a worm, abject and futile in the face of wholly incomprehensible immensities. 'The silence of those infinite spaces frightens me.' You may feel as Pascal felt. Or, alternatively, you may feel as M. Paul Valery has said: 'The silence of those infinite spaces does not frighten me.' For the spectacle of that moon need not necessarily make you feel like a worm. It may, on the contrary, cause you to rejoice exultantly in your manhood. There floats the stone, the nearest and most familiar symbol of all the astronomical horrors; but the astronomers who discovered those horrors of space and time were men. The universe throws down a challenge to the human spirit; in spite of his insignificance and abjection, man has taken it up. The stone glares down at us out of the black boundlessness. But the fact that we know it justifies us in feeling a certain human pride. We have a right to our moods of sober exultation. (307 words)

6. Culture is the cultivation of a plant or garden, not the eradication of its roots; it is an understanding of the roots and seeds, their patient care, and instructed nourishment. Culture is not knowledge, nor is it art, still less is its acquaintance with literature or art. By culture I mean first of all what the anthropologists mean, the way of life of a particular people living together in one place. That culture is made visible in their arts, in their social system, in their habits and customs, in their religion. It is an aggregate of customs, institutions, manners, standards, tastes, morals, and beliefs. These are transmitted rather by the family than by the school, hence when family life fails to play its part, we must expect our culture to deteriorate. It is a delusion to think that the maladies of the modern world can be put right by a system of instruction. On the contrary, universal education by lower standards and morals taste to a common denominator. It is due to sharpening the wits rather than disciplined character that tend to break down existing checks and balance. Education should be the drawing forth of potential values; it should not be the destruction of the safeguards that tradition places around young egos naturally inclined to wilful and precarious flights. (216 words)
7. How often one hears children wishing they were grown up, and old people wishing they were young again. Each age has its pleasure and pains, and the happiest person is the one who enjoys what each age gives him without wasting his time in useless regrets. Childhood is a time when there are few responsibilities to make life more difficult. If a child has good parents, he is fed, looked after, and loved, whatever he may do. It is improbable that he will ever again in his life be given so much without having to do anything in return. In addition, life is always presenting new things to the child—things that have lost their interest for older people because they are too well known. A child finds pleasure in playing in the rain, or in the snow. His first visit to the seaside is a marvellous adventure. But a child has his pains; he is not so free to do as he wishes as he thinks older people

are; he is continually being told not to do things, or being punished for what he has done wrong. His life is, therefore, not perfectly happy.

When the young man starts to earn his own living, he becomes free from the discipline of school and parents; but at the same time he is forced to accept responsibilities. He can no longer expect others to pay for his food, his clothes, and his room, but has to work if he wants to live comfortably. If he spends most of his time in playing about in the way that he used to as a child, he will go hungry. And if he breaks the laws of society as he used to break the laws of his parents, he may go to prison. If, however, he works hard, keeps out of trouble, and has good health, he can have the great happiness of seeing himself make steady progress in his job and of building up for himself his own position in society. (337 words)

8. To a greater or less degree all the civilized communities of the modern world are made up of a small class of rulers, corrupted by too much power, and of large class of subjects, corrupted by too much passive and irresponsible obedience. Participation in a social order of this kind makes it very difficult for individuals to achieve that non-attachment in the midst of activity, which is the distinguishing mark of the ideally excellent human being; and where there is not at least a considerable degree of non-attachment in activity, the ideal society of the prophets cannot be realized. A desirable social order is one that delivers us from avoidable evils. A bad social order is one that leads us into temptation which, if matters were more sensibly arranged, would never rise. Our present business is to discover what large-scale changes are best calculated to deliver us from the evils of too much power and of too much passive and irresponsible obedience. It has been shown that economic reforms too, so dear to 'advance thinkers', are not in themselves sufficient to produce desirable changes in the character of society and of the individuals composing it unless carried out by the right sort of means and in the right sort of governmental, administrative, and educational contexts; such reforms are either fruitless or actually fruitful evil. In order to create the proper contexts for economic reform, we must change our machinery of government, our methods of public administration, our system of education, and our metaphysical and ethical beliefs. (262 words)
9. There are some men who seem to be always on the outlook for trouble and, to tell the truth, they are seldom disappointed. Listening to such men one would think that this world is one of the stormiest and most disagreeable places. Yes, after all it is not such a bad place and the difficulty is often in the man who is too thin-skinned. On the other hand, who goes out expecting people to be like himself, kind and brotherly, will be surprised at the kindness he meets even in the most unlike quarters. A smile is apt to be met with a responsive smile while the sneer is just as apt to provoke a snarl. Men living in the same neighbourhood may live vastly different lives. But it is not the neighbourhood which is quarrelsome, but the man within us. And we have it in our power to change our neighbourhood into a pleasant one by simply changing our own ways. (163 words)
10. The direct telecast of the matches helps the people all over the country to watch the match. Even people who are living in remote areas are not able

to reach the venue of the game for want of time or money, are also able to watch the performance of their favourite heroes. They get inspiration. National feelings have come to be linked with the game of cricket. In a way cricket promotes national integration. Quite a number of youngsters, who watch cricket on TV, begin to play the game in their humble surroundings. Heroes grow out of these young aspirants.

The direct telecast of matches also creates an adverse feeling among cricket fans. Some of them begin to realize what they are losing by constantly watching cricket matches and then start taking interest in other things. This leads to a general decline in interest in the game of cricket. Moreover, the potential players, who watch the performance of their favourite players on the TV and want to emulate them, remain ignorant of the trials and tribulations which the players have gone through to gain eminence. The young aspirants see only the glamorous part of the game and begin to dream of similar glamour without actually taking adequate pains for the realization of their dreams. The result is that in the end their hopes are frustrated. (226 words)

11. Man's own survival depends not on his capacity to deal with the thermonuclear explosion but also on his capacity to stop the careless plunder of the planet. He must start applying the science of ecology to himself so that he can learn, before it is too late, that he is a part of the intricate relationship between all living things. Nature is a vast treasure-house of knowledge but it is as yet hardly explored. Some species are becoming extinct before they can be properly studied.

    Wildlife is valuable asset as a renewable natural resource, particularly in developing countries, and can contribute to the economy, especially through tourism. Already, in some countries of Africa, for example, tourism may soon become the leading industry and is an important source of overseas currency. People from all over the world come to see and photograph wildlife. If the animals vanished, many of the tourists would stay away. Wildlife, if intelligently managed and husbanded, can also be a valuable source of much needed protein.

    When there is an unavoidable collision between the survival of man and the survival of wildlife, human interest is likely to prevail. But such collisions are rare and in most cases a little thought, ingenuity and good will permits coexistence of man and wildlife. We must first learn to recognize that these dangers exist and we ourselves shall be the losers if we do nothing about it. We must make sure that everyone everywhere understands the threat, accepts the responsibility, and appreciates that it is in the interest of human progress to avert it. What is needed now are more and more larger areas set aside for wildlife reserves, more sanctuaries, and national parks; more reservation legislation—better laws and better law enforcement; more conservation research to find out exactly why species and habitats are threatened and on animals in captivity so they can be returned to their natural habitats; more conservation education and campaigns to make the world aware of the existing problem and to avert specific disasters; and, most important of all, more money for those various activities which will help to save the world's wildlife and places with wildlife. (357 words)

12. William Caxton did a yeoman's job for mankind by inventing the printing machine in 1469. However, the Romans are credited with bringing out the first newspaper in the form of wallpapers which carried the edicts of their kings and were displayed prominently at the market place. Since then newspapers have trodden a long and eventful path. A newspaper today is not merely a piece of paper carrying some news; it is a powerful medium of mass communication and a mighty force which cannot be easily ignored. It is the custodian of truth and a sentry of human rights and liberties. It spreads ideas and educates the public at large regarding the various issues involving public interest and morality. It comments on and criticizes government's policies and actions. That is why the Press means a lot to the masses.

    A newspaper has become part and parcel of our daily life. It gives us all kinds of news about our country and the world. A regular reader of a newspaper remains in touch with public affairs; it educates him by providing a lot of information on almost all walks of life. A newspaper keeps people informed about the latest happenings in the world of politics, business, sports, art, culture, and so on. Newspapers help both the consumers and the producers with advertisements, they help in keeping the prices uniform by publishing market rates, and they also reflect the financial health of the country by publishing the index of various stock markets. Sports fans get all the news they want through the newspaper. The various sports are given due coverage in its columns. In fact, it caters to the needs of all. (278 words)

13. Life without discipline is like a ship without a rudder. As it is impossible for a ship to sail without a rudder, it is impossible for a man to pass through life without discipline. It is discipline, indeed, that helps a man to sail on course through the ocean of life and brings him safe to the heaven of peace and prosperity. Without discipline, life is sure to become a hopeless wreck.

    The first lesson in discipline is obedience. Man must obey the rules of the society or the organization where he is working. The second lesson is how to behave—how to avoid the conduct which is considered unbecoming and wrong, and how to acquire good habits. The training given to a child is a good example of discipline. To be a useful member of society, a child has to be trained by its parents and teachers from very beginning.

    The methods of training are patient instruction, example, encouragement, and punishment. A child has to be imparted proper instruction to discriminate between right and wrong. It must be made to understand the distinction between good and bad. It must be told not only what to do, but also what not to do. But sometimes, all teaching is futile. A child learns not through instruction but through example. It imitates and hero-worships. The parents and teachers present it with an example which it finds easy to follow. Thus the child must be presented with a role model which, in other words, means that the elders too should be disciplined.

    Encouragement and punishment also play a significant role in disciplining the child. When a child shows discipline, he must be encouraged, patted on the back, and if possible, rewarded. But if he violates the norms of discipline, an occasional dose of punishment does help. (302 words)

14. The Indian economy is chiefly based on agriculture. Ironically, we are in an age of science and technology, yet we are frequently hit by famines, especially in Orissa, Bihar, and Gujarat. Why is India subject to famines?

India is a vast country where the irrigation system hardly benefits twenty percent of the land. Agriculture in India, therefore, depends mainly on the monsoons. If the monsoons break at the appropriate time and bring sufficient rains, the crops are abundant; if the monsoons fail, the crops also fail and agricultural activities are brought to a halt. The result is famine with all its terrible consequences.

The condition of a famine-stricken region is miserable. A visit to such an area brings before us all the horrors of life. Day after day, the sun blazes overhead, and there is not a drop of water anywhere. Pools, tanks, and streams all dry up. Wells and hand pumps are rendered useless. The land becomes parched and dry. Vegetation also dries up. Cattle grow lean and thin, and die. Men, women, and children die of starvation. People even sell their children for paltry amounts. There is a great exodus in search of new pastures.

Such is the horrible condition of the people during the days of famine. Some sort of relief is provided, but it is meagre. Food is rushed to the famine-stricken area, yet even this affords little relief to the poor. They are too poor to be able to buy grain at any price. The programmes such as 'Work for Food' are launched, but all these are nothing but temporary measures.

The government no doubt comes forward to help the poor. Famine relief funds are started. Subscriptions are raised by the people and food is provided free of charge. Modern transportation is employed to provide relief promptly. But all this seems to be an exercise in futility. Can such programmes eradicate droughts forever? Why can't we have proper planning to alleviate the misery of the people? (335 words)

15. 'Women's Lib' can be called the most important movement of this century. It seeks to liberate women from the age-old shackles of male-dominated society. In fact, it is a protest against male chauvinism. In some Western countries it is acquiring more extreme forms. In India there is greater need for women's liberation as they have been treated like slaves for ages. Though they have been acknowledged as 'ardhangini', that is, the other half of man, there has been a wide gulf between preaching and practice. That is why great social reformers such as Dayanand Saraswati, Vivekananda, Raja Ram Mohan Roy, and Mahatma Gandhi aimed at women's liberation especially through education.

Women must be liberated in the sense that they should be allowed to play responsible roles in different walks of life. It is an established fact that in most Oriental, African, Latin, and Arab countries, women continue to be neglected; in general, there are fewer women than men who have the benefits of higher education or who pursue suitable careers. Their place is still in the kitchen, playing the traditional role of serving men and looking after children.

The neglect of women costs the world a great deal both in economic and in social terms. A family without an educated mother is, in most cases, a deprived family. Such families suffer on other social counts also because the mother is unable to help the children in their education and training for life. Needless to say, an educated and enlightened mother can make all the difference to the family. (259 words)

16. The term 'labour' includes both bodily and mental work. But when we talk of the dignity of labour, it always means physical or manual work. Mental work; however, is regarded respectable and dignified, whereas manual labour is looked down upon as unsuited to a man of intellect. A white-collar worker is generally esteemed as a man of achievement, while the man who works with his hands is regarded low.

    There is, however, a great difference between the two categories in terms of its relevance to social needs. The basic needs of life such as food, clothing, and shelter require manual labour much more than mental labour. A farmer toils hard in tilling, sowing, reaping, and winnowing the harvest to grow food. For our shelter, we again depend upon the manual work of masons, carpenters, and builders. Weavers and tailors help us in providing clothes. Since life cannot go on without manual work, labour cannot be anything but dignified.

    There is another side to the coin. Sophisticated tasks require mental rather than manual work. Behind the builders stands the architect, behind a tailor is the designer, and behind the successful farmer the agriculture researcher. Without their help no progress would be possible. But the argument appears to be lop-sided when we ponder on the value of each particular role.

    In short, the adviser requires the practitioner as much as the latter needs the former. There has to be complete harmony between the two. Moreover, it is wrong to presume that the engineers, doctors, architect, and designers are merely thinkers. To be good they too must combine action with thinking, and work with their minds as well as with their hands. It is indeed true that mental and manual work are complementary to each other. It also means that society must change its attitude towards the manual labourer. This change can be brought about through appropriate education. Even Gandhiji envisaged the importance of labour in his concept of basic education. (327 words)

17. Freedom comes as naturally to man as flight to birds and leaves on trees. Man indeed is born free but it is also true that everywhere he is found to be in chains. Sometimes, outside agencies such as society, religion, and the State put him in shackles; sometimes man chooses his own fetters.

    Indeed life is reduced to a meaningless drift if man does not enjoy freedom. Man must enjoy freedom of speech and thought, freedom to act, freedom to move freely, and, in the ultimate analysis, freedom of conscience which envelops all other freedoms. This, however, seems to be an idealist's version. The reality, harsh as it is, points a contrary view. Freedom eulogized by each and every philosopher and statesman is still a philosophical chimera that can never turn into reality.

    Political thinkers have wrestled with this problem; their conclusion is that the existence of society and the concept of freedom are antithetical to each other. The society which creates an agency to govern itself has perforce to create certain rules. The emergence of these rules marks the beginning of the end of individual freedom. Society defends these rules by insisting that they are in the larger interest of the people.

    Political thinkers emphasize that the tyranny of the State turns human beings into mere machines. They become 'Unknown Citizens' whose only job is to meekly obey the law. Thus, the State becomes an agency to suppress the individual's craving for freedom; the individual must obey or perish. The state becomes so powerful, and•the use of force so naked that an individual dares not express his views for fear of reprisal.

Even in a democracy, freedom is merely a decorative word. All the political parties swear by it, but once in power they unscrupulously curb it. If we go deep into Rousseau's dictum, we shall concede that the trammels of social decency and social laws, including customs and conventions, besides the all-powerful State, can never allow man to remain free. (332 words)

18. I strongly believe in the old maxim—money makes the mare go. I dream of money day in and day out. I do so because I am a pauper and from morning till evening I am tormented by the fact that I am very, very poor.

This constant thought of poverty becomes so harrowing on occasions that I want to escape into a world of fantasy. I want to ease myself into sheer affluence.

I start daydreaming about what I would do if I had a billion rupees. Maybe such abundance of money would disorient me altogether; it is also possible that this unimagined wealth might make me share the grievances of other people like me.

But if there is such a windfall, one may be sure of one thing. First, I will have a truly luxurious mansion on the beach, the likes of which I frequently see in the Hindi films. The mansion will be richly decorated with genuine works of art. It will have a library with the classics from the old world and the new. These books will be no mere pieces of decoration. No, with the accursed poverty being over, I shall be free to spend my days as I deem fit. In fact, there will be a fleet of liveried servants to take care of each whim that comes to my fancy.

My house will have a vast garden enriched with exotic flora and fauna. The beauties of nature will relieve me of the occasional anxiety I might face in life. I will possess a fleet of cars, air-conditioned, cushioned, and glittering to transport me from the world of one fancy to another. I may even think of possessing a private aircraft to soar high among the clouds. My billion rupees will come handy to realize this dream. (300 words)

19. The Indian women has waged a long and relentless battle for a dignified existence and equality with her male counterparts. Still her life is fraught with insecurities and risks. The birth of a female child even today heralds a spell of gloom and anxiety for the parents. She is discriminated against in matters of health, education, and occupational opportunities. As a young woman she is subjected to sexual harassment from chauvinistic males. Her entire existence, despite the much vaunted slogans of liberation, symbolizes nothing but degradation and humiliation.

Ironically, the ultrasound device, which was originally invented to detect any ailment or abnormality within the human body, is being used by unscrupulous people to detect the sex of the child in the womb so as to destroy it in case it is female. Huge hoardings unabashedly announce the easy availability of pre-natal tests and murderers in white coats roam freely aborting female foetuses.

This raises serious social and moral questions which all enlightened people should think about. We have to ponder what makes men and women take a conscious, deliberate decision to destroy the foetus. One reason, of course, is the traditional notion that woman is inferior to man in all respects. While this may be an altogether irrational notion, there are several problems such as the evil of dowry and sexual harassments that women frequently encounter in an increasingly desensitized world.

The question is: Are these reasons good enough to justify a patently immoral and criminal act? Haven't women proved themselves equal to their male counterparts in all respects, and that too against tremendous odds? The myth of the continuation of lineage is irrational and is eroding fast. Again, in the rapidly crumbling social order it is more often than not the daughter who comes to the rescue of the old parents. (300 words)

20. It goes without saying that education is a lifelong process. Gandhiji has aptly stated that the education of an individual commences from his birth and lasts till his death. It is, however, imperative to differentiate between education and literacy. Even an illiterate person can be educated if he has learned his lesson from the 'school of life'. In short, an educated man is liberated from the narrow confines of ignorance and superstition. That is why, education aims at bringing humanity into the light of knowledge from the darkness of ignorance. 'Tamso Ma Jyotirgamaya' is the very root of our educational philosophy. Moreover, education aims at the all-round development of an individual enabling him to be a good citizen. It is a pity that we are far from these cherished goals of education even after nearly five decades of freedom.

The present system of education in India, by and large, is a legacy of the English. Lord Macaulay introduced this system of education to produce 'white-collared' clerks. Unfortunately, we have not been able to change this slavish mentality even today. As such, our present education does not fulfil the aspirations of our society. Our educational system has rapidly expanded since Independence with the result that we have sacrificed quality at the altar of quantity. The mushrooming growth of schools, colleges, and universities has created a wide gulf between those educated and corresponding job opportunities, leading to unemployment. Unfortunately, we have woefully neglected skill education and work experience in our present set-up, with the result that our youths fail to imbibe the spirit of dignity of labour. Moreover, a university degree is regarded as a passport to a job. Therefore, our educational system has been rendered merely examination- and career-oriented. A student soon learns to distrust knowledge and contrives to pass the examination by fair or foul means. (306 words)

5.3 ESSAY WRITING: AN ART

'The pen is mightier than the sword,' however, the pen is not sufficient to make one a writer. One needs to learn tips to write an essay.

5.3.1 The Art of Essay Writing

Essay writing is basically an art. Like any other art this too cannot be mastered overnight. It demands a flair for writing, a thorough knowledge of grammar, and an analytical approach of mind. Students must, therefore, learn the art of essay writing right from the early stage of their educational career.

Like any other art such as painting, sculpture, music, singing, and so on, an essay too is a vehicle of self-expression. The writer pours out his inner feelings into his essay. Essay is thus the most innocent way of putting down one's thoughts and feelings in black and white on any subject. Dr Johnson had echoed this sentiment when he said that 'An essay is a loose sally of the mind; an irregular, indigestible piece.'

Gradually by constant practice the students can learn to write essays of fairly high level. Today essays have come to be regarded as a test of a man's intellectual calibre. This is the basic reason why these days essay writing is included in most of the competitive examinations to judge the suitability of candidates for various posts.

An essay is always marked by a personal touch. In the words of Ben Johnson, 'An essay is a thing someone does himself and the point of the essay is not the subject but the charm of personality.'

In reality, an essay is a literary composition. Bacon, Hazlitt, Lamb, Stevenson, Johnson, Swift, and many more wrote literary essays which are regarded as the greatest treasures of the English language of those times. These essays are real masterpieces of great minds.

Of course, the essay written in a college or competitive examination is quite different from an essay as understood in the literary sense. In a competitive examination, the essay attempted should be precise, balanced, coherent, and objective.

5.3.2 What Is an Essay?

An essay is, actually a 'unified, coherent and logically constructed literary composition'. It is, generally, a short composition which treats a particular subject in 'a methodical and orderly manner'. It is usually a written attempt, within certain limits of time and space, to describe and elaborate upon a certain object, a person, a thing, or a thought which forms the theme of the essay. In fact, it is an organic piece of writing having a beginning, middle, and an end. An essay, consequently, has unity, that is, it deals with one main subject, and all the parts are clearly related to the subject. Its coherence implies the logical sequence of thought. The paragraphs are interlinked so as to give the impression of a single whole. Relevance in the essay means that the necessary and appropriate information related to the subject is supplied. No unnecessary digressions are permissible. Proportion involves the treatment of the more important points accordingly.

5.3.3 Structure of an Essay

An essay generally consists of three parts:

i. The introduction
ii. The body
iii. The conclusion

The Introduction

The introduction in a short essay must be brief. It should be striking and interesting, for 'well begun is half done'. Most beginnings are either halting or irrelevant. For instance, an essay titled 'Sweet Are the Uses of Adversity' should not begin with the definition of the word 'adversity' which is well known. Such definitions might be acceptable in reflective essays involving abstract terms. Again, you must plunge straight into the subject without beating about the bush. The beginning should invariably be related to the theme which naturally should lead to the body of the essay. The other ways an essay can begin are: with a quotation, with a proverb, or with some general statement leading to the subject. In short, the opening of the essay must arrest the attention of the readers.

The Body of the Essay

It is, indeed, its backbone. Your subject matter should be divided into a number of points. You may then develop each of these points into a paragraph of suitable length. Take care that one paragraph leads to another in thought. In this way, your essay will become a chain of which the various paragraphs will form the links. This will make your essay an orderly piece of composition, possessing continuity. Avoid repetition of facts and ideas. Let your essay be the expression of your individuality; let it reflect your mind, your thoughts, your opinions, your feelings, and your experiences.

The Conclusion

An ending should be natural and not abrupt. The reader should not feel that the essay has ended as the writer has run out of ideas. Let the conclusion arise out of the main theme. It should, like the beginning, be carefully attended to. It should be convincing and impressive. The conclusion should be such as to win the readers' approval of the ideas and opinions expressed in the essay. There are a number of ways in which an essay can end:

a. A striking quotation often forms the most effective ending.
b. The arguments put forward in the essay may be summed up.
c. It can be ended with a sentence that expresses the main points in a nutshell.

5.3.4 Style in Writing

You must pay attention to the following 'dos' and 'don'ts':

i. Don't use a word or phrase the meaning and usage of which you do not thoroughly understand.
ii. Avoid using flowery language and too many adjectives.
iii. Don't use the same sentence constructions again and again.
iv. Don't use many allusions.
v. Let your words suit the sense and your style suit the subject matter. A serious subject should not be treated in a light manner, nor should a light or humorous subject be treated in a heavy style.
vi. Stick to the main theme of the essay and do not digress.
vii. Be clear, simple, and natural.

5.3.5 Different Kinds of Essays

Essays may be divided into roughly six categories in accordance with their subject matter. But it must be remembered that there may be essays which include the characteristics of more than one class. For instance, a narrative essay may contain a good deal of description, and a descriptive essay may contain in it much of reflection. The following are some of the major categories of the essay:

The Narrative Essay

In a narrative essay an event or a series of events are narrated. The happenings must be narrated in the order in which they occur. These essays include historical events, legends, biographies, accidents or natural calamities, journeys, or stories—real or imaginary. For example, 'A Street Quarrel', 'A Festival', 'The Celebration of a Marriage', and 'Life of Sachin Tendulkar'.

The Descriptive Essay

A descriptive essay aims at the description of something—a person, place, or thing. Usually, the description is factual and objective. In certain cases it can be subjective also. A descriptive composition may deal with such subjects as towns, courts, ships, buildings, animals, and so on, as also natural phenomena such as volcanoes, the monsoons, and so on.

The Reflective Essay

It requires reflection on the part of the writer on some topic which is generally of an abstract nature. Here the writer develops his thoughts on a certain subject in a reflective manner, ignoring the descriptive or narrative aspects. The topics may include habits, hobbies, patriotism, discipline, poverty and education, and so on.

The Expository Essay

An essay which supplies an answer to the questions—how and why—is termed an expository essay. Scientific, literary, and financial topics are covered under this category.

The Imaginative Essay

In an imaginative essay, the writer is called upon to draw ideas from his own imagination. For instance, 'If I Were the Prime Minister', 'If I Were Rich', 'The Journey of a Hundred Rupee Note', and so on come under the purview of the imaginative essay.

The Argumentative Essay

An argumentative essay is written to prove or disprove a certain idea. It is common to put forth arguments for and against the subject under consideration, and then to substantiate the particular point of view. For instance, topics such as 'Should India Manufacture Nuclear Bombs?', 'Should English Be Abolished?', 'Should Sex Education Be Introduced?', and the like would come under this category.

PRACTICE EXERCISE E

Develop the outlines given below into a full-fledged essay.

Topic: **Student Unrest in India**

Introduction

a. Who is a student?—One who pursues the path of knowledge. A sacred occupation, but is the student conscious of what he is?—No.
b. He is neither conscious of his strength nor of his values, hence, he is out of control—parents and educational authorities are helpless.

Some characteristics of the modern student:

a. Indiscipline—shows little respect to parents, teachers, and elders; indifference towards study—does not attend lectures, uses abusive language.
b. No sense of hygiene. Comes to college in ruffled clothes or with uncombed hair.
c. Misbehaviour in and misuse of public systems.
d. Smoking, drinking, use of narcotics presuming that these habits mean sophistication and 'progressive' thinking.
e. Mobile addiction, anti-social behaviour on and off campus.

Students and Strikes

a. Sociopolitical reasons for going on strike
b. Indisciplined behaviour during the strikes—shouting, uproar, slogans, stone throwing, and the like
c. Students' energy and idealism exploited by political parties

Reasons for their indiscipline

a. Energy and enthusiasm of youth are not given any direction—'Indisciplined and untamed energy is always destructive' (Russell).
b. In our society, wealth dominates character and education—a wealthy man commands much respect. Motives, methods, and modes of behaviour may be warped.
c. Uncertainty about future after completion of studies—selection in service and jobs based on considerations rather than on the merit and efficiency of a candidate—the unemployment problem. 'Moral values are money-governed.' (Marx)

Suggestions

a. Students should be made aware of their potential.
b. Students should be made to feel secure of their future by introducing more and more job-oriented courses.
c. There should be fair selection in service and jobs on the basis of individual merit.
d. Student problems should be tackled on priority.
e. Students should refuse to become tools in the hands of political parties. They should be aware of the national–international political scenario, but they should concentrate more on acquiring skills and knowledge in order to equip themselves for a career.

5.3.6 Sample Essays

Drug Abuse: A Serious Public Health Problem

From time immemorial drugs have been used by mankind for medical purposes. But never before had the abuse of narcotics caused such unprecedented worldwide concern and posed an alarming menace to the society. According to World Health Organization, it is estimated that 1 in 20 adults, or a quarter of a billion people aged 15–64 years, used at least one drug in 2014. Even the Eastern Hemisphere is no longer secure from the drug network. Drugs have scanned the planet at jet-speed and proved once again that the earth is a small place to live in. The abuse of drugs is now an international problem that bothers Indians and Americans alike.

Taking a drug other than for medical reasons in amount, strength, frequency, or manner that damages the physical and mental functioning is drug abuse. Drug abuse is a painful problem for the addict, for his family, and for all those who touch his life. It is mostly the youngsters who fall prey to drugs. Adolescence is a period when many choices must be made. At this stage, the youngster is especially vulnerable to pressure from friends.

The future generation is virtually being crippled by the abuse of drugs. Drug abusers are completely self-centred and care least about others. His consciousness is clouded, and he loses his will-power, concentration, memory, and judgement capacity. When in need of money, he does not hesitate to steal or indulge in other antisocial activities. 'More drugs, more crime' shows the graph. A new addict develops friendship with fellow addicts, and gradually enters the so-called 'drug subculture'. He is then regarded as an outcaste in the society, and there is little chance that he shall again lead a healthy life.

To start with, the addict takes a pill to alleviate pain or get a 'thrill' at the persuasion of his friends. Quickly he develops a mental dependence to the 'thrill'. Gradually he becomes physically dependent too, requiring increasing dose daily, in absence of which he shows 'withdrawal symptoms'. Ultimately, the addiction becomes a habit, when the sheer thought of taking drugs thrills him. Enquiries have attributed the addiction of a subject to his health, mentality, environmental factors, and even genetic factors. In fact, drug habit has become a fashion among young people in the country's principal urban centres. In order to be 'modern' and 'march with the times', students having generous pocket money take to drug habit. In want of money, these addicts gradually take to drug pushing, and the network widens. Some others get addicted to overcome frustration and mental agony. Children of quarrelling parents are found to be prone to addiction. Studies conducted in the United States, United Kingdom, and Japan have shown that the fathers of the addicts are generally indifferent or mentally weak. Besides, the lack of healthy education, uninspiring lectures by teachers, and unhealthy books and cinemas degrade moral values of the youth and may lead to addiction. Minor tranquilizers (like Benzodiazepine) prescribed by doctors may also lead to addiction if taken regularly for a considerable length of time. The total permissiveness in Indian society, on Western lines, is also responsible for the fast-spreading drug menace. Gone are the days when the Eastern and the poor or developing countries were free from drug abuse. Record seizures of various intoxicants in the recent police raids have turned the spotlight on drug abuse in India also. But the seizures are only the tip of the iceberg. In fact, drug traffic is now considered as second only to armaments, and even more lucrative than oil business. The Asian drug circuit and American mafias work in coordination, as the 'Golden Crescent' (the junction of Iran, Pakistan, and Afghanistan) and 'Golden Triangle' (the junction of Thailand, Burma, and Laos) serve as prime source of narcotics. The role of India as a major transit route for international drug traffic has also caused much concern around the world. The overwhelming magnitude of the looming calamity requires the voluntary indulgence of the youth to apprise the masses of the ill-effects of drug and the symptoms of an addict.

The medical treatment for detoxification is not sufficient, unless supplemented by Group Therapy. Under this treatment, the medically treated addict must be brought in regular connection with an anti-drug community, where former addicts shall instil confidence in them. 'Aversion Treatment' by Behavioural Psychotherapy may also come to help. The addicts may also be helped to change their negative outlook by Logo Therapy. At the same time, the cultural growth of seeking professional help for drug addict is itself a healthy sign. It means that we recognize the problem and want to set it right. That's half the battle won. Addiction should be considered as an illness and not a sign of moral weakness or lack of willpower. Nor is it a crime. It is an illness that can be treated by professionals with full understanding of drug abuse.

The patient should be motivated to seek treatment. The treatment includes detoxification and after-care. When the body is dependent on drugs for its normal functions, detoxification is needed. Toxins are poison like drugs in the body, which must be got rid of under medical care, so that a person is able to achieve a drug-free condition. However, it is the patient's willpower and support and understanding from near and dear ones that will help him remain drug-free and overcome his craving for drug. It must be remembered that the addict is fighting a constant drug temptation.

In order to tame and trample the monster of drug abuse, we must go back to the root of the problem and make the user of drugs more human, tolerant, understanding, appreciative, sympathetic, and helpful. This is a 'social responsibility' underscoring the dictum 'No man is an island.' Social workers, teachers, and above all, parents, especially mothers, can play a vital role in this direction. Many counselling and dead diction centres have contributed greatly to create a national awakening. More such efforts are required from all walks of the society.

We Live in Deeds and Not in Years

We should live in deeds and not in years. Life, ordinarily, is oak-like. One crowded hour in a glorious life is worth more than an age without a name. Life should, therefore, be full of deeds studded with achievements.

Long life is desired by all. Nobody likes to die early. But age is a matter of living not years. We read in newspapers of men who lived one hundred years or more. If these men left no noble account of their lives behind them, we may ask whether their life was worth living. They do not live in the memory of man. If their memory is not cherished by men, their long life has no value. They are soon forgotten by men because they lived in years, not in deeds.

The value of life is measured by noble deeds and not by long years. When a man fulfils the long mission of life, he lives a true life, no matter whether he dies early or lives long. Life's mission is not simply to eat, drink, and be merry. A man must have a noble aim. He must do something good for his countrymen and the world. A self-centred man may be rich and may live long but nobody cares to show any regard for him or remember him after his death.

A man's true wealth is the good he does in the world to his posterity. So long life should not be the only aim of our life. We may try to live long, but at the same time we must make our long life purposeful. We must count our life by deeds, not by years. We must do noble deeds which will make us immortal. Man is born to work out than rust out. Death is a must. Let the body fall in serving a noble cause. Therefore, the problem now is not to add years to our life but to add life to our years.

Fruitful is the birth even of that grass growing on the banks of a river which provides a hold for the hand of a drowning man. Blessed are those who die for their beliefs. For their blood shall fertilize the soul of man.

In India, it has been a recurring experience that we talk high philosophy and live very ordinary lives. Actually life is an exciting business and most exciting when it is lived for others. It is a fact that respect is earned by actions and not acquired by years. But we must manage our time as we manage our money. We cannot control the length of our life but we can control its depth and height. So as long as we live, we should keep learning how we live.

Death comes to all but great achievements build a monument which shall endure until the sun grows cold. The wise generally die after they have lost their reason; fools before they found it. We could rather die on our feet than live on other's knees. Our only insurance against tomorrow is what we do today.

In this world many great men died rather early in life. During the short span of life, they did so much work for the good of others that people cherished their memory even after their death. Such a life is worth living though it may be painfully short. Such men gain immortality in their death. In the history of the world, there are many instances of such men. Shankaracharya died early. But his countrymen cannot forget him. During his short life he did enough for the good of his countrymen. Swami Vivekananda died rather early. He did not reach even 40. We have read what he had done for the Indians in America and Europe and in India also. His life has been an inspiration to many. Can we ever forget him? He will live forever in his deeds though he died early. Can lovers of English poetry forget the names of Shelley, Byron, and Keats? All of them died early but their poetic works have made them immortal. The rose is a beautiful flower. It does not last long but as long as it lasts, its beauty and sweet smell give joy to man. In this way, the short-lived rose fulfils the mission of its life and we remember it forever. A tree may live long but it does not please man as the blooming rose does. So the short life of a rose is far superior to the long life of a tree without beauty and fragrance.

In conclusion, thus we find that the worth of a thing depends upon quality and not quantity. A successful life is measured by noble deeds and not by years. Of course, there were born men who lived long. During their long life they did many noble deeds for the good of their countrymen and the world. They are remembered not for their long life but for their noble deeds. We may mention here the name of the great poets Rabindranath Tagore and Sarojini Naidu. They will be remembered forever by people for their achievements and not for their long life.

Importance of Learning English

English language as a medium of instruction was introduced in India in the nineteenth century by Lord William Bentinck, the then Governor General of India, for imparting Western system of education.

The underlying objective of the British rulers in introducing English language in India was to inculcate mental slavery among the Indians and to make them clerks or *Babus*. It was also an attempt to convert the Indians to Western culture.

Introduction of English, however, proved a boon for India. In fact, Raja Ram Mohan Roy, a famous religious and social reformer, was an ardent supporter of this language. Other leaders such as Dadabhai Naoroji, Pt Moti Lal Nehru, and Pt Jawahar Lal Nehru were also educated in English. This language enabled our leaders to take up the cudgels with the foreign rulers on the public platform and in the legislature in their own language.

English played a great role in our freedom movement. It served as a link language among Indians belonging to different regions and provinces. Again, it is through this language that India became aware of great strides made by the Western civilization, science, and culture. Not only that, it brought us closer to people of other countries.

In the present scenario, English is no longer a language of Britain. It has grown into an international language. Even countries such as China, Japan, South Korea, and Thailand, and many other countries of West Asia and Africa are learning the English language.

English is one of the important working languages of the United Nations Organization (UNO). Indians who are well versed in this language have, therefore, greater scope for getting jobs in the various offices and agencies of UNO. In fact, UNO has more Indians serving in its various offices and establishment than is warranted by India's share. The main reason for this is that a large number of Indians possess the knowledge of the English language. India is very fortunate that its people learned this language. Knowledge of this language has helped India to develop close relations with the English-knowing countries. It has given India an important place in international affairs.

It is a well-known fact that the advanced knowledge of science, technology, space research, nuclear field, medicine, engineering, and the like is abundantly available in English language. By learning the English language, the Indians have been able to gain access to this vast treasure of knowledge in the fields of science and technology.

India has a number of languages. After India became free, the country was reorganized into states on the basis of languages spoken by the people. Hindi was spoken by the majority of people and as such it was declared the national language of India. But its imposition was opposed tooth and nail by the southern states of India. These states were assured by the then Prime Minister, Pt Jawahar Lal Nehru, that Hindi would not be imposed on them. As a result, English has virtually become the link language of India. It is serving as a link between the northern and southern states. It has enabled us to preserve the unity of India.

However, protagonists of Hindi language are not in favour of the continued use of English even as a link language. They want that with the end of British rule in India, English language should also be thrown out because, whatever its merits, it is a foreign language. Our love for this language is nothing but a sign of our slavish mentality.

But the supporters of the Hindi language should not forget the fact that English also belongs to the same Indo-European languages family to which Sanskrit and Hindi belong. English has been in use in India for as many as 200 years. It has virtually become an Indian language. It cannot and should not be discarded in haste.

We should look at the language problem dispassionately. Hindi is no doubt our national language. It should be encouraged, developed, and popularized. Till such time as it is accepted by the southern states, English should continue to be used as the official language along with Hindi. English is the repository of all modern scientific and technological knowledge. We should not lose it. The most prudent course for us is to let Hindi and English languages flourish together and enrich each other.

Freedom of Expression: Advantages and Disadvantages

Since ancient times, man has attached great importance to his fundamental right of expression. He regarded this right as his proud possession. He defended this right with all his might. If necessary, he even laid down his life to uphold this precious right. History is replete with examples of thousands of men, women, intellectuals, philosophers, artists, writers, politicians, and so on having fought and sacrificed their lives for the sake of this freedom.

In ancient times, Socrates was accused of misleading and corrupting men of Athens by spreading the gospel of truth and his famous dialectical method for acquiring knowledge. Socrates sacrificed his life by drinking hemlock for the sake of his freedom of expression. Lord Christ was crucified because he spread the message of God to the people.

Galileo, a scientist, declared on the basis of research and study that the earth is not the centre of universe and that it revolves around the sun and not vice versa. But Galileo had to embrace death for expressing a view which went counter to the popular belief of the church at that time.

During the medieval ages, the scholastic church establishment did not allow the airing of the non-conformist ideas. Those who had the courage to express what they felt were accused of blasphemy and awarded deterrent punishments such as stoning to death, death by drowning in the river, or burning alive. Many others were condemned for the rest of their life like 'The Prisoner of Chillon'.

During the Mughal rule in India, the Sikh Gurus preached what they thought was right but the Mughal rulers did not relish this freedom. They persecuted the Sikh Gurus for their beliefs. Thus Guru Arjun Dev, the fifth Guru of the Sikhs, was made to sit on hot iron plates. Bhai Mati Das was sawed into two. Guru Tegh Bahadur was beheaded in Delhi. The young sons of Guru Gobind Singh were buried alive inside a wall.

During the British rule in India, many Indians expressed themselves openly against the tyranny of alien rule and fought for the independence of the country. Freedom fighters were put behind bars, made to sleep on ice slabs or broken pieces of glass, lathi and forced to do manual labour. Lala Lajpat Rai, the Lion of Punjab, died in a police lathi charge while demonstrating against the Simon Commission. Hundreds of Indians lost their lives at Jallianwala Bagh as a result of brutal and indiscriminate police firing while expressing their views in public.

George Orwell, the famous British writer of celebrated novels such as *Animal Farm* and *1984,* criticized denial of freedom to express one's ideas. In his 'Essay on Liberty', J. S. Mill, the English political philosopher, also advanced the view that there should be no limitations on the freedom of expression of one's opinion and ideas. He declared that even if there are 10 cranks, we should not limit their free opinion because it is just likely that out of 10 cranks might turn out to be a genius.

Similarly, even if one person wishes to express an opinion different from the opinion of the whole society, he should be allowed to do so. Sometimes, even the whole society can be wrong as it was when Socrates, Christ, and Galileo gave their individual opinions. Later on, it was proved that they were right whereas their opponents were wrong.

In the modern age, Popper in his famous book *Open Society and Its Enemies* criticized the concept of a closed society where human beings are reduced to the position of robots and subhumans.

But freedom of expression also carries with it a duty or responsibility towards the society. It cannot be an unbridled expression. It has to be subject to such reasonable restrictions as the society may deem fit in the larger interest. Article 19 of the Indian Constitution gives to every citizen the right of freedom of speech and expression. This right is not absolute. Reasonable restrictions on the exercise of this right can be imposed on the grounds of (i) the security of the State, (ii) friendly relations with foreign States, and (iii) incitement to offence, public order, decency or morality, defamation, and contempt of court.

Thus, the right to freedom of expression is a valuable right of man. It is a fruit of democracy. It should be enjoyed, nurtured, and preserved. However, it should not be allowed to be misused as a license by any person.

Superstitions Lead to Death of a Thinking Mind

Superstition is the religion of the feeble mind. It means an irrational or blind belief. It imports ominous significance to an otherwise innocuous happening, coincidence, or circumstance. Superstition is a worldwide phenomenon. Every country has people who believe in one superstition or the other. In some cases, superstitions are more deep-rooted because they form part and parcel of the religious beliefs. Though there is hardly any scientific justification for superstitions, yet people continue to cling to them.

Superstitions are not a recent phenomenon. They have come down to us from ancient times. The primitive people of the bygone ages were a mute witness to a number of natural events or happenings. They did not understand the causes of physical changes taking place around them. They also did not know why they sometimes met with success and at other times with failure. They had no inkling of why various diseases inflicted them. They were overawed by forces of nature such as fire, wind, water, clouds, storms, and the like. It is this element of fear which gave rise to superstitions. The urge for material well-being also led people to either do or not do certain things. Repeated coincidences strengthened these beliefs.

Most of the people in India are uneducated. Therefore, they are prone to entertain superstitious beliefs. In fact, if a comparative study is made, it will reveal that the maximum numbers of superstitions are prevalent among the people in India. Let us see what these superstitions are like. If someone sneezes just when you are about to go out, you are likely to fail. If you are about to go out for some work and someone interrupts you by asking 'Why or where you are going?' you start believing that you will meet with a failure now.

Some superstitions, it is thought, enable one to ward off the evil eye. For example, when some people build a new house, they hang an earthen pot with an ugly face painted on it on the facade of their house. Similarly, owners of new cars or scooters ward off the evil eye of other people by hanging women's braids at the back of their vehicles.

Strangely enough, sometimes one superstitious belief contradicts the other. According to one most commonly held belief, Brahmins are high-caste people and Sudras are regarded as low caste. But if you go by the superstition, meeting a Sudra on your way brings success, but meeting a Brahmin is likely to result in your failure.

Certain birds and animals are regarded as the worst omens. If a black cat comes across your path, you will either fail or meet with an accident. Wailing of a dog foreshadows death; hooting of an owl spells disaster.

Sometimes people go to the extent of not celebrating a festival throughout their life simply because someone in their family died on the day of that festival. One may believe or not, but it is a fact that in India if soon after a marriage someone dies in the family, the poor bride is blamed for it.

Some superstitions are supposed to bring good luck or happiness. If you find a horseshoe and bring it home, it could bring luck to you and your family. Breaking of crockery on the occasion of a marriage ceremony is regarded as auspicious.

Superstitions are not only prevalent in backward countries, but even the advanced Western countries have not remained unaffected by this irrational phenomenon. For instance, people in the Western countries believe that the number '13' is an unlucky number. They will not do anything important on the 13th of a month lest they should come to grief. Inmates of a house carrying this number will dread disease. Passengers do not like to travel in a taxi with a number plate of this number.

Surprisingly, even when a particular superstition does not come true in actual life, people do not give that up. On the contrary, they cling to it for whatever it is worth. The hold of superstitions on our mind is so strong that even if nothing happens to a man after a black cat cuts across his oath, or he meets with success in spite of a sneeze, he will not stop believing in these superstitions.

There is nothing wrong in sneezing. In fact, it is a biological necessity. It can come to a person at any time of the day. So if it comes when a person is about to go out, one need not raise any eyebrow. Similarly, when a person is about to leave, it is but natural for the other person to ask questions to know as to where he is going. One should not read too much into such spontaneous questions raised by people who are curious to know.

Superstitions lead to mental disorders. A person believing in superstition is always haunted by unknown fears and anxieties. He suffers from strain and stress. Sometimes he may even suffer a nervous breakdown. A superstitious person loses self-confidence. Education alone can play a positive role in convincing people about the futility of superstitions.

A Little Knowledge Is a Dangerous Thing

The essence of human life since its appearance on earth has been man's insatiable hunger for knowledge—knowledge of the self, of the skies above, and the domain below. As knowledge expanded, so did its utilization. Hitherto inexplicable events become intelligible when viewed from a scientific perspective.

However, knowledge cannot be designated as a mere awareness of facts; it is to be considered thorough understanding of facts and their implications achieved through an analytic attitude. From this viewpoint a knowledgeable person is meticulous and hard-working, quite different from the half-wit claiming to be learned.

We can classify the half-wits in two categories—the first consisting of those who are ignorant and cannot claim to be knowledgeable, and the second consisting of those who are half-read yet claim to be very knowledgeable. People in the first category are fools who bask in their ignorance and lead the happy and contented life of an ignoramus. They are, in a sense, harmless. But a person in the second category is a half-wit and is dangerous for the society. Throughout his life, he clings to his conviction of being scholarly. He, therefore, lives in a fool's paradise. It is such an individual who tends to be a bigot, who shuts his mind to any change for fear of someone shattering his paradise, his long held illogical beliefs, and half-baked notions.

And with this attitude, the self-complacent fool enters the arena of society. If the selection mechanism is faulty, such an individual might come to occupy an important position in the society. He then becomes more harmful because, with his half knowledge, he is not able to discharge his duties efficiently. He takes the wrong decisions and is a barrier to the smooth functioning of society. Moreover, such a person is generally jealous of his well-read contemporaries and tries to create problems for them. Consider a teacher whose cognizance of his subject is nothing beyond a mere smattering. Armed with his closed mind and lack of erudition, he is likely to become a pedagogue with a narrow vision and a dogmatic viewpoint. His students will never get the opportunity for analysis and self-learning, restricting the horizon of their knowledge and killing their creativity. These students shall never be able to contribute anything to their subjects.

The unscholarly economist who seeks to reform his nation's economy would inevitably lead it to a quagmire, and destruction shall ensue due to his unlearned mind mingled with self-opinion.

A bureaucrat who is half-read harms the society because of his inefficient mode of working. He promotes corruption by misusing his powers. An unscholarly doctor is dangerous for his patients.

In fact, a half-knowledgeable person in any important position in society is harmful for it. The wiseacre has great faith in his intelligence and derives conclusions without actual verifications. This way being easier to claim to be an intellectual is adopted even by the young people these days. Such a trend is disheartening as it pollutes the academic life of a nation.

The half-read individual does not hesitate to indulge in the adulation of selectors if they can assure him of a good office. They then further corrupt and damage the system. The solution is to make the system of selection rigorous so that the meritorious are retained and the half-wits eliminated. This would give people an incentive to be proficient in their fields, because only that would ensure their economic security, and half-learnedness would decrease considerably.

In conclusion, one can say that half-knowledge is indeed worse than ignorance because a half-wit, while living in his mental prison, is intolerant and is harmful to society. The immortal remark of Pope states this very appropriately:

'A little learning is a dangerous thing;
Drink deep, or taste not the Pierian Spring.'

Relevance of Religion in Modern Society

Religion is as old as man. It is based on the instincts of man. It gives him solace and contentment. It is food for his soul. Every religion has a set of beliefs and a code of customs, rituals, and ceremonies. The followers do not question the veracity of these beliefs. In fact, they develop a blind faith in these beliefs. Though the progress of science has made people doubt the relevance of religion in today's world, yet the protagonists of religion are not prepared to give it up. They cling to it more firmly. Thus, religion continues to survive in the world side by side with science.

In the past, cruelties and barbarities have been committed in the name of religion. Fierce clashes between followers of different religions resulted in great loss of life and property in many countries of the world. This menace is continuing even today. In India, religious differences have been the root cause of communalism. These differences led to the partition of our country in 1947. Though India has declared itself as a secular state, communal clashes do take place in one or the other part of India every year.

Unfortunately, followers of every religion have forgotten the essence of their religion. They confuse religion with its rituals and ceremonies. Most people think that religion consists of going to a temple, mosque or a church, fasting, going to places of pilgrimage, wearing a holy thread or cross, obedience to pandits, priests, or mullahs, giving donations to religious institutions, lying prostrate before idols of gods and goddesses, worshipping the holy books, reciting prayers, and so on.

Saints like Kabir and Nanak taught us that rituals and ceremonies are not true religion. What makes a man truly religious is truth, non-violence, meditation and compassion. They pleaded that people should follow the essence and true spirit of their religion rather than its form.

The essence of all religions is love. Christ's famous precept 'Love thy neighbour' implies ideal of service and self-sacrifice. A person with a religious bent of mind is always inclined to relieve human misery and increase happiness. He is full of compassion and benevolence. He is honest to the core. He hates cunningness, hypocrisy, cruelty, and the like.

According to Pope, 'An honest man is the noblest work of God.' Honesty is more valuable than all the rituals, ceremonies, and practices of all the religions of the world. In reality, a person can be truly religious without calling himself a Hindu, Muslim, or Christian. If a man does not go to a temple, mosque, or a church, it does not mean that he cannot be a religious man. Similarly, it is also not necessary to believe in or follow any dogma. A true religion has nothing to do with them. For example, belief in a personal God, belief in heaven and hell, belief in immortality of the soul, or form and content of any prayer are dogmas.

Religion makes people believe in destiny and fate. People stop making efforts for progress. They do not aspire or struggle for anything in life. It is for this reason that Karl Marx condemned religion. He called it opium of the masses.

Science has no doubt made tremendous progress but it has still not been able to unravel many secrets of life and nature. Meditation can help us to turn inward and introspect. This is what self-realization means. We should not meditate or pray in a mechanical way. Our whole personality should be involved in it.

Most religions commend people to abstain from pleasures of life. Religion has come to mean self-denial, detachment and renunciation. Such a puritanical approach to life does not sustain interest in life. It divests life of all its charm. This is a negative approach. True religion is one which gives equal importance to body and mind.

Religion is a way of life. It is a matter of one's faith and conviction. When religion embraces fanaticism, it loses its soul. Followers of one religion become the arch-enemies of the followers of another religion. Instead of bringing people together, religious fanaticism divides them.

What is more disturbing is that religion has started making inroads into politics. It has got intertwined with political squabbles. Some countries have gone to the extent of making the religion of the majority population as their state religion. Though India is a secular state, we have in India many religion-based political parties which are wedded to one or the other religion.

If we believe in the essence of religion, we should imbibe the qualities of truth, non-violence, honesty, love, compassion, and the like. We should not give undue importance to any rituals, ceremonies, or dogmas of any religion. We should cultivate universal brotherhood. We should not dilute the purity of religion by injecting politics into it.

Good Manners: Polite and Well-Bred Social Behaviour

Good manners play a very important role in the life of the boys and girls. Though good manners are a very valuable possession for developing social relations, yet they cost nothing. They help a person to win friends. The social standing of a man is judged by the manners he possesses. Polished and polite manners create a healthy impact.

Good manners go a long way in making a person cultured and civilized. A man without good manners remains a savage. Normally good manners are inherited from parents. But these can also be learned from others. It is, therefore, essential that all children are taught good manners from the childhood itself. Ill-mannered children bring disgrace to their worthy parents.

Children with good manners are liked by one and all. They are appreciated even by strangers. All-round development of a child is possible only if a child is groomed in good manners. Therefore, the public schools lay great emphasis on the cultivation of good manners in their students. It is no exaggeration to say that a man without manners is an animal.

If a person is well dressed it does not mean that he must be possessing good manners as well. We find that more often than not, even good looking children lack good manners. The moment such children speak, they expose themselves.

It is a matter of regret that some parents go on meeting the demands of their children but do not care to teach them good manners. These parents spoil them but when such children bring a bad name to them, they repent. But then, it is too late. Therefore, if we want that our children should possess good manners and behave well, we must catch them young.

Courtesy and politeness are the key to good manners. Biographies of great men can also help us in learning good manners. Use of polite words such as 'Sorry', 'Please', 'Thank you', 'Beg your pardon', 'Sir', and so on create a healthy impact on the minds of others. No doubt these are little words but if they are spoken at the right moment and in a soft and sweet voice, they are bound to work wonders. Even if we have to say 'No' to someone, we should say so in a polite manner so that his feelings are not hurt.

Good manners not only demand courtesy and politeness but also respect for the feelings and opinions of other people. We should not criticize others for holding views different from us. We should avoid acrimonious discussions at the social gatherings. They help no one. We should also steer clear of heated discussions on controversial and sensitive political issues to avoid bad blood with others. We should not ridicule a blind or a lame person. It shows bad manners. We should be considerate to our elders, ladies, children, and sick persons. While travelling in a bus or train, we should always offer them a seat. It is a pity that in buses we sometimes find men occupying even the seats reserved for ladies. We should help an old lady or a blind person to cross the road safely. We should not talk loudly or shout at others. While riding in a car or a scooter, we should not blow horn unnecessarily especially near a hospital, school, or a library. We should not pluck a flower from any public garden. Flowers are meant to please our eyes and not to be plucked. If we go on talking to others but do not listen to what they have to say, it is a sign of bad manners. While coughing or sneezing we should always cover our mouth with a handkerchief. We should not throw away banana skins on the roads. Someone might slip and sustain an injury. Similarly, the habit of writing obscene things on the walls or on the books smacks of bad manners. We should regard a foreigner as our most honoured guest. Whenever he needs our assistance, we should extend it to him. We should not jeer at him. Certain unscrupulous elements try to cheat foreigners of their money and belongings. This spoils the image of our country and its people in the eyes of the world. While waiting for a bus, we should always stand in a queue. We should not try to break the queue even when we are in a hurry. All public property belongs to the nation. We should not damage it under any circumstances. These days political parties have made the act of damaging public property such as buses, trains, bridges, and so on a political weapon to press their demands or to air their grievances. This tendency needs to be curbed. We must treat public property as our own.

All great men are humble. They do not brag about their achievements. We should be happy over the achievements of others and not jealous. If we know these people, we should congratulate them on their achievements. Criticizing a person behind his back is not good manners.

A well-mannered person is always the centre of attraction. He is loved and respected by all. Good manners bring joy and success in his life. He becomes a gem among his fellow men. We should acquire good manners and enrich our personality.

My Ambition in Life

A person without any ambition in life is like a ship without a rudder. He has no destination. He does not have any urge to make a start. He reaches nowhere. He is tossed about like a straw in the wind. He achieves nothing in life.

So everyone should have an ambition in life. But simply having an ambition is not enough. Whatever be the ambition it must be backed up by continuous efforts to achieve it. If a person sets an ambition before him, but does nothing to achieve it, his ambition is no more than an idle dream or a pious resolution.

Different persons have different ambitions. The nature of ambition varies from man to man, depending upon his family background, upbringing, social status and economic condition, and so on. Thus, some people's only ambition in life is to amass wealth by fair or foul means. It is with this end in view that people demand fabulous dowry on the marriages of their sons. Sometimes they also take to anti-social professions like smuggling to make quick money. Corruption has struck deep roots in India because of this ambition.

Wealth is not everything in life. Man does not live by bread alone. The ambition of some persons is to earn fame so that even after their death their name lives on. Thus, we find people striving to become top artists, journalists, educationists, sportsmen, and the like even though these pursuits may not enable them to earn much wealth.

There are others who want neither wealth nor fame but want to serve humanity. They believe that service of mankind is the service of God. Mahatma Gandhi and Swami Vivekananda have laid great stress on alleviating the sufferings of the poor people. Mother Teresa rendered a yeoman's service to the poor and the destitute people who were in need of love and care.

Some young boys and girls would like to become film stars. If a person succeeds in this profession, it will enable him to earn both wealth and fame and lead a glamorous life. These days a number of persons also wish to go and settle down in advanced countries where they can earn more and lead a luxurious life.

As for myself, I want neither wealth nor fame. I do not want to become an actor. I have no liking for politics also because it is said to be the last resort of a scoundrel.

My ambition in life is to become a teacher. There are a number of reasons for my choice. First, about 50 per cent of people in India are illiterate. They are steeped in ignorance. They are governed by superstitions. By becoming a teacher, I will be able to remove illiteracy, ignorance, and superstitions to some extent.

Second, though the teachers of our country are ill-paid, yet it is one of the noblest professions. This profession will enable me to translate into my life the Gandhian principle of simple living and high thinking.

Third, this profession will enable me to serve the cause of education. According to Plato, education is the turning of the inner eye towards light. By adopting the profession of teaching, I can hope to perform this stupendous task.

Fourth, teaching profession calls for a missionary zeal and a sense of dedication. I possess both these qualities in ample measure. I have aptitude for this profession. Therefore, if I join this profession, it will give me job satisfaction. It will mean fulfilment of my cherished ambition.

Fifth, the students of today are the citizens of tomorrow. This profession will enable me to make my humble contribution in the building of my nation by instilling the spirit of nationalism and patriotism in my students.

In view of the foregoing reasons, I am convinced that my preference to become a teacher is a step in the right direction. I will, therefore, spare no efforts to achieve this ambition of my life.

PRACTICE EXERCISE F

Write essays in approximately 800–1000 words on the given topics:

1. Current taxation system
2. Military service and the role of gender
3. Do all religions have a right to exist?
4. My favourite music
5. Global climate changes
6. Bollywood celebrities in politics
7. Corruption
8. Politics is everywhere and always a 'dirty' game
9. Are cell phones too harmful?
10. Dangerous, violent video games
11. Does participation in sports keep teens out of trouble?
12. The role of uniform in colleges.
13. Pros and cons of globalization.
14. Technology and communication
15. Teenagers and crime
16. What makes a criminal?
17. Family size
18. Role model
19. Prevention vs. cure
20. Autobiography of a 100 rupee note

5.4 E-MAIL WRITING

Electronic mail, popularly known as e-mail, has now become the most preferred means of communication in the Internet age.

5.4.1 Composition of an E-mail

To: Write the recipient's e-mail address here.

CC: Carbon Copy (CC) is used to send the message to additional recipients beyond the primary recipient mentioned in *To*.

BCC: Blind Carbon Copy (BCC) is used to send messages to several addresses without revealing it to all. The e-mail address of the recipients specified in this field cannot be seen by the recipients in the *To* or *Cc* fields, and they will not know that a copy of the email has been sent to these address.

Subject: Use a brief and precise line to tell the recipient clearly what the mail is about.

Body: The main message is to be written here. Reading from the computer screen is harder and slower than reading a print out of the same text. So the message must be kept short, covering all the vital information.

Attachment: One can attach files created with other programmes such as MS Word or a zip file, along with the e-mail.

Signatures: Your e-mail account can automatically add these data to the bottom of the email:

Full professional name, job title, business phone/fax numbers, business street address, business website (if any)

5.4.2 Writing Effective E-mails

Although it is possible to send an email without a proper subject line, it is not recommended to send such e-mails. Providing an appropriate subject to the e-mail will ensure that the recipient can easily identify the topic of the e-mail, without even opening the mail. So equip your mail with a subject line that gives the reader an accurate idea of the content of your mail.

E-mails, like letters, should have a proper beginning and ending in both formal and informal contexts.

Formal Opening	*Formal Ending*
Dear Ma'am/Sir	Yours faithfully
Dear Professor Pandey	Yours sincerely
Dear Dr Patel	With regards
Dear Organisers	Best regards

Informal Opening	*Informal Closing*
Dear Harshit	Best wishes
Hi Bhawna	Thanks
Dear Mom	Kind regards
Hello Anjali	Cheers

In case of a long e-mail, break it into paragraphs, with each paragraph dealing with a separate point.

Or you may break up your e-mail into points so that it is easy to read it out. The way text is arranged on screen greatly affects its readability.

Dear Aman,

We regret to inform you that your paper 'Misuse of Laws on Women in India' has not been recommended for publication by our reviewers on the following grounds:

1. The topic has not been adequately researched.
2. Rather than making general statements, elaborate comparisons have to be made between laws of other countries.
3. Refer and cite actual judgments.
4. The paper requires complete restructuring and scholarly inputs.

We encourage you to revisit your paper in the light of the above and resubmit for our subsequent issues.

Best regards,
Meera Agarwal
Editor
Journal of Law

Dear Mr Frank,

Sequel to the 'White Wedding' project you assigned me, I have written a proposal on it. I need you to approve the disbursement of the funds needed to carry it out.

I e-mailed the proposal to you a week ago and you have made the necessary corrections. Also, you have green-lit the commencement of the project. The event will be held a month from now and some fund is needed to make a reservation for the proposed venue for the event. The management of the event centre requires booking and an advance payment, at least two weeks, before the proposed date.

The approval of the disbursement of the fund will facilitate the swift and early execution of this project, which is the edge we have over our rivals.

I await your positive response.

Yours faithfully,
Tina Green
Event Producer

5.4.3 Netiquette

This refers to the good practices and customs that are commonly observed while sending e-mails.

To be an effective e-mail communicator, the following etiquettes should be observed:

a. Respond to e-mail messages in a timely manner.
b. Provide clearly worded subject lines for all messages with no more than 6–7 words.
c. Use shorter sentences and paragraphs to communicate your message.
d. Use upper- and lower-case letters. All caps is considered as 'shouting', which should be avoided.
e. Avoid trivial messages which only clutter the e-mail system.
f. Avoid adding too many attachments to your e-mail.
g. Use spell check to ensure correct spellings.

5.4.4 Email Abbreviations and Acronyms

Provided below is a list of common abbreviations and acronyms used to keep e-mail messages short:

Abbreviations/Acronyms	*Expanded Form*
ASAP	As soon as possible
BTW	By the way
FYI	For your information
LOL	Laughing out loud
NBD	No big deal
OTOH	On the other hand
NRN	No reply necessary
IMO	In my opinion
BBL	Be back later
AFAIK	As far as I know

5.4.5 Limitations of an E-mail

Some limitations of email include:

a. Space available on e-mail screen is less than that of a page. Hence long-typed e-mail messages are annoying.
b. Senders of messages have no assurance that the intended receiver will check his mail and respond.

c. E-mails are more prone to grammatical and spelling mistakes as they can be prepared and sent more quickly than most other means of communication.
d. Spam and junk mail represent messages that clutter the user's inbox. While junk mail often comes from opt-in services, such as from businesses, spam refers to messages that the user did not opt to receive. Spam mails are useless for the receivers and it only results in filling up of the mailbox.

PRACTICE EXERCISE G

1. Draft an e-mail applying for a vacancy.
2. Send an e-mail to your friend recommending reading a book you liked.
3. Draft a complaint to the Electricity Board regarding the frequent power outages in your locality.
4. Send an e-mail to the customer care section of a mobile company whose mobile you have purchased but it is not functioning properly.

5.5 BUSINESS MEMOS

Like a business letter, a business memo is a positive functional instrument of professional exchange of business ideas, opinions, decisions, policies, and information. However, a business memo differs from a business letter in several important ways:

- Memos are used to send information inside an organization unlike letters, which are used as a means to reach out to people outside an organization.
- A memo is written in a specific format, which is different from the letter format.
- Memos are less formal than letters.
- Memos are less structured than letters.
- The tone of memo is conversational than that of a letter.
- Memos contain less background explanation and information than letters.

Memos play an important role in decision-making process in an organization by facilitating the flow of information within its various parts and units. Some of the vital characteristics of a memo are discussed below.

5.5.1 Clarity

In order to maintain clarity in memos, the following points must be remembered:

- Clear references should be used.
- Simple, familiar, and specific words and expressions should be used.
- Clichés and overused proverbs and phrases should be avoided.
- Short sentences and paragraphs should be used. Ideas should be separated into paragraphs.
- Appropriate linkers and transitional signals should be used.

5.5.2 Conciseness

Concise and direct memos are more effective. A memo should contain only essential information. Unnecessary explanations, repetitions, wordy expressions, and exaggeration must be avoided in order to ensure that the memo makes its point with the fewest words possible.

5.5.3 Unity of Theme

A memo, which does not have unity of theme, ceases to be purposeful.

An important way of ensuring unity in a memo is to make sure that it deals with only one topic. A single topic is developed, and related ideas are subordinated. Focusing on a single topic unfolds the theme logically.

5.5.4 Informal Tone

Although a memo is a formal business document, its tone is usually informal and conversational. Personal tone may be used as a very formal tone might sound intimidating.

5.5.5 Form and Structure

Writing memos is a professional activity that demands effort and sincerity. The memo should be divided into four segments to organize the information and to help achieve its purpose. Standard memos contain four parts: (a) Heading, (b) Opening, (c) Body, and (d) Closing.

Heading

The heading segment of a memo includes four elements, that is—

Date: Complete and current
To: Name and designation of the recipient
From: Name and designation of the sender
Subject: Topic of the memo

Opening

Most memos begin with a short paragraph describing the problem that led to the need for the memo and the basic purpose of the memo. The opening segment thus mentions the central idea which may include the context, the specific assignment or task, and the purpose of the memo. The context being the circumstance or background of the problem, the assignment describes the efforts to solve the problem. The purpose gives the reason for writing the memo. The opening of the memo must answer the following questions:

- What is the problem?
- What led to the need for memo?
- What is the purpose of memo?

Body

The body of a business memo contains the message of the memo. It describes, explains, and discusses the central idea of the memo, and includes all the details that support the sender's ideas. It may begin justifying the importance of the main point, and the next few paragraphs may contain more information and supporting details. The body may also contain a brief statement of the key recommendations the sender has reached. Appropriate graphic techniques and non-verbal data may be used in order to highlight the main parts of the memo.

Closing

Memos should be closed with a courteous ending, stating what action the reader is required to take. The closing segment of a routine memo contains action information seeking action-oriented response specifying the action, while complex and long memos may also contain a summary of the main ideas.

5.5.6 Sample Memos

AFRON PHARMACEUTICAL IND.
Ansari Road, Daryaganj, New Delhi 110002
www.afronpharma.ac.in

Date: 15 January 2008
To: M. David
District Manager
From: Kapil Khadelwal
Regional Manager

Subject: New procedure for stock verification

We are starting a new procedure for stock entry and verification. Instead of keeping three different registers for recording stock of expired medicines, past stock, and new arrivals, we will use only two registers for the three types of entries—one register for expired medicines and one for past stock and new arrivals.

The change will make it easier to record and verify existing stock. This will avoid the present confusion created by triple entries and will save time, space, and energy. District managers will continue to be the stock verification officers for their respective district.

This change will go into effect from 30 June 2008. I am sure the change will make stock entry and verification in our company more organized and logical.

Kapil Khandelwal

SKP Ship Management
Remi Bizourt, VD Road, Andheri (W), Mumbai 400 053

Date: 7 August 2004
To: Ashish Kumar, Training Manager
From: Jerry Massey, Managing Director

Subject: Special workshop 'Ship Management and Modern Technology'

Please refer to your memo dated 31 July 2004, containing the proposal to organize a special workshop 'Ship Management and Modern Technology' for the junior executives of our company. I am pleased to inform you that the Executive Board has approved your proposal.

You may send us the final list of resource persons to be invited in the workshop. You may consider including the names of a few senior executives working in the ship management industry. This may help us in making the workshop more focused and need-based.

I would like to express my appreciation for the effort that you have put in to design the structure of the workshop. Keep up the good work and keep these ideas coming.

Jerry Massey

National Tours and Travels Pvt. Ltd
M-15/6, South Extension, New Delhi 110 049
www.nationaltours.com

Date: 15 June 2005
To: Preeti Biswas, Training Organizer
From: P. R. Mehta, General Manager

Subject: Special training courses in sales and marketing

As you know that Sarna Corporate Training Pvt. Ltd, Delhi, has proposed to conduct special training courses in sales and marketing for our field staff involved in aggressive selling of tour packages. I would like you to select the appropriate course for our sales trainees.

I am sending you the following information as an attachment to enable you to choose the right course for them.

- List of the courses
- Duration of each course
- Structure and content of each course

I would like to discuss this matter with you at your earliest convenience. We need to take a decision by the end of this month.

P. R. Mehta

Syndicate Consultancy Services Pvt. Ltd
Nayadeep, Andheri (W), Mumbai 53

Date: 16 June 2006
To: All employees
From: Arunabh Bhattacharya, Director (Sales and Marketing)

Subject: New Health Scheme

The company is introducing a new health scheme called SCS Health Plan. You will receive your new medical card and a booklet outlining the terms and conditions of the scheme by 30 June 2006.

The main features of the SCS Health Plan include:

- Medical reimbursement for treatment at private hospitals and clinics

- Direct payment of medical expenses to AIIMS and other important national hospitals
- Medical facilities for retired staff
- Token system at SCS Hospital

SCS Health Plan is compulsory for all the employees of the company. The use of the medical card is mandatory.

I am sure the new health scheme will improve the existing medical facilities and would benefit our employees. We encourage you to use your new medical card whenever you visit the health centre and follow the guidelines contained in the brochure. Your cooperation in this matter will be greatly appreciated.

Arunabh Bhattacharya

PRACTICE EXERCISE H

1. You work as a clerk in the personnel department. For the past six years you have taken your vacation in the usual summer months. This year, however, your sister is getting married and you will need to travel out of town and would like to take your two-week vacation in October. You are aware that vacation leave is not normally granted at this time of year, but feel your reasons are valid. Write a memo to your unit head, Mr Roberts, to inform him of your situation and request your vacation for October.
2. You are the training coordinator. You have been asked to make arrangements for a half-day seminar at the Conference Centre. The seminar is for 25 division chiefs from various departments. Write a memo to the director of the Conference Centre, Mary-Ann Downs, making arrangements for space, tables, audiovisual equipment, and refreshments.
3. You are employed in the accounting department for a large company. Your department paper shredder has been causing problems because it gets used so much. Write a memo to the purchasing manager explaining the problem and requesting the purchase of a new, larger-capacity paper shredder. Provide a rationale for the expense.

5.6 LETTER WRITING

Everybody will have to write various types of letters for different purposes. Letters help bring people together, share joys and sorrows, communicate requests, arrange for selling/buying and even promote general good will among the people of a community. It is unfortunate that the increasing use of telephone has led to the disappearance of the art of letter writing. But even in the hustle and bustle of modern life, one is called upon to write letters for transacting official/business work. Generally speaking, there are two types of letters:

1. **Informal Letters**
   Letters written to parents, relatives, and friends are personal, intimate, chatty, and informal. The emotions of the writer are expressed in these letters. They need not be centred round any specific topic. They can be rambling, inconclusive, and anecdotal. The informal letters will be colloquial and even slangy.

2. **Formal Letters**
   Business and official letters are more polite and formal than personal letters. Business letters are written by official departments and businessmen to their counterparts. Official letters are addressed to senior officials and bureaucrats by individuals.

Business Letters

These letters are the main means of establishing business relations with the external agencies or persons. It should be effective and in order to be effective it has to be written with a learned skill. These letters should convey a good impression to the recipient and on this depends the continued cordial and mutually profitable relation between the business organization and the recipients. Through business letters, a modern businessman is able to maintain good relations with all his contacts and is able to represent the business interest of his company. His letters make friends for his company and for himself. It acts as a communication between the firm and its customers. A good business letter can be written when the writer understands something about human relations. The language must be concise, to the point, and easy to read. Short, direct, simple statements covering the main points and stating them carefully in an organized order make very good letters. A business letter is certainly more effective if it stresses the 'you' instead of 'I'. There are different types of business letters, some of which have been discussed below:

1. **Enquiries and Replies**
   Enquiries are among the most common types of business letters. If an enquiry is properly written it may bring valuable business information and also realize a glorious business opportunity. The clearer and more complete the enquiry is, the most satisfactory the answer will be. It is by this kind of letter that business may originate. These are written asking for information regarding the financial position, credit reputation, and business methods of traders and firms, and also to estimate the worth of a product.

2. **Complaint and Adjustment Letters**
   After the order has been executed and the goods have been sent by the seller to the customer, the Salesman should not think that the job is over. It is just possible that something may go wrong and as its results,

it may bring a letter of complaint, and claim from the customer. After all every businessman is likely to make mistakes and therefore he should be tolerant when his mistakes are pointed out. A good businessman should always look upon letters of complaints as a means of discovering and removing the defects in goods and services. He must treat it as an opportunity to satisfy the customers by winning their goodwill.

3. **Sales Letters**

   A sales letter is nothing but an advertisement aimed at a carefully selected group. It requires some skill to get a customer interested in an article for which he has never asked or maybe he might have never heard about it. It can also be used to arouse interest in the prospective customers, so that they are induced to visit the store and make purchases. A sales letter can also carry season's greetings and simultaneously announce some new conveniences and services that have come. It cultivates customer relationship which is sure to bear fruit in the long run.

Sample Letters

1. Write a letter of an enquiry from a student (research scholar) on special distribution problems in the milk industry.

From
The Research Scholar
Institute of Business Management
New Delhi

Dated:

To
The Manager
Milk Industry
New Delhi

Sir,

I am a student working towards a Bachelor of Science degree in business administration at the Institute of Business Management, New Delhi. To fulfil the requirement of a team project/report in my marketing course, I have chosen the topic 'Special Distribution Problems in Milk Industry'. As your company has such a long record of successful accomplishments in this field, I request you to furnish me with pamphlets, booklets, or other information on this subject. I shall greatly appreciate your cooperation.

Thanking you
Sincerely,
XYZ

2. Write a letter of enquiry regarding insurance premium.

To
The LIC of India
Divisional Office
Asif Ali Road
New Delhi 1

Sir,

I am an agent of LIC policy. Will you please tell me what happens to a policyholder if he does not pay his premium on time. I have heard a lot of conflicting statements from the public and thought you might help me.

Thanking you
Sincerely,
XYZ

3. Write a letter of an enquiry for a particular type of commodity.

To
Messrs Kapoor Watch Company
Station Road
Ajmer

Sir,

We have an enquiry for wrist watches in stainless steel case with luminous dial (brightness of a watch) and unbreakable glass. Please send us an offer quoting your best terms and discount for cash payment. We should be grateful for an early reply.

Sincerely,
XYZ

4. Write a routine reply to a trade enquiry.

To
Messrs Hindustan Motors Pvt. Ltd
Scindia House
Connaught Place
New Delhi

Sir,

In reply to your catalogue No. 124, we enclose a copy herewith and we hope you may find it useful. You will find an order form inside to assist you in choosing the items you may require.

Truly yours,
ACME Company

5. Write a letter of complaint to the manager of a departmental store about the rude and uncivilized behaviour of one of their salesmen at the counter.

To

Kapoors
Footwear Specialists
Lucky Range
Allahabad
Civil Lines

Sir,

About a fortnight back, I visited your showroom and wanted to have some good quality shoes for my friends. In the shoe department I was attended to by one of your salesmen, who called himself No.1 in your organization. He sold me a pair of shoes, the sole of which has given way in a week's time only. I think that fellow to be a highly inefficient person. He did not have the courtesy even to offer us seats and then sold us a shoe with such a rotten sole. I am afraid your customers will dwindle (become less/smaller), no respectable person will dare come to your shop. I do not think it would be possible for you to send me another pair of shoes. He would make better as a sole of my shoe while your shoe department will do well without him.

Faithfully yours,
Judge (High Court)

Adjustment of Complaint Letter

To

Shri H. J. Moothan
Judge, High Court
1 Tagore Road
Allahabad

Dear Justice Moothan,

We are very sorry to find that a salesman of our shoe department has been the source of complaint to you. We further regret the inconvenience caused to you first when our salesman could not give you proper attention during the rush of customers, and then when inadvertently a defective shoe was passed on to you. Please accept our apologies on this account. We have examined our salesman from all angles and we feel rather reluctant that he would not make a good sole for your shoe. We are further sending you another pair of shoes. If the original one arrives, we would appreciate having it returned to us. We might have to use it, at a pinch, as a salesman. We hope to continue to be assured of your custom and patronage.

Faithfully yours,
Kapoor Footwear

PRACTICE EXERCISE I

1. Write a letter to the editor of a newspaper on the topic 'Street Light Problem'?
2. Write a letter to the bank manager on delay in receiving your bank statement.
3. Write a letter to your customers inviting them for a presentation organized in your company.
4. Write a letter of requisition to the CEO for promotion and hike in pay.

5.7 TECHNICAL REPORT WRITING

A report is an important part of the genre of transactional writing; that is, writing that is intended to convey factual information. In higher education and work, formal reports communicate information to others without the need for meetings. If you are required to explain your work to others in this way, effective reports are vital. Effective reports will give you a professional image and get others to take your work seriously.

Report writing in higher education: You may be required to produce written reports as part of your course, so you will have opportunities to enhance your report-writing skills. Reports can form a regular part of assessed work and can be needed if you're involved in extracurricular activities with societies or external groups.

Report writing at work: Reports are a way of informing and persuading people as well as initiating change. You might prepare or contribute to annual, project, or progress reports. A well-structured report that has clear objectives will get more attention and is more likely to produce the intended results.

5.7.1 Types of Reports

Reports are mainly divided into two types:

Informal Report

The purpose of an informal report is to inform, analyse, and recommend. It usually takes the form of a memo, letter, or a very short document such as a monthly financial report, research and development report, and the like. This report is shorter and informal than a formal report. It is written according to an organization's style and rules. The informal report is generally more conversational in tone and typically deals with everyday problems and issues of an organization. Sales reports, lab reports, progress reports, service reports, and the like are a few examples of this kind of report. An informal report usually consists of:

- Introduction
- Discussion
- Recommendations and reference

Introduction

Mention the general problem first so that the readers can understand the context. Then state the specific question or tasks arising from the problem that you will be dealing with. Finally, explain the purpose of the essay and its expected results. Since this is an informal and short report, this part does not need to be long. Two or three sentences will be sufficient.

Discussion

Present your findings clearly and briefly, in an appropriate method. You can use lists, tables, charts, and so on with adequate explanations. Present your results in descending order of importance. This way the most important information will be read first. This will be the longest part of your report since this contains the major information.

Conclusions and Recommendations

The conclusion of a report, depending on its intention, should remind the reader what actions need to be taken. Recommendations section might not be needed unless it is requested. It depends on the company's/organization's policy.

Types of Informal Reports

There are many embodiments of the informal report:

Incident Report	a report describing something that has happened
Accident Report	a report describing how someone was hurt or something was damaged
Sales Report	a report describing how many goods or services were sold, and the reasons for any differences from the plan
Progress Report	a report describing how close you are to completing something you planned
Feasibility Study/Report	a report on how practical a proposal is
Recommendation Report	a report on what your organization should do
Site	a report on what has happened in a place, and how close your organization is to finishing construction

Formal Report

The purpose of a formal report is collecting and interpreting data and reporting information. The formal report is complex and long, and may even be produced in bound book volumes.

Types of Formal Report

They can be categorized as: informational reports, analytical reports, and recommendation reports.

Informational Reports
Informational reports present results so readers can understand a particular problem or situation. Informational reports might

A. present information on the status of current research or of a project.
B. present an update of the operation in your division.
C. explain how your organization or division does something.
D. present the results of a questionnaire or research.

Example: Manager of a city's website might prepare an informational report for the city council; the report would provide statistics on the number of people who pay their city water and sewage bills online, and so on.

Analytical Reports
Analytical reports present results, analyse those results, and draw conclusions based on those results. These reports attempt to describe why or how something happened and then to explain what it means. Like informational reports, analytical reports can be formal or informal. Explain what causes a problem or situation. Present the results of a traffic study showing accidents at an intersection—the report explains what it means. Explain the potential results of a particular course of action. Suggest which option, action, or procedure is the best.

Recommendation Reports
This type advocates a particular course of action. This usually presents the results and conclusions that support the recommendations. This type is identical to analytical report. For example, your analytical report suggests using treatment X is more efficient than treatments Y and Z. However, that does not mean that you will use treatment X as cost and other considerations might recommend treatment Y. What should we do about a problem? Should we or can we do something? Should we change the method or technology we use to do something?

Case Studies
A case study is a task which aims to teach how to analyse the causes and consequences of an event or activity by creating its role model. Such assignments show

how complexities may influence various decisions and that is what makes case studies so important.

A case is basically a story. It recounts events or problems in a way that students can learn from their complexities and ambiguities. The students can learn from the original participants in the case, whether it is business people, doctors, or other professionals.

Some recommendations which will be helpful in completing a case study are as follows:

- Use real-life examples. If you are free to choose a topic on your own, try to take it from real life. However, avoid real names.
- Finish every part of your study with points for discussing. They will engage your reader and help them orient themselves in the study.
- Provide credible information on the topic.
- Make sure the story is believable, that is, it consists of sequence of time and events, problems and issues to solve, identities, and so on.

The most important parts of the case study are:

1. The case study's questions
2. The study's propositions
3. How information and data will be analysed
4. The logic behind the propositions
5. How the findings will be interpreted

The case study is two-parted. One part is the case itself, and the other part is the discussion of the case. Case studies are chosen for teaching based on how rich the narrative is, and whether the people in the study are required to make a decision or solve a problem. When using case studies, the focus is not on the data or the analysis but to analyse the case and try to find ways to find solutions and solve problems.

Reports have their own structure and this is distinct from the form of an essay. Essays are mainly used to allow you to demonstrate your ideas and arguments to others. Written reports provide specific research-based information which results in a course of action being decided and acted on. Reports are designed to give information concisely and accurately. A formal report has an impersonal and objective 'tone of voice'. The main argument is clear and uses a minimum of words. Accurately presented facts are in the main body of the report—your evaluation of these is in the 'conclusion' and 'recommendations' sections.

A report differs from an essay in that a report

- presents information, not an argument.
- is meant to be scanned quickly by the reader.
- uses numbered headings and sub-headings.
- uses short, concise paragraphs and dot-points where applicable.

- uses graphics wherever possible (tables, graphs, illustrations).
- may need an abstract (sometimes called an executive summary).
- does not always need references and bibliography.
- is often followed by recommendations and/or appendices.

Reports tend to follow a standard structure but much depends on the circumstances in which they are being written. It helps to ask your lecturers, employers, or mentors what they expect—there may be an accepted way of writing a report appropriate to your course, employment or professional body.

A formal report should generally include the following sections:

[Sections marked with an asterisk (*) are essential; others are optional depending on the type, length, and purpose of the report.]

- Letter of transmittal
- Title page*
- Table of contents
- List of abbreviations and/or glossary
- Executive summary/abstract
- Introduction*
- Body*
- Conclusion*
- Recommendations
- Bibliography
- Appendices

Letter of Transmittal

This is a letter to the person who commissioned the report, in which you effectively hand over your work to that person. Include:

- The purpose of the letter (e.g., Here is the final version of the report 'Underwater Welding' which was commissioned by your organization.)
- The main finding of the report
- Any important considerations
- An acknowledgement of any significant help
- An expression of pleasure or gratitude (e.g., Thank you for giving us the opportunity to work on this report.)

Title Page

This must contain

- the report title which clearly states the purpose of the report.
- full details of the person(s) for whom the report was prepared.
- full details of the person(s) who prepared the report.
- the date of the presentation of the report.

Table of Contents
(Usually only if the report is longer than, say, 10 pages)

This is a list of the headings and appendices of the report. Depending on the complexity and length of the report, you could list tables, figures, and appendices separately. Make sure the correct page numbers are shown opposite the contents. Up-to-date word processing packages can generate a table of contents for you.

Abbreviations and/or Glossary
If necessary, you should provide an alphabetical list of the abbreviations you have used in the report, especially if they may not be familiar to all readers of the report.

If you have used a lot of technical terms, you should also provide a glossary (an alphabetical list of the terms, with brief explanations of their meanings).

Acknowledgements (If Appropriate)
This is a short paragraph thanking any person or organization which gave you help in collecting data or preparing the report.

Abstract (Summary or Executive Summary)

An abstract is quite different from an introduction. It is a summary of the report, in which you include one sentence (or so) for every main section of your report. For example, you can include

- the context of the research;
- the purpose of the report;
- the major findings (you may need several sentences here);
- the conclusions; and
- the main recommendations.

Write the abstract after you have written the report.

Introduction

- Give enough background information to provide a context for the report.
- State the purpose of the report.
- Clarify key terms and indicate the scope of the report (i.e., what the report will cover).

Body
The content of the body depends on the purpose of the report, and whether it is a report of primary or secondary research.

A report of primary research (based on your own observations and experiments) would include:

- Literature review (what other people have written about this topic). The literature review should lead towards your research question.
- Method (summarizes what you did and why). Use the past tense.
- Findings or results (describes what you discovered, observed, and so on in your observations and experiments). Use the past tense.
- Discussion (discusses and explains your findings and relates them to previous research). Use the present tense to make generalizations.

A report of secondary research (based on reading only) would include:

- Information organized under appropriate topics with subheadings. It is unlikely that your report will discuss each source separately. You need to synthesize material from different sources under topic headings.

Analysis/discussion of the sources you are reporting.

Conclusion
Sum up the main points of the report. The conclusion should clearly relate to the objectives of your report. No surprises please! (That is, don't include new information here.)

Recommendations (If Appropriate)
These are suggestions for future action. They must be logically derived from the body of your report.

Bibliography

Appendices
An appendix contains material which is too detailed, technical, or complex to include in the body of the report (for example, specifications, a questionnaire, or a long complex table of figures), but which is referred to in the report. Appendices are put at the very end of the report, after everything else. Each appendix should contain different material. Number each appendix clearly.

Format of Writing a Case Study
There are usually eight sections in a case study:

Synopsis/Executive Summary

- Outline the purpose of the case study.
- Describe the field of research—this is usually an overview of the company.
- Outline the issues and findings of the case study without the specific details.
- Identify the theory that will be used.

- Here the reader should be able to get a clear picture of the essential contents of the study.
- Note any assumptions made (you may not have all the information you'd like, so some assumptions may be necessary example: 'It has been assumed that…', or 'Assuming that it takes half an hour to read one document…').

Findings

- Identify the problems found in the case. Each analysis of a problem should be supported by facts given in the case together with the relevant theory and course concepts. Here it is important to search for the underlying problems; for example, cross-cultural conflict may be only a symptom of the underlying problem of inadequate policies and practices within the company.
- This section is often divided into subsections, one for each problem.

Discussion

- Summarize the major problem/s.
- Identify alternative solutions to this/these major problem/s (there is likely to be more than one solution per problem).
- Briefly outline each alternative solution and then evaluate it in terms of its advantages and disadvantages.
- There is no need to refer to theory or coursework here.

Conclusion

- Sum up the main points from the findings and discussion.

Recommendations

- Choose which of the alternative solutions should be adopted.
- Briefly justify your choice explaining how it will solve the major problem/s.
- This should be written in a forceful style as this section is intended to be persuasive.
- Here integration of theory and coursework is appropriate.

Implementation

- Explain what should be done, by whom, and by which time.
- If appropriate include a rough estimate of costs (both financial and time).

References

- Make sure all references are cited correctly.

Appendices (if any)

- Attach any original data that relates to the study but which would have interrupted the flow of the main body.

Sample of Reports

1. Imagine that you are the chief engineer of Vijayabharati Constructions. Due to an accident a bridge collapsed killing five people. Draft a report to the chairman about the accident.

<u>Report Submitted to the Chairman</u>

From
XYZ
MS (UK)
Chief Engineer
Madhya Pradesh

Dated:

To
The Chairman
Vijayabharati Constructions
Andheri, Bombay
Maharashtra

Sub: Regarding collapse of bridge on river Narmada, death of five persons

Dear Sir,

You are aware that a bridge is being constructed by our Vijayabharati Constructions on the river Narmada in Madhya Pradesh. The construction was in progress when there was a sudden heavy rainfall in the upper regions of the river. Thereby the water gushed from upstream in a flood. The bridge under construction could not bear the sudden force of the flood waters and gave in at the fifth pillar. The workers who were near the pillar tried to escape but five of them came under the collapsing column. Their bodies were fished out of the river with the help of a crane. As we have to pay compensation to the nearest kin of the deceased I am contacting the insurance company for the same.

This for your information.

Sincerely,
(signature)
XYZ

2. Write a technical report on the need to construct a low-cost housing colony in your native place.

Report Submitted to the Principal Secretary

From
XYZ
Hyderabad

Dated:

To
The Principal Secretary
Weaker Sections Welfare Department
Government of Andhra Pradesh
Hyderabad

Sub: Report regarding the need to construct a low-cost housing colony

Dear Sir,

House is essential for every person. The minimum requirements of a person are food, clothing, and shelter. During winter and rainy seasons it is absolutely necessary to have a shelter where one can protect one's self from the bitterness of winter and from the drenching of rains, respectively. When the rich live in palatial buildings the poor should have at least a small dwelling place. In my village there are nearly 500 people who do not have even a proper hut to live in. They are unable to bear the bitter cold and rainy weather.

Therefore, I request the government and philanthropists to come forward to construct a low-cost housing colony for the poor in my native place with *Shramdaan* of the beneficiaries in the construction work. Each house can be constructed at a cost of ₹20,000/- with an attached toilet and bath. (For information and necessary action)

Sincerely,
(signature)
XYZ

3. Prepare a report on the feasibility and desirability of introducing cooking gas in place of petrol and diesel in automobiles.

Introduction

Due to growing need or demand of the growing population, petrol and diesel are getting exhausted. If we continue to use petrol and diesel at the same consumption rate, the day is not far away when all the reserves of these oils get exhausted and the world faces severe fuel crisis. Therefore, it is advisable to slowly shift to the use of cooking gas in place of petrol and diesel.

Market Study

It is found that cooking gas is more economical than diesel or petrol. It is also observed that cooking gas is a less pollutant than petrol or diesel. Therefore, many people prefer to use cooking gas in place of petrol or diesel.

Availability of Men and Material

To supply cooking gas in place of diesel and petrol, special gas filling stations have to be started. Gas dealers and suppliers have to be appointed. Gas cylinders have to be manufactured or the present fuel tanks in the vehicles have to be suitably altered and strengthened to store cooking gas. A conversion kit has to be provided in the vehicles.

Conclusion and Recommendations

To reduce pressure on diesel and petrol and also to reduce environmental pollution, it is desirable to use cooking gas in vehicles. It is also feasible to use it as a substitute for diesel and petrol.

4. You are an electrical engineer in Asian Constructions, your company has undertaken the job of rewiring a shopping complex in Hyderabad. Write a report on the progress of your work.

From
Asian Constructions
Koti
Hyderabad

Dated:

To
The Secretary
Twin Cities Shopping Complex
Hyderabad

Sub: Regarding rewiring of shopping complex

Dear Sir,

The rewiring programme of Twin Cities Shopping Complex is in progress. The cost of some articles is higher than quoted earlier. However, we expect to complete the work within the estimated cost. As the work is progressing speedily, we hope that the labour charges will be reduced. We have paid 5 lakh towards equipment so far. The cost of the labour will be around 1.25 lakh. It is hoped that the remaining expenditure will not be more than 75,000.

The rewiring of three floors has been completed. The replacement of lighting fixtures started two days ago. We shall complete the rewiring of the remaining two floors within 25 days. We would be able to complete the whole work within 35 days from today.

Sincerely
(signature)
XYZ

5. The management of a newspaper wants to start a weekly magazine and has nominated a committee to conduct a study of magazine readership in the state.

From
The Project Leader
Place

Dated:

To
XYZ
The Hindu

Sub: Regarding introduction of weekly magazine and its readership

Dear Sir,

Introduction
As per your instruction to conduct a survey on weekly magazine and readership. I have collected some information on the above. As per my survey, I have found that a magazine catering to the women folk and children will be a good idea. As women are free in the afternoon, a magazine which will cater to their needs may be introduced. The magazine will be well received by children too if we add a few stories appropriate for them in between.

Abstract
The need of the hour is a magazine that caters to women's need. The magazine should include gossips on film stars and TV personalities, stories, cooking, and useful tips. It should also cater to children by including puzzles, comics, latest trends, and so on.

Procedures Followed
A survey was conducted in three most populated zones. A list of magazines was taken and noted the contents. When we go through this survey, many people have suggested to start a magazine for women.

Findings

The magazine should have photographs including those of women and cater to the taste of teens, so it should have fashion as a priority on its list.

Recommendations

The cost should be less so that middle-class people can afford it. Introduce various competitions which will involve housewives and children. Offer generous prizes to boost the sales.

PRACTICE EXERCISE J

1. Imagine that you are an expert in the field of environment. You are approached by the government to suggest ways of checking the air and water pollution in your city. Write a report focusing on the possible solutions to the problem of pollution.
2. Imagine yourself as the collector of your district and accordingly draft a report on the progress of office automation in your district including audio, video, and teleconferencing facilities.
3. Prepare a report on the desirability or otherwise of promoting separate professional colleges for women.

FURTHER READING

1. Eiche, Sabine. 'Column: A Little Learning Is a Dangerous Thing; More Is Better'. Richmond News. 27 August 2014. http://www.richmond-news.com/opinion/columnists/column-a-little-learning-is-a-dangerous-thing-more-is-better-1.1331349 (accessed on 27 September 2018)
2. United Nations Office on Drugs and Crime. 'World Drug Report: Illicit Drug Markets: Situation and Trends'. http://www.unodc.org/doc/wdr2016/WDR_2016_Chapter_1.pdf (accessed on 27 September 2018)
3. Puri, G. K., and Saroj Puri. *100 Important Essays for All*. New Delhi: IIMS Publications, 1999.
4. IELTS Liz. http://ieltsliz.com/common-essay-topics-for-ielts/ (accessed on 27 September 2018)
5. Clathacker. http://clathacker.com/profiles/blogs/practice-from-past-years-paper (accessed on 27 September 2018)
6. *Comprehensive Workbook: Interact in English*. New Delhi: Laxmi Publications, 1994.
7. Hart, Steve, Aravind R. Nair, and Veena Bhambhani. *Embark: English for Undergraduates*. New Delhi: Cambridge University Press, 2016.
8. Chhabra, T. N. *Business Communication: Concepts and Skills*. New Delhi: Sun India Publications, 2016.

9. Woculus. https://www.woculus.com/category/professional-emailing/ (accessed on 27 September 2018)
10. Task-Based Activities for LBS. taskbasedactivitiesforlbs.ca/content/write-business-memos (accessed on 27 September 2018)
11. WriteExpress. https://www.writeexpress.com/request.htm (accessed on 27 September 2018)
12. *University of Newcastle Library guides. libguides.newcastle.edu.au/report_writing/types-of-reports/short-report* (accessed on 27 September 2018)
13. https://www.slideshare.net/.../report-writingtypes-format-structure-and-relevance (accessed on 17 September 2015)
14. Wordpandit. https://wordpandit.com/practice-reading-comprehension/ (accessed on 27 September 2018)
15. Universal Class. https://www.universalclass.com/articles/business/case-studies-types.htm (accessed on 27 September 2018)
16. Tilak, Raghukul. *Rajhans English Essays.* Meerut: Rajhans Prakashan, 1967.
17. Puri, G. K., and Saroj Puri. *100 Important Essays for All.* New Delhi: IIMS Publications, 2010.
18. Miglani, Seema, and Shikha Goyal. *English for Professionals for B.Tech.* New Delhi: Vayu Education of India, 2010.
19. Gupta, Tanu, and Titiksha Mittal. *English for Engineers.* Chandigarh: Wonder Publications, 2009.

6

UNIT

Oral Communication

6.1 EFFECTIVE LISTENING SKILLS

Listening refers to the process of hearing a person, with attention being paid to his words, tone, and body language. The process starts with hearing but goes beyond. It involves hearing with attention. In other words, listening has to do with the ears as well as with the eyes and the mind. Hearing is physical, while listening is intellectual, involving both the body and the mind. The process of listening involves:

Hearing
This is the first process in listening. It relates to sensory perception of sounds.

Decoding
The second process involves sensing and filtering verbal messages. Sense of appeal and sense of judgement come into play during sensing and filtering the message.

Comprehending
The third process involves understanding the message. The filtered message assumes a meaning. The listener tries to absorb, grasp, and assimilate the message. In doing so, the listener brings into play their own knowledge, experience, perception, and cognitive power.

Remembering

Memorizing the message therefore assumes significance. It relates to a process whereby the comprehended message is stored in memory to facilitate future call.

Responding

The process of response takes place at the end of the verbal communication. This may take the form of prodding, prompting, or reassuring that the message is being well received.

6.1.1 Barriers to Effective Listening

1. **Physical barriers:** This has to do with poor or outdated equipment used during communications, background noise, poor lighting, or temperatures that are too high or too low.
2. **Attitudes:** Emotions like anger or sadness can taint objectivity. Also, being extremely nervous, having a personal agenda, or 'needing to be right no matter what' can make communications less than effective. This is also known as 'emotional noise'.
3. **Language:** This can seem like an easy one, but even people speaking the same language can have difficulty understanding each other if they are from different generations or from different regions of the same country. Slang, professional jargon, and regional colloquialisms can even hurt communicators with the best intentions.
4. **Physiological barriers:** Ill health, poor eyesight or hearing difficulties, pain.
5. **Problems with structure design:** Companies or institutions can have organization structures that are not clear, which can make communications difficult. Also to blame for faulty communications are bad information systems and lack of supervision or training of the people involved.
6. **Cultural noise:** People sometimes make stereotypical assumptions about others based on their cultural background.
7. **Lack of common experience:** It's a great idea to use examples or stories to explain a point that is being discussed. However, if the speaker and the audience cannot relate to these examples because they do not have the same knowledge or have not shared the same experiences then this tool will be ineffective.
8. **Ambiguity and abstractions overuse:** Leaving things half-said, using too many generalizations, proverbs or sayings, can all lead to communications that are not clear and that can lend themselves to misinterpretations.

9. **Information overload:** It takes time to process a lot of information and too many details can overwhelm and distract the audience from the important topics. Keep it simple, sweetie!
10. **Assumptions and jumping to conclusions:** This can make someone reach a decision about something before listening to all the facts.

Active listening is the most desirable type of listening. There are some skills which help you to be proficient in effective listening, which are discussed as follows.

1. **Suspended judgement**
   This skill consists of
   - Keeping an open mind. That is, not having any preconceived notions about the speaker or the subject, and filtering out any likes or dislikes about the style, delivery, and so on.
   - Concentrating on understanding the speaker.
   - Hearing the complete message without interruption.
   - Not agreeing or disagreeing with the speaker.
   - Not asking any questions.
   - Not giving any advice.
   - Not starting to solve problems.
2. **Attending skills**
   This gives a response to the speaker while speaking by doing the following:
   - Maintaining eye contact
   - Head nods
   - Making suitable sounds
   - Making verbal responses
3. **Clarification**
   This means doing two things:
   - Checking the meaning of words you do not understand
   - Checking with the speaker whether you have followed the subject correctly
4. **Summarization**
   After the speaker finishes speaking, repeat to him in a very short manner the main points of what he has delivered.
5. **Paraphrasing**
   In paraphrasing, you capture the essence of what the speaker has said. In effective listening, paraphrasing is done for two reasons:

- To check whether you have understood what the person has said
- To show the speaker that you are trying to understand

Paraphrasing has two positive uses:

1. If you have paraphrased the other person wrongly, he will have the opportunity to correct you, and the misunderstanding will be removed.
2. If someone asks you a difficult or unclear question, and you cannot answer at once. Paraphrasing will give you time to think and answer.

How to paraphrase?

While paraphrasing, avoid names, criticisms, harsh words, and controversy. Stick only to the facts. Avoid the emotional content of the statement. Start paraphrasing by using the words 'In other words', 'I understand that', 'It appears that', and the like, and repeat the facts shortly to the speaker.

Example: 'My boss, Mr Raghavan, is a real tyrant. I have to work daily from 6 AM to 9 PM. I am not able to pay any attention to my children. I am sick and tired of working in this factory.'

Let us analyse each sentence:

1. My boss, Mr Raghavan, is a real tyrant: contains a name, criticism, and hard words
2. I have to work daily from 6 AM to 9 PM: contains facts
3. I am not able to pay any attention to my children: contains facts
4. I am sick and tired of working in this factory: contains criticism, hard words, and controversy

PRACTICE EXERCISE A

Paraphrase the following situations:

1. I wasted a lot of time in attempting the first question, and as a result I had to hurry while answering the other questions. I don't know if the answers are good enough for me to pass the exam.
2. My parents interfere a lot whatever I want to do. They always keep advising me about everything. It's as if parents never want us to do what makes us happy.

PRACTICE EXERCISE B

Comprehension Check (TOEFL Model)

1. **Listen to the conversation your teacher reads out and answer the questions:**

   Sangitha, a visitor, introduces herself to the boss of the organization where her father works.

   Sangitha: Good morning, madam.
   Boss: Good morning. Please get in.
   Sangitha: I'm Sangitha, daughter of Mr R. S. Kumar.
   Boss: Oh, you're my colleague's daughter! Nice to meet you, Sangitha.
   Sangitha: I'm pleased to meet you, madam. Could you permit me to speak to my father for a while?
   Boss: Your father sits in the next room. I think he's free there. Please go and meet him.
   Sangitha: Thank you.
   Boss: You're welcome.

   1. Whom did Sangitha want to meet in the office?
   2. Was Sangitha permitted to meet the person she wanted to?
   3. Where is her father's room in the office?
   4. What is her father's name?

2. **Listen to the conversation and answer the questions:**
   Ramu introduces Rahim to his friend Robert.

   Ramu: Robert, this is my friend Rahim.
   Robert: I'm glad to meet you, Rahim.
   Rahim: Pleased to meet you, Robert.
   Robert: Have you been here before?
   Rahim: Of course, I've visited this place twice, but I know nothing except Abids Road and Hyderabad airport.
   Ramu: Shall we go sightseeing tomorrow since it's Sunday?
   Robert and Rahim: That would be wonderful!

   1. How does Ramu begin the conversation?
   2. Has Rahim visited Hyderabad earlier?
   3. What do they plan to do on Sunday?

3. **Listen to the following bits of dialogue and complete the following sentences given below:**

   Praveen: Can you give me a lift to my office in your car?
   Peter: I'm sorry. The rear wheel is punctured and I've given my car for servicing.

   1. Praveen asked ________________________________
   2. Peter could not ________________________________

   Teacher: I'm sorry to say this, but you know, your son hasn't been attending classes regularly.

Father: Thank you for informing me. I will ask him about this.

1. The teacher informed the father ________________________
2. The father told the teacher ________________________

Krithika: Let me congratulate you on your getting selected for the IAS.
Meena: Thank you. It's been my dream that I should become an IAS officer.

1. Krithika congratulated ________________________
2. Becoming an IAS officer ________________________

Customer: I'm afraid I've got a complaint about the TV I bought from you yesterday.
A man in service department: I'm sorry, sir. I'll send the technician with you now.

1. The customer came ________________________
2. The man in the service department apologized saying ____________

4. Listen to the conversation and answer the questions:
Two old friends bump into each other at the airport.

Harsha: Excuse me. Are you Dr Nithin by any chance?
Nithin: Yes. I am. How do you know me?
Harsha: It surprises me that you don't know who I am.
Nithin: Well, your face looks familiar to me. Are you Harsha?
Harsha: That's right. I'm your old friend and currently a film actor in the Telugu film industry. Haven't you seen me in Telugu films?
Nithin: No, Harsha, believe it or not, after becoming a cardiologist, I haven't watched a single Telugu movie. Anyway, I'm glad that my doctor friend has become a film star.
Harsha: I'm also very happy that my friend has become a devoted cardiologist. I think it's time for the flight. Let's check in.

1. Name the two participants in the conversation.
2. What are they by profession?
3. Does Dr Nithin watch Telugu movies regularly?
4. Where do they meet each other?
5. Did Dr Nithin recognize his friend immediately?

PRACTICE EXERCISE C

Listening Tasks for Practice

1. Use of minimal pairs (pairs of words which differ only in one sound), e.g., pat–bat
2. Identification of the words with different stress patterns, e.g., ˈconduct–conˈduct
3. The teacher gives commands and students follow them.

4. Reading out the listening passage and asking a few questions to check if the students have listened and understood correctly.
5. The teacher plays a tape containing a recorded speech and asks the students to listen to the tape keeping in view the questions already written on the blackboard.

6.2 EFFECTIVE SPEAKING SKILLS

Good speaking is a prerequisite skill which makes communication effective. Effective speaking makes one an effective leader. Speaking is a fine art that can be cultivated which needs conscious effort on the part of the speaker. *Practice, observation,* and *hard work* can turn an ordinary speaker into a good speaker. Good speakers mesmerize the audience with their mastery over language, depth of the subject, power of expression, fluency, and style.

The art of speaking is made up of five elements:

6.2.1 Invention

It introduces new ideas and techniques, and relates to ideas, creativity, and innovativeness.

6.2.2 Arrangement

It refers to sequencing and order of presentation. Going back and forth and speaking in a rambling manner will have to be avoided.

6.2.3 Style

It refers to the stamp of individuality and abundant supply of words using with judgement.

6.2.4 Memory

It comes into priority when the speaker is not consulting any notes. Extempore speakers depend much on their memory.

6.2.5 Delivery

It refers to the manner of speaking. For the development of effective delivery style, there are two primary areas of importance, namely *accent* and *voice modulation*.

The following elements of voice modulation need to be kept in mind for giving an effective delivery:

Tone

- It should express appropriate emotion.
- It should be pleasant.
- It should be polite and courteous.
- It should display interest, concern, and empathy.
- It should sound energetic and enthusiastic.
- It should reflect one's attitude, whether positive or negative.

Pitch

The high pitch and low pitch in speech brings about better expression and improves the process of communication. A high-pitched voice sounds shrilled and tense, while a low-pitched voice sounds monotonous and dull. Maintaining a medium level of pitch is a comfortable way to communicate and bring effectiveness.

Volume

It is also important to speak in a comfortable medium volume, which should sound neither too loud nor too soft. Lack of audibility could lead to disinterest and inattention.

Clarity

To bring about clarity in one's speech use correct speech sounds, speak slowly using appropriate rate of speech, speak fluently using appropriate pauses when any new term or phrase is being introduced.

Rate of Speech

It is extremely important for good communication. A fast rate of speech results in confusion, as it causes words to run into each other, reduces the vowel sounds, and softens the consonant sounds by making the word endings unclear. A slow rate of speech can be very frustrating and results in impatience and total loss of attention from those around you. A medium rate of speech is always preferable, which also reflects your personality. Practising voice technique is just like practising a sport.

6.3 CONVERSATIONS: SITUATIONAL DIALOGUES

Most of us are comfortable talking with our friends and family, but find it difficult to converse with a stranger or indulge in a small talk with people we do not know well. As we step out of college and move into the professional world, there will be an increasing need to converse with different people in different situations. One has to understand how and when to switch roles—from being a listener to a speaker.

6.3.1 Initiating a Conversation

One has to be very much aware while taking care of the situations and the kind of people we meet so that the language used may also differ accordingly. There are two ways of involving ourselves in conversation with various people we come across.

Formal Conversation

It takes place between officials, superiors, and strangers where the intimacy level is very less. One has to be polite, courteous, sophisticated, fluent, and expressive in using the language.

Informal Conversation

It takes place between friends, neighbours, relatives, and family members where the intimacy level is very high and it happens by way of talks and chats without being extra polite or respectful in using the language. One of the best strategies to start a conversation with known or unknown ones is ISRF:

Initiate, respond, sustain, and *follow-up.*

Greeting and Introducing

- How do you greet people?
- What are the different greetings for different occasions?
- How do you introduce yourself and others?

There are some useful expressions for greeting and introducing:

I. Greeting People

Informal/Friendly	*Formal/Business*	*Formal Conversation Beginners*
Hello!	Good morning!	How do you do?
Hi!	Good evening!	How are you?
Responses to Conversation Beginners	*When Meeting Someone after a While*	*Phrases to Close a Conversation*
How do you do?	Good to see you again.	Good night!
Very well.	It's been a long time.	See you later.
Fine, thank you.		

II. Greeting on Different Occasions

Congratulations!
Merry Christmas!
Pleased to meet you!
It's celebration time!
Well done!
Good luck!
Welcome to our team!
Happy New Year!
All the best for your exams!

III. Introducing Oneself and Others

There are some useful phrases in introducing.

Introducing Oneself

I would like to introduce myself
I am ___

My name is ___ and I am from ___
Hi, I am ___

Introducing Others

This is ___
I would like to introduce ___ from ___
Here's ___
I feel privileged to introduce ___

When Meeting for the First Time/On Being Introduced

Pleased to meet you
Nice to meet you.
Glad to meet you.
It's pleasure meeting you.

Responding to a Greeting

Pleased to meet you too.
Nice meeting you too.
Glad to meet you too.

Some sample conversations which contain the kind of language we use in everyday life.

I. Two friends greet each other at the college

Kavya: Hi, Bhavya.
Bhavya: Hi, Kavya. How are you?
Kavya: I am okay. Which subject do we have in the first hour today?
Bhavya: It's English.

II. Two friends greet each other at Christmas

Rita: Good morning, Jim. Wish you a Merry Christmas!
Jim: Very good morning, Rita. Merry Christmas! I am surprised you are awake this early.
Rita: It's my pleasure to wake early for a person like you.
Jim: Thanks a lot.
Rita: See you later!
Jim: See you. Bye!

III. Nita introduces her friend Gita to her father

Nita: Dad, may I introduce Gita to you?
Father: How do you do?
Gita: I am fine. How do you do, sir?
Father: Where are you from, Gita?
Gita: I am from Kanpur. I have come to Hyderabad recently.
Father: How do you find Hyderabad and its people?
Gita: I am greatly fascinated by Hyderabad but I don't think I can comment on the people here for I have been here only a few weeks.
Father: I appreciate your frankness, Gita.
Nita: You keep talking. I will be back with mom in a minute or two.

IV. A professional meeting a well-known individual

Professional: I am pleased to meet you.
Individual: The pleasure's mine.
Professional: I have heard Ravi speak about you often.
Individual: Only good things, I hope.

V. Conversation between a customer and a salesperson at a busy shopping place.

Customer: I am looking for a nice shirt to go with my black jeans. (initiate)
Salesperson: Please take a look at this blue shirt. (respond)
Customer: I have two blue shirts already. (sustain)
Salesperson: Let me show you a few other colours to choose from. (follow-up)

Apologies and Responses

When we make a mistake, do something wrong, or someone is inconvenienced with our actions, it is brought to our notice. We may not be responsible for the situation or we may not have done intentionally but the first thing to do is to apologize.

Some useful phrases for making apologies

- I am sorry.
- Oops! I am sorry about that.
- Sorry to bother you.
- I am sorry for the inconvenience caused.
- I apologize for the inconvenience caused.
- My sincere apologies.

Some common expressions that help to carry on the conversation smoothly

- Please allow me to offer my apologies. (apology)
- Please don't worry. (response)

- I can't tell you how sorry I am about that lapse.
- Let's forget it.

- Please forgive my ignorance.
- There's no need to apologize.

- Pardon me, please.
- That's all right.

- Oh! I am very sorry.
- That's okay.

- It was foolish of me to have talked so irresponsibly.
- Please don't feel bad about it.

- We are extremely sorry for troubling you like this.
- Doesn't matter at all.

Giving Directions

Giving directions in finding a location and responding appropriately is one of the effective means of communication. The following factors have to be considered in giving directions:

- Mention the landmarks, stoplights, statues, and buildings.
- Give actual distance between the landmarks and the location in km.
- Mention the crossroads or the significant things one can trace if he goes too far.

- Give your mobile number and address to contact if one goes wrong in finding the location.
- Use appropriate phrases in giving directions.

Useful Phrases and Expressions

Asking Directions	*Giving Directions*
How do I get to...?	Go straight on (until you come to)
What's the best way to...?	Turn back/go back
Is there a...near here?	Turn left/right (into...street)
Can you help me find...?	Go along....
How far is....?	Around the corner
How do I find...?	At the crossroads/junction
Where is...?	It's on the left/right
	Take the first/second road on the left
	At the end/on the corner
	In front of/behind traffic lights
	It is next to/opposite to/in between

Making a Short Formal Speech

A short formal speech prepared and delivered before an audience has to be very and expressive and challenging. It is made to welcome a guest at a function, to bid farewell to someone leaving an organization, or to propose a vote of thanks at the close of any important event. A short formal speech involves three processes—*planning, writing,* and *delivery.*

Planning

The content and delivery of speech will depend on three important factors:

- Occasion/situation
- Audience
- The purpose of speech

Writing

This stage involves:

- Creating an outline
- Collecting the material required
- Preparing the first draft
- Editing for correctness, cohesiveness, and so on

Delivery

While delivering a speech the following guidelines are to be practised:

- Appearance
- Clarity and audibility
- Appropriate pauses when necessary
- Maintaining eye contact with audience to win their confidence
- Natural gestures and postures
- Adjusting pace of delivery which should be moderate
- Welcoming the guests: naming them, giving their position/ designation
- The sequence in welcoming: chief guest, guests of honour, and other dignitaries. The head of the organization is invited last as she is the host.
- Appropriate qualifiers should be used before dignitaries: esteemed, respected, His/Her Excellency (e.g., Governor/President)

Useful Phrases and Expressions

Opening Courtesies	*Introducing Theme/Purpose*
Good morning/afternoon/evening.	This gathering offers us a diverse platform to ...
Let me first welcome ...	Let us take the first step towards ...
I feel privileged to welcome.	The initiative to ... will go a long way in creating ...
I would like to welcome ...	Today's function marks ...
It is a great pleasure to welcome ...	This meeting or conference stands for ...
I take this opportunity to welcome ...	This gathering presents ...
I extend a warm welcome to ...	This event showcases a window of opportunity to ...
I welcome you all to....	The occasion offers a unique platform for ...

Vote of Thanks

A formal function/occasion normally involves a formal closing with a vote of thanks for all those who organized and participated in the event.

Useful Phrases

- I have the task of delivering the vote of thanks to this august gathering here.
- My thanks to distinguished....
- I am also grateful to....
- I must also thank the other members of....
- It's a great honour to have this opportunity to thank all of you.
- We are deeply indebted to....
- In this connection, we would like to make particular mention of....
- We thank you very much for your patience....
- Thank you so much.

Telephonic Conversation

Telephonic talks have become an integral part of business communication and people at various levels have to learn to talk effectively over telephone. In order to be an effective communicator on the telephone, it is important to understand this medium of communication well. Unlike face-to-face communication, in telephone conversation the participants cannot see each other. Voice plays a central role in telephone communication. It is important to be aware of differences in the language, etiquette, and manners to be observed while making calls for different purposes. Make sure your voice, language, tone, and information are receiver-friendly.

Some noteworthy points relating to telephone talk are as follows:

1. Telephone is not a status symbol, it is a means of communication.
2. Lift the receiver and answer calls within three or four rings.
3. Switch off TV/radio or minimize the volume when calling or taking calls.
4. Greet the caller appropriately by announcing your name.
5. Have a pen and pad ready to note down important information.
6. If the call is to be directed, make sure the caller is not made to wait on the line for long.
7. If the person is not available, avoid saying, 'He is in the conference/ meeting./He is out for lunch/coffee./I don't know where he is.' A better approach would be to say, 'He/She is unavailable at the moment.' Make a note of the caller's name, number with extension (if necessary), and the message, and communicate to the person at the earliest.
8. Keep personal talk on the official line to the minimum.
9. Keep the distant calls as short as possible and cost effective.
10. Speak clearly at a moderate pace with sufficient loudness.
11. Teach yourself to speak slowly with appropriate pauses to separate one piece of information from another.
12. End the conversation with appropriate expressions such as 'Thank you' and 'Please'. Or a 'Good day'.
13. Put down the receiver gently in its right place after the call is over.

Useful Phrases

Stage	*Phrase*	*Response*
Opening	Good morning! Hello!	Good morning! Who's calling?
	This is....	Nice to hear from you.
Warming up	I'd like to speak to	Just a minute. Hold on please.
	Can I speak to...?	I'm sorry she's not in. The line is busy. Will you hold?

Stage	*Phrase*	*Response*
Giving the message	I'm calling about...	
	Could you give her a message?	I'll give her a message.
Rounding off	Thanks for your help.	Thank you for calling.
	OK. I'll look forward to your call.	OK/right/fine.
Closing	Goodbye for now.	Goodbye.

Conversations for Practice

I. A: Hello!
Is that 2272-5533?
B: Yes.
A: Can I speak to Sundar? I'm Kapil, a friend of Sundar's.
B: Please hold on. Sundar, a call for you.

II. A: Hi! This is Manju. Is Nisha there?
B: No. She has just stepped out.

III. A: Good afternoon. It's Sunitha Mishra here. Can I speak with Aarti, Please?
B: Yes, just a moment.

IV. A: I am Geetha here. I'd like speak to Anju Reddy, please.
B: Hold the line, please. I'll see if she's in.

V. A: Sundaram here.
Good morning, Mr Sundaram. Sorry to bother you.
I am Narayanan. I have an appointment with you tomorrow.
I am sorry I won't be able to make it.
B: I see. Thank you for calling.
A: Could I possibly see you same time Thursday instead?
B: I'm not too sure. You may contact my PA later in the day.

Greetings

Informal Dialogue

Neetu meets Sheetu, who used to be a classmate at school, at a supermarket after a long time and they exchange a few words of greeting.

Neetu: Hello! What a lovely surprise! Good to see you after so long.
Sheetu: Hello! It's pleasant to see you too.
Neetu: How are you?
Sheetu: Just fine, thanks. How're things with you?
Neetu: Everything's okay, thanks. Where have you been?
Sheetu: I was away in Mumbai for the past three months.
Neetu: We haven't met for quite some time, have we?
Sheetu: We must meet and catch up on what's happening.
Neetu: Yes, we must do that.
Sheetu: Wish I could have stayed longer, but I must run.
Neetu: That's all right. I hope we can meet again soon.

Sheetu: I do hope you will excuse me.
Neetu: Yes, I hope so too.
Sheetu: Sure, see you sometime. Bye, bye!
Neetu: Yes, please do come over sometime. Bye!

Formal Dialogue

Nita is on her way to violin class. She meets Dr Prakash, her father's boss, outside the music school. The two persons greet each other and exchange a few words before taking leave.

Nita: Good morning, sir. How're you?
Dr Prakash: Good morning, Nita. I am very well, thank you. What about you?
Nita: I am fine, thanks.
Dr Prakash: Where are you going?
Nita: I am on my way to violin class.
Dr Prakash: Please have a lift in my car, Nita. I'll drop you at your violin class.
Nita: Thank you so much, sir. It's nearby. I can go on foot.
Dr Prakash: How's your father's health? Recently he has been unwell.
Nita: He is slowly recovering, sir.
Dr Prakash: Hope that he may recover soon.
Nita: Yes, I hope so too.
Dr Prakash: Well, it's nice meeting you. I hope we can meet again soon.
Nita: Please do come over sometime to our home, sir.
Dr Prakash: Sure, with pleasure sometime. Bye, bye!
Nita: Bye, sir!

Congratulations

Formal Dialogues

Aditi has been selected as a member of NCC contingent that will take part in the Republic Day parade in Delhi. Her principal congratulates her.

Principal: Aditi, congratulations on your selection for the Republic Day parade.
Aditi: Thank you very much, sir.
Principal: It is a big honour for the college as well.
Aditi: I believe that being a student of this college with its NCC department is really what helped me.
Principal: It was also your determination and hard work.
Aditi: It is all because of the encouragement and help I have always got from you.
Principal: Not entirely. It's a result of your perseverance.
Aditi: It's very kind of you.
Principal: We are really proud of you. I am sure you will keep up the good work.

Aditi: Surely, I promise, sir.
Principal: You will really deserve this honour.
Aditi: Thank you, sir.
Principal: Very well done! Keep it up! Best wishes for the event!
Aditi: Thank you very much for your blessing.

Chetan's essay on global warming wins the first prize in an international competition organized by UNESCO. His supervisor, Mr Raju, congratulates him on his achievement.

Mr Raju: Chetan, I just heard a wonderful news.
Chetan: What's it about, sir?
Mr Raju: You have bagged the first prize in the essay competition organized by UNESCO.
Chetan: It's incredible, sir!
Mr Raju: Congratulations on your remarkable achievement.
Chetan: Thank you very much, sir.
Mr Raju: Everyone in the department is really proud of you.
Chetan: It's all because of your assistance and motivation.
Mr Raju: It's a consequence of your creativity and effort.
Chetan: It's very kind of you.
Mr Raju: The university too wants to honour you on 15 August.
Chetan: I am feeling happy for the recognition I am about to be given.
Mr Raju: You really deserve this honour. Keep it up.
Chetan: Thank you, sir.

Thanking People

Formal Dialogues

Veena thanks her neighbour Sravya for lending money when she needed it.

Veena: Sravya, could I ask a favour of you?
Sravya: Could you please?
Veena: I am direly in need of money now.
Sravya: Sure. I'd be glad to help.
Veena: I don't want to leave Ram alone in the hospital and go to an ATM.
Sravya: Certainly I could be of help.
Veena: I am sorry to trouble you, but I need your help.
Sravya: Of course, by all means.
Veena: Would you mind helping me with this? Hope it isn't a problem.
Sravya: Not at all. I had withdrawn some extra cash early this morning.
Veena: Thanks a lot.
Sravya: You're welcome.
Veena: Thanks again, Sravya.
Sravya: You are most welcome.

Vinay asks his friend Aman if he could get an application form from the passport office.

Vinay:	Aman, I wonder if you could do me a favour, please.
Aman:	It's no problem at all.
Vinay:	I would like you to pick up a passport application form for me on your way back from office.
Aman:	Sure, I'll do it today.
Vinay:	Hope it won't be a problem.
Aman:	Of course not! No problem at all.
Vinay:	Thank you very much!
Aman:	It's OK.
Vinay:	I am sorry to trouble you once again.
Aman:	Not at all.
Vinay:	Thanks again.
Aman:	That's all right.
Vinay:	It's nice of you.
Aman:	You're welcome.

Inviting

Formal Dialogues

Mrs Matthew invites two heads of the departments in her college to her daughter's wedding.

Mrs Matthew:	Good morning, Dr Kaur. Can I come in, please?
Dr Kaur:	Sure, Matthew. Please sit down.
Mrs Matthew:	Thank you, sir. Good morning, Professor Kulkarni.
Professor Kulkarni:	Good morning, Matthew. How are you?
Mrs Matthew:	I'm fine, thank you, sir. My daughter, Jonice, is getting married next week. I'll be happy if you both come with your families to her wedding reception.
Dr Kaur:	Thanks for the invitation, and congratulations. When and where is the wedding reception?
Mrs Matthew:	Next Sunday at the Defence Club. Let me give you the invitation cards.
Dr Kaur:	I'll certainly be there for the wedding reception.
Mrs Matthew:	Thank you, Dr Kaur. I look forward to having you with us.
Professor Kulkarni:	Congratulations, Matthew, and thank you for inviting me. I'm sorry I won't be able to come.
Mrs Matthew:	Why, sir? What's the problem?
Professor Kulkarni:	I'd love to come but I'm going to Varanasi for a conference next Sunday.
Mrs Matthew:	What a pity you won't be able to come!
Professor Kulkarni:	It can't be helped, I suppose. But I'll make it up some other time.

Mrs. Matthew: That's all right. I understand, sir. But we'll miss you.

Sangeetha invites her friends Raghav and Roshni to her tea estate for the weekend.

Sangeetha: Hi, Raghav! Hello, Roshni!

Raghav and Roshni: Hi!

Sangeetha: I'm leaving for our tea estate in Kotagiri this weekend. Would you both like to accompany me?

Roshni: Oh, I'd love to!

Sangeetha: It'll be a great pleasure.

Roshni: It's a long weekend, and besides, I've heard so much about the place. Thanks, Sangeetha.

Raghav: I'm sorry, but I don't think I'll be able to make it.

Sangeetha: What's the reason?

Raghav: I have CAT on Saturday. Thanks for asking me.

Sangeetha: I'm disappointed that you won't be there.

Raghav: We'll make it up some other time.

Sangeetha: You are most welcome. It's a pity, but we'll go again some other time.

Roshni: I'll accompany Sangeetha for this weekend.

Sangeetha: That's great. I'll ask my cousin to take us around.

Offering Help and Instructions

Formal Dialogues

Offering help to a colleague on a new project

Kamal: I was wondering if you need any help on your new project.

Preetam: Sure! That would be great! Are you good at writing or would you rather do the computer work?

Kamal: I would like to help with the computer work.

Preetam: Great! We are going to be working in teams of three. Are you OK working with others?

Kamal: Yes, I like working in team.

Preetam: We will begin next Monday. Would you be available then?

Kamal: Yes, I can be there.

Preetam: Well, if you could send me your basic background information before next Monday, it would be useful.

Kamal: I will be sending the information to you by evening.

Preetam: Well then, thanks for your help. Have a great day!

Kamal: I enjoy offering help to others.

Preetam: Our first meeting is next Monday. I look forward to working with you.

Kamal: I'll enjoy working with you!

A friend offering instructions in making cookies

Tommy: Hi, David. You look busy? What are you doing?

David: I'm trying to figure out how to make these cookies, but I lost the instructions that came with the box.

Tommy: Making cookies from a box is easy. You want me to help you?

David: Yes, these have to be done in an hour.

Tommy: Okay, first, pour the cookie mix from that bag into a large bowl.

David: Is this bowl big enough?

Tommy: No, you need a bigger one. You're going to be adding more ingredients. Use that one.

David: Okay, now what?

Tommy: Next, add two eggs and a cup of milk to the bowl and beat until very creamy, with no lumps.

David: What should I mix it with, a fork or spoon?

Tommy: You could use either, but if I were you, I'd use an electric mixer.

David: That's done, what next?

Tommy: Now, grease the cookie sheet with butter. Then put one tablespoon of cookie dough per cookie on the cookie sheet. You should space the dough evenly around the cookie sheet, leaving at least an inch between each cookie.

David: Got it. Now they go in the oven, right?

Tommy: Yes.

David: Okay, they're in. How long will it take before they're done?

Tommy: Cook them at 325° and for about 35 minutes.

David: Thanks for offering instructions in making cookies.

6.4 ORAL PRESENTATION

Presentation is a relatively recently developed form of interactive communication. Presentations are made in classrooms, seminars, workshops, conferences, and to a group of persons on certain scheduled topics. The main objective is to present all the relevant details to the interested target audience on a specific topic or concept in a participative manner. Presentations help when technical and other relevant features have to be explained by means other than oral or written communication. Presentation skills are extremely important for a number of reasons. First of all, it demonstrates your ability to communicate your ideas clearly and precisely. Second, it is a good way of assessing whether we are confident. The starting point in planning oral presentation is to formulate a precise objective. The purpose may be to inform, persuade, or report but we should not have more than one main objective or else we will lose focus.

6.4.1 Difference between a Presentation and a Speech

Although there may be similarities between a presentation and a speech, they differ mainly in the aim of the speakers, the type of audience and their expectations, the extent of information presented and the level of interaction with the audience. In the case of a presentation, the audience is generally homogenous, and the speaker and the audience have a clear and common focus. Therefore, a topic of common interest to the speaker and audience is dealt with thoroughly. However in the case of public speech, the audience is mostly heterogeneous who expect to listen to a general talk without getting into too many details. In presentation, the speaker uses visual aids such as an overhead projector (OHP) or a LCD and interacts with the audience whereas in public speaking such aids are not generally used and is less interactive.

6.4.2 Structure of Presentation

A typical presentation would have the following parts and sections: introduction, main body, conclusion, questions, and responses.

Introduction

If the total time available for your presentation is 20 minutes, your introduction should not take more than 6 minutes. Here are some useful phrases to be used during introduction:

1. Greet the audience	Good morning, ladies and gentlemen/one and all
2. Introduce yourself	I am/My name/This is....
3. Announce the topic	Today I am going to speak to you about/on the topic....
4. Explain the purpose	The reason why I am here....
5. Length of presentation	My presentation will take about 20–30 minutes
6. Questions	I'll be happy to try and answer any questions at the end.
7. Presentation outline	I've divided my presentation into four parts—first/finally...

Main Body

It is the most important part of the presentation and one must devote to it 60 per cent of time available. We should take up each of the points outlined in the introduction one by one and develop them logically and rationally showing the relationship between the themes and arguments. Here are some useful phrases:

1. Ending introduction	That's all for introduction
2. Beginning the main body	So to begin with/Now to take up the first aspect/point
3. Ending parts within main body	So that's all then regarding the first aspect
4. Beginning a new part	Let's move on to/So now we come to the question of...

Conclusion

We end or conclude a presentation by summing up the main points, reiterating the central message, offering comments/suggestions, or making recommendations. Remember the audience of the stated objective and check if it has been achieved. Thank the audience for listening to you and invite questions from them. Here are some of the useful phrases:

1. Summing up	So to sum up/Let me sum up
2. Concluding	So I'd like to conclude by saying/Let me end by saying/Finally, I'd like to....
3. Offering suggestion	So I'd like to suggest/recommend
4. Closing	Thank you for listening/your attention
5. Questions	If you have any questions, I'll be glad to try and answer them.

6.4.3 Tips to Make Effective Presentation

1. Do not read out your presentation from a prepared manuscript. It might take away from the spontaneity of the delivery. An effective presentation is extemporaneous and is most effective when you speak making a complete eye contact with the audience.
2. Some of the popular visual aids such as Microsoft PowerPoint, OHP, flipcharts, and whiteboards enhance the quality of presentation. They enable the listeners to remember and recall main points and reduce the amount of time a speaker spends presenting information.
3. Body language plays a vital role to make positive impact on the audience. Use positive gestures and hand movements. Maintain positive posture by standing erect and do not slouch/fidget.

4. Be enthusiastic about what you say. Only then the audience will be able to share enthusiasm with you and enjoy your talk.
5. Modulate your voice appropriately. Neither be too feeble nor too loud.
6. Be well prepared. Rehearse your presentation with someone who can give sound feedback. If you can make a video recording of your presentation and watch it yourself, it will help you to reflect on your performance.

Like the art of good speaking, presentation skills are perfected through regular practice. Communication through multimedia presentation is bound to gain much greater popularity in business as well as training in the days ahead. Visual/audiovisual messages and the material prepared beforehand act as aide memoire and the communicator finds it easier to put across the message forcefully and a ready rehearsal helps in ready recap of the points to be elaborated before the commencement of presentation which mesmerizes the audience.

Practice Activities

1. The teacher will ask you to speak on a topic for one minute. You will be given 10 minutes to think and plan your talk. After 10 minutes you should speak on the topic without stopping. A normal pause is allowed but it should not be extended. Each student will be given different topics. Topics such as my best friend, my best pet, my best movie, my source of inspiration, my best picnic spot, and my best sport can be used for presentation.
2. Your teacher will ask you to make a presentation on the topic of your choice. Select a topic to make the presentation.

Some Topics for Presentation

1. Use of plastic in daily routine
2. India is a popular tourist destination in the world
3. The country or a city I would like to visit the most
4. Technology: A double-edged weapon
5. Tourism and biodiversity

6.5 GROUP DISCUSSION

Group discussion (GD) constitutes an important facet of group communication. Unlike a meeting or conference, which is well-structured with specific roles being assigned to the participants, GDs are less formal and unstructured. We can refer to two types of GDs in an organizational context.

The first type of GD is where a group of persons meet informally and exchange information, or discuss and deliberate on a topic of common interest. The participation of the members is voluntary and every member is free to express views and react to the issues brought out during the deliberations. There is no chairperson or hierarchy and participants enjoy freedom of expression. GDs involving participants from different departments, functional areas, and hierarchical levels conducted effectively and in a formal manner help in seeking collective wisdom on the issues of concern. We may also note in this context the types of GDs that take place on TV channels, where experts invited air their views on the topic with a moderator being present and facilitating the smooth flow of deliberations.

The second type of GD comprises those where the job-seeking candidates invited for discussions participate as part of the selection process. Performance in the GD thus becomes vital for the candidate in the selection process.

6.5.1 Procedure of GD

Generally GD is conducted in the following manner:

1. A group, usually consisting of 8 to 10 members, is arranged to sit in a semi-circle or full circle. Each participant in the group has to address themselves through their names or else sometimes they have to address by the given numbers.
2. The topic for discussion is usually suggested by evaluator or sometimes the group may be asked to choose a topic for discussion. The topic may or may not have relevance to the job or to the candidate's area of specialization.
3. The time limit for a discussion is usually 30 minutes.
4. It is expected that everyone in the group participates in the discussion by presenting his/her views and ideas on the topic. If any candidate has not participated in the discussion the person is generally given an opportunity to speak on the topic towards the end.
5. Finally, one of the candidates in the group is expected to summarize and present the group's viewpoint on the topic at the end.

6.5.2 Characteristics Judged in a GD

1. **Content**
   Content is a combination of knowledge and the ability to create logical ideas on the basis of that knowledge.

2. **Communication Skills**
   Communication is a two-way process. Besides listening, you also need to have the ability to

- express your ideas in a clear and concise manner.
- build on others' points.
- sum up the discussion made by the entire group.

3. **Group Dynamics**

   As GD is a formal peer group situation, it tests your behaviour as well as your influence on the group. In addition, you need to have

   - Willingness to listen and discuss various points of view. Try not to take strong views in the beginning itself; try and analyse the problems of a situation.
   - Learn to disagree politely, if required. It is far better to put forward your point of view without specifically saying 'I disagree' or 'You are wrong'.
   - Show appreciation for good points made by others. You can make a positive contribution by agreeing to expand an argument made by someone else.
   - Seize the opportunity to make a summary near the end.

4. **Group Leadership**

   Leadership is all about giving direction to the group in terms of content. One of the most common misconceptions about leadership is that it is all about controlling the group. A good leader is one who allows others to express their views and channels the discussion to a probable decision or conclusion on the given topic. The leader is one who initiates discussion if the group is frozen in the beginning. He is one who listens as much as he speaks. He also plays an important role in ensuring that everyone in the group gets a chance to speak. He also helps in maintaining the psychological and emotional health of the group in the case of disagreements and controversies. He must also offer alternative perspectives and solutions to the differences of opinion among the members.

6.5.3 Negative Points in a GD

- Dominating nature
- Disagreeing beyond reason
- Being irrelevant
- Losing temper
- Impatient attitude
- Poor communication skills
- Ignorance about the topic given
- Non-participation

6.5.4 Guidelines for GD

1. We must speak clearly, sensibly, and also let others speak.
2. We must be our natural self so that our responses are spontaneous and not artificial.
3. Listen carefully if someone else takes the initiative and do not pick up a fight with that person for grabbing the initiative.
4. In a GD the topic must be discussed from all points of view and all aspects must be taken into account before a final conclusion is reached.
5. GD should not turn into a debate.
6. If someone interrupts you when you are speaking ask the person to wait till you complete. If the interruption continues even then, give that person a chance to speak and you can resume from where you stopped after the other person completes. You gain marks and the other person loses the marks.
7. While participating in discussion on controversial topics, do not change your viewpoints after you have already taken a stand or viewpoint. The type of frequent change of your views creates an impression that you do not have concrete ideas and hence you can easily be influenced.
8. Keep track of the time. The time allotted for GD makes it essential to present the views briefly and lucidly.
9. It is better and most advisable to stop the discussion about 30 seconds before the deadline and summarize the salient features or viewpoints of the group. So this is one where you can score over others.
10. While speaking we must establish eye contact with each and every member of the group. This will not only involve them in what we are saying but also indicate the persons who are receptive to our arguments.
11. We must try and appear friendly and not overbearing or intimidating. Smile is the most important body language to win friends and allies.
12. The amount of time we speak for is not as much important as the quality of what we have said and its impact on the group. Let us not try to dominate by speaking for a long period of time. Our aim should be to make the discussion meaningful by adding substance and content.

Finally, always remember that the four practical skills needed for any GD are as follows:

- Active listening
- Asking effective questions
- Reflecting
- Analysing what the other person is saying

GD Topics

1. BPO: Boon or bane
2. Entrance cancellation
3. Indo-China competition
4. India in world cricket
5. Olympic medal: Why not for India?
6. Bribery: Cause, effect, and remedy
7. Religion and society
8. Indian economy and business
9. Nuclear deal: Boon or bane
10. Iraq War and Saddam Hussain
11. Terrorism: Cause and remedy
12. Product- and service-oriented: Stable economy?
13. Education system and reforms required
14. Dowry system
15. Bhopal Gas Tragedy: Root cause
16. Westernization is a culture degradation?
17. Mobile phones: Merits and demerits
18. MBA vs. engineering
19. Constitutional changes required
20. Effect of films on youth
21. Industrial growth in India
22. Indian vs. Western engineering
23. IT industries and its effects on culture
24. Ethics for engineers

6.6 INTERVIEW SKILLS

6.6.1 Interview Process

There are many and different types of interviews designed to serve different purposes or situations. Regardless of the type of interview, most will incorporate the following stages: establishing rapport, exchanging information, and closing the interview. Pay attention to the job titles of the interviewer(s). This can help you decide how much technical detail to provide in your responses.

Establishing Rapport

This is a very important part of the interview because it is while establishing rapport that first impressions are made, and the tone of the interview is set. Some people suggest that the decision to hire is greatly influenced by the first five minutes of the interview. A good interviewer will introduce him/herself, and take the lead. Follow his or her lead—if they are chatty, be chatty; if they are formal, be formal. Some employers use what seems to be casual conversation to get to know you on a more personal level—this may be crucial to a hiring decision!

- Smile and maintain eye contact. This is one way of communicating confidence, even if you don't feel it.
- If the interviewer offers his or her hand, shake it firmly. If they don't, it is appropriate to offer yours.
- Wait until the interviewer sits or offers you a seat before sitting down.
- If the interviewer is making small talk, participate. Keep your answers short and positive.

Exchange of Information

This is the bulk of the interview. It is your opportunity to let the interviewer know what you have to offer, and your chance to learn more about the organization.

When you answer a question, look the interviewer in the eye.

- Be aware of the interviewer's reactions. If he or she looks confused, ask if you can clarify anything.
- Be aware of what your body is saying. Avoid closed postures. Sit upright, but not stiffly. Try to find a comfortable position as that will make you feel more relaxed.
- Control your nervous habits. Don't swing your foot, talk with your hands (to an extreme), or fiddle with jewellery, buttons, pens, and the like.
- Show that you are interested in the job by asking questions.
- Try not to appear bored or anxious. Don't look at your watch.

Closing the Interview

When the interviewer is done gathering the information that is needed, he or she will ask if you have anything to add, or if you have any questions. This is your opportunity to mentally review your inventory of skills and make sure that you have communicated everything that you wanted to. If any of your questions have not been addressed during the course of the interview, now is the time to ask them.

- Thank the interviewer for his/her time and consideration.
- Ask when you can expect to hear from him/her.
- If it is not known when a decision will be reached, ask if you can phone in a week's time to inquire about the progress.
- If the interviewer offers his/her hand, shake it firmly. Otherwise, it is fine to offer yours first.

- If not already discussed, you can offer to leave a sample of your work or portfolio, if you have one.

6.6.2 Types of Interview

Panel/Board Interviews

Candidates are interviewed by two or more individuals. This process is commonly used by governments and large organizations. It is important to maintain eye contact with the person asking the question and give an answer with an example to support it. Always acknowledge the other interviewers' presence by making eye contact while answering rotating questions. Direct your attention at the beginning and end of your response to the person who asked you that question. The questions asked in the interview are often set out in advance. The board may already have decided which answers they will accept/prefer for the questions. Ignore note-taking by board members. Obtain employers' names prior to the interview and use them during the conversation.

One-on-One Interviews

Candidates are interviewed by one person. These interviews tend to be more informal, however, it always depends on the employer's style. The interviewer will often have a series of prepared questions, but may have some flexibility in their choices. It is important to maintain eye contact with the person interviewing you.

Impromptu Interviews

This interview commonly occurs when employers are approached directly and tends to be very informal and unstructured. Applicants should be prepared at all times for on-the-spot interviews, especially in situations such as a job fair or a cold call. It is an ideal time for employers to ask the candidate some basic questions to determine whether he/she may be interested in formally interviewing the candidate.

Second Interviews or Follow-up Interviews

Employers invite those applicants they are seriously considering as prospective employees following a screening or initial interview. These interviews are generally conducted by middle or senior management, together or separately. Applicants can expect more in-depth questions, and the employer will be expecting a greater level of preparation on the part of the candidate. Applicants should continue to research the employer following the first interview, and be prepared to use to their advantage any information gained through the previous interview.

Telephone Interviews

Have a copy of your resume and any points you want to remember to say nearby. If you are on your home telephone, make sure that all roommates or family members are aware of the interview (e.g., avoid loud stereos). Speak a bit slower than usual. It is crucial that you convey your enthusiasm verbally, since the interviewer cannot see your face. If there are pauses, don't worry, the interviewer is likely just making some notes.

Group Interviews

Employers bringing several candidates together in a group situation to solve a problem are testing your ability to work in a team environment. They want to know how you will present information to other people, offer suggestions, relate to others' ideas, and work together to solve a problem. In short, they are testing your interpersonal skills. It is difficult to prepare for this type of interview except to remember what is being tested and to use the skills you have to be the best team player and/or leader you can be. Some employers will take you to meet the staff who would be your co-workers if hired. This is a very casual type of interview, but leaving a positive and friendly impression is no less critical.

6.6.3 Interview Preparation

Research is a critical part of preparing for an interview. If you haven't done your homework, it is going to be obvious. Spend time researching and thinking about yourself, the occupation, the organization, and questions you might ask at the end of the interview.

Know Yourself

The first step in preparing for an interview is to do a thorough self-assessment so that you will know what you have to offer an employer. It is very important to develop a complete inventory of skills, experience, and personal attributes, which you can use to market yourself to employers at any time during the interview process.

In developing this inventory, it is easiest to start with experience. Once you have a detailed list of activities that you have done (past jobs, extracurricular involvements, volunteer work, school projects, and so on), it is fairly easy to identify your skills. Simply go through the list, and for each item ask your own self 'What could I have learned by doing this?' 'What skills did I develop?' 'What issues/circumstances have I learned to deal with?'

Keep in mind that skills fall into two categories: technical and generic. Technical skills are the skills required to do a specific job. For a laboratory assistant, technical skills might include knowledge of sterilization procedures, slide preparation, and scientific report writing. For an outreach worker, technical skills might include counselling skills, case management skills, programme design, and evaluation skills. Generic skills are those which are transferable to many work settings. Following is a list of the 10 most marketable skills. You will notice that they are all generic.

- Analytical/Problem-Solving
- Flexibility/Versatility
- Interpersonal
- Oral/Written communication
- Organization/Planning
- Time management
- Motivation
- Leadership
- Self-Starter/Initiative
- Team player

- How have I demonstrated the skills required in this position?
- What are my strong points and weak points?
- What are my short-term and long-term goals?
- What can I offer this particular employer?
- What kind of environment do I like? (e.g., How do I like to be supervised? Do I like a fast pace?)
- What do I like doing?
- Apart from my skills and experience, what can I bring to this job?
- What are the trends in the area? Is technology changing the job?

Know the Occupation

The second step in preparing for an interview is to research the occupation. This is necessary because in order to present a convincing argument that you have the experience and skills required for that occupation, you must first know what those requirements and duties are. With this information uncovered, you can then match the skills you have (using the complete skills/experience inventory you have just prepared) with the skills you know people in that occupational field need. The resulting 'shortlist' will be the one that you need to emphasize during the interview. It is also in your best interest to identify the approximate starting salary for that position, or those similar. There are several ways to find out about an occupation:

- Acquire a copy of the job description from the employer (Human Resources/Personnel) or check with Student Employment Services. If you are responding to an advertisement, this may also supply some details.

- If you belong to a professional association related to the occupation, use its resources. These associations often publish informative newsletters and sponsor seminars. It is also a good way to meet people working in the field.
- Conduct information interviews with people working in the field.
- Read articles about people in the occupation, and articles written by people in the occupation. Sources include newspapers, magazines, and the Internet.
- Find out what are the future trends in the area. Is technology changing the job?

Know the Organization

The more you know about an organization, the better prepared you will be to discuss how you can meet its needs. Some of the characteristics that you should know about an organization are:

- Where is it located?
- How big is it?
- What are its products and who does it serve?
- How is the organization structured?
- What is its history?
- Have there been any recent changes, new developments?

There are a number of ways in which you can access this information. Most medium- to large-sized organizations publish information about themselves. You can access this in a number of ways:

- On campus at the Student Employment Services (company literature and business directories) or at the Drake Centre Library.
- The Winnipeg Centennial Library has a business microfiche with information on over 5,000 Canadian companies and business directories.
- Many companies have Internet home pages which you can locate by searching by industry and company name.
- Finally, you can visit or phone the organization and request some information on their products, services, or areas of research.

Prepare Questions

If the organization is fairly small, or fairly new, there may not be much information published. In this case, it will be necessary to do an information interview.

- Contact someone within the organization, introduce yourself, explain that you are considering moving into the field, and ask if it would be possible to meet with him/her to inquire about the company/organization and about what exactly the position would involve.
- Try to think of questions for which the answer was not readily available in company literature. Intelligent, well thought-out questions will demonstrate your genuine interest in the position.
- Pick your questions with care—this is your chance to gather information, so ask about what you really want to know.
- Avoid sounding critical by mentioning negative information you may have discovered. This is one of the most effective ways to compare different employers, so for issues of particular importance to you (for example, whether they support staff upgrading), you should ask the same questions of each employer.
- It is very important to ask the last question because employers want to hire individuals who are interested in the position, and asking this question definitely helps to demonstrate interest on your part.
- Exercise judgment when asking questions to an employer. When being interviewed by a large company that has a high profile, one would not ask the question 'What is the history of the company and how the company was started?' You can find the answer to this question in the company's annual report or articles in magazines/newspapers. This question is appropriate if you have exercised all other ways to find out the answer.

6.6.4 Sample Questions and Answers

Q. **Was there ever a time that you were challenged or put under pressure?**
A. Yes. I recently had to meet a very tight project deadline for an important customer. Would you like for me to go on?

Q. **Yes, please do. What were the circumstances?**
A. One of our top customers wanted complex product modifications in only a week, including matching changes to the standard user manual. It was my job to customize the user manual by working with the engineer who was to make the modifications. During our first project meeting, I recommended that I write an addendum to the user manual, which would be quicker than editing the entire manual. The project team and our customer thought it was a good idea, so that's what I did.

Q. **Good recommendation. When did you feel challenged or under pressure?**
A. Well, I felt pressured right away; because I knew that the deadline was tight even for an addendum, and this particular customer was so very important to our business.

Q. **How did you cope with the pressure?**
A. I turned the pressure into challenge. A good challenge makes me determined, and determination gives me the energy to meet the challenge.

Q. **Can you give me an example to help me better understand what you mean?**
A. Sure. It's like when I challenge myself to jog a little further than I have before. I'm determined to do it, which in turn gives me the energy to do it. The same thing happened on the project.

Q. **Good analogy. How did you go about accomplishing the project?**
A. To save time, I started with the same template I initially created for the standard manual. It took only a few tweaks to modify it for an addendum. Then I worked extra hours in my office or took my laptop home with me after office hours and worked on it there.

Q. **What was the outcome?**
A. I met the deadline on time. Our customer was so pleased with the addendum that my manager gave me an out-of-cycle promotion. Our CEO took the project team out to dinner at a nice restaurant, where he presented Gold Achievement Award to all of us.

Q. **Tell me about yourself?**
A. This is the dreaded, classic open-ended interview question and likely to be among the first. It's your chance to introduce your qualifications, good work habits, and so on. Keep it mostly work and career related.

Q. **Why do you want to leave your current job?**
A. Be careful with this. Avoid trashing other employers and making statements like, 'I need more money.' Instead make generic statements such as 'It's a career move.'

Q. **What are your strengths?**
A. Point out your positive attributes related to the job.

Q. **What are your weaknesses?**
A. Everybody has weaknesses, but don't spend too much time on this one and keep it work related. Along with a minor weakness or two, try to point out a couple of weaknesses that the interviewer might see as strengths, such as sometimes being a little too meticulous about the quality of your work. (Avoid saying 'I work too hard.' It's a predictable, common answer.) For every weakness offer a strength that compensates for it.

Q. **Which adjectives would you use to describe yourself?**
A. Answer with positive, work-oriented adjectives, such as conscientious, hard-working, honest, and courteous, plus a brief description or example of why each fits you well.

Q. **What do you know about our company?**
A. To answer this one, research the company before you interview.

Q. **Why do you want to work for us?**
A. Same as above. Research the company before you interview. Avoid the predictable, such as 'Because it's a great company.' Say why you think it's a great company.

Q. **Why should I hire you?**
A. Point out your positive attributes related to the job, and the good job you've done in the past. Include any compliments you've received from management.

Q. **What past accomplishments gave you satisfaction?**
A. Focus more on achievement than reward.

Q. **What makes you want to work hard?**
A. Naturally, material rewards such as perks, salary, and benefits come into play. But again, focus more on achievement and the satisfaction you derive from it.

Q. **What type of work environment do you like best?**
A. Tailor your answer to the job. For example, if in doing your job you're required to lock the lab doors and work alone, then indicate that you enjoy being a team player when needed, but also enjoy working independently. If you're required to attend regular project planning and status meetings, then indicate that you're a strong team player and like being part of a team.

Q. **Why do you want this job?**
A. To help you answer this and related questions, study the job ad in advance. But a job ad alone may not be enough, so it's okay to ask questions about the job while you're answering. Say what attracts you to the job. Avoid the obvious and meaningless, such as 'I need a job.'

Q. **How do you handle pressure and stress?**
A. This is sort of a double whammy, because you're likely already stressed from the interview and the interviewer can see if you're handling it well or not. Everybody feels stress, but the degree varies. Saying that you whine to your shrink, kick your dog, or slam down a fifth of Jack Daniels are not good answers. Exercising, relaxing with a good book, socializing with friends, or turning stress into productive energy are more along the lines of the 'correct' answers.

Q. **Explain how you overcame a major obstacle.**
A. The interviewer is likely looking for a particular example of your problem-solving skills and the pride you show for solving it.

Q. **Where do you see yourself five (10 or 15) years from now?**

A. Explain your career-advancement goals that are in line with the job for which you are interviewing. Your interviewer is likely more interested in how he, she, or the company will benefit from you achieving your goals than what you'll get from it, but it goes hand in hand to a large degree. It's not a good idea to tell your potential new boss that you'll be going after his or her job, but it's okay to mention that you'd like to earn a senior or management position.

Q. **What qualifies you for this job?**

A. Tout your skills, experience, education, and other qualifications, especially those that match the job description well. Avoid just regurgitating your resume. Explain why.

Q. **Why did you choose your college major?**

A. The interviewer is likely fishing to see if you are interested in your field of work or just doing a job to get paid. Explain why you like it. Besides your personal interests, include some rock-solid business reasons that show you have vision and business sense.

6.6.5 Interview Purpose

The interview is an opportunity for both the employer and the applicant to gather information. The employer wants to know if you, the applicant, have the skills, knowledge, self-confidence, and motivation necessary for the job. At this point you can be confident that the employer saw something of interest in your resume. He or she also wants to determine whether or not you will fit in with the organization's current employees and philosophy. Similarly, you will want to evaluate the position and the organization, and determine if they will fit into your career plans. *The interview is a two-way exchange of information.* It is an opportunity for both parties to market themselves. The employer is selling the organization to you, and you are marketing your skills, knowledge, and personality to the employer.

Mistakes

Oversell	Trying too hard to impress, bragging, acting aggressively.
Undersell	Failing to emphasize the fact that you have related skills; discussing experience using negative qualifiers (e.g., 'I have a little experience ...').
Body language	It is easy to create a negative impression without even realizing that you are doing it. Are you staring at your feet, or talking to the interviewer's shoulder? Beware of what your actions say about you.

Lack of honesty	The slightest stretching of the truth may result in you being screened out.
Negative attitude	The interview is not an opportunity for you to complain about your current supervisor or co-workers (or even about 'little' things, such as the weather).
Lack of preparation	You have to know about the organization and the occupation. If you don't, it will appear as though you are not interested in the position.
Lack of enthusiasm	If you are not excited about the work at the interview, the employer will not assume that your attitude will improve when hired.

6.6.6 Rejection

Keep in mind that rejection is a normal part of every job search. For every position, if 100 people apply, 99 will be rejected. If you are rejected, it does not mean that you are not a good applicant. It simply means that you were not the best applicant for that particular job at that particular time. Don't get discouraged. Rejection happens to everyone and is not a reflection of you. Consider each new application a new opportunity.

- Walt Disney's idea for Disneyland was rejected by six major banks before being accepted. They said no one would come.
- A record company which had the opportunity to sign the Beatles rejected them. They felt that electric guitar music was only a phase.

PRACTICE EXERCISE D

Job Interview Conversation 1

Mike: Good morning, John. I am Mike.
John: Good morning.
Mike: How are you doing?
John: I am doing fine. Thank you.
Mike: How was the traffic coming over here?
John: I am so glad that the traffic was light this morning. No traffic jam and no accidents.
Mike: That is good. John, let's start the interview. Are you ready?
John: Yes, I am.
Mike: First of all, let me properly introduce myself. I am the finance department manager. As you know there is an open position in my department, and I need to fill this position as soon as possible.
John: Please tell me a little bit about the position.

Mike: It is an entry-level position. The new employee will have to work closely with the accounting department. He will also have to deal with the bank on a daily basis.

John: What type of qualifications do you require?

Mike: I require a four-year college degree in finance. Some working experience would be helpful.

John: What kind of experience are you looking for?

Mike: Doing office work is good. However, since this is an entry-level position, I do not require a lot of experience. I am willing to train the new person.

John: That is great!

Mike: John, tell me a little bit about yourself.

John: I was a student at West Coast University, and I just graduated with a bachelor's degree in finance. I have been working part-time as a payroll clerk for the last two years.

Mike: What are you looking for in a job?

John: The job should help me see what finance is all about. I have learned a lot of finance theories at school, and now it is time for me to put them into practice.

Mike: Anything else?

John: I also hope that it will help me grow in my field.

Mike: What are your strengths? Why should I hire you?

John: I am a hard-working person and a fast learner. I am very eager to learn, and I get along fine with people.

Mike: OK. Now, let me ask you a few quick questions. You do not mind working long hours, do you?

John: No, I do not.

Mike: Can you handle pressure?

John: Yes, I can. When I was going to school, I took quite a few courses each semester while working at least 20 hours every week. And I handled that situation very well.

Mike: Do you still have any questions for me?

John: No, I think I have a pretty good understanding of the job. I believe that I can handle it with ease, and I hope to have the opportunity to work for you.

Mike: John, nice meeting you. Thank you for coming.

John: Nice meeting you too. Thank you for seeing me.

Job Interview Conversation 2

Here is a dialogue between an interviewer and an interviewee. Act out this as a role play with your partner.

Interviewer: Good morning, Ms Regita Sofyan.

Interviewee: Good morning, Mr Bima Suseno.

Interviewer: You are applying for the position of a public relations officer, aren't you?

Interviewee: Yes, sir.

Interviewer: Could you tell me a little about your educational background?

Interviewee: I have a degree in public relations from Gadjah Mada University.
Interviewer: Can you tell me about your last job?
Interviewee: I'm a receptionist in a developing company.
Interviewer: Could you tell me what your duties are?
Interviewee: I receive guests and incoming phone calls.
Interviewer: I would like to know whether you know your responsibilities if you are accepted here.
Interviewee: As far as I know, a PR officer is responsible for building a good relationship not only between the company and its employees, but also among employees and between the company and customers or colleagues.
Interviewer: How would you describe your relationship with your present company?
Interviewee: Our relationship is very good. We communicate well.
Interviewer: So I would like to know why you are leaving your job.
Interviewee: I want to get a more challenging job which is relevant to my educational background.
Interviewer: I wonder if you could tell me something about what kind of person you are.
Interviewee: I'm diligent and sociable. I'm also a good communicator.
Interviewer: What would you say about your weaknesses?
Interviewee: Some people say I'm a perfectionist.
Interviewer: What is your goal for the future?
Interviewee: Working for a well-developed company like this company.
Interviewer: OK, Ms Regita Sofyan.
That's all for the interview today. I'll call you for the results later.
Interviewee: Thank you for the interview.

Job Interview Conversation 3

Candidate May I come in, sir/ma'am?
Interviewer: Yes, come in.
Candidate: Good morning.
Interviewer: Good morning. Please take a seat.
Candidate: Thank you.
Interviewer: Well, I have seen your CV. It was impressive, and that's why we have selected you for this interview. Tell me, why did you opt for this job?
Candidate: Because I believe that I possess excellent knowledge regarding it and I have three years of experience working in the same field too. Besides, working for a reputable company is what I always wanted, which is why I opted for this job.
Interviewer: Nicely put. Why did you leave your previous job?
Candidate: I want to expand my career as much as I can. I don't want to stick to the same position forever unless it is a reputable organization.
Interviewer: Well, thanks for coming. You will be informed in two weeks if you get selected.
Candidate: Thank you so much. Goodbye.
Interviewer: Goodbye.

Job Interview Conversation 4

Here is a dialogue between a company representative and a job seeker. Enact a role play.

Ram: Hello, can I speak to Ms Gita?
Gita: This is Gita. May I know who's calling?
Ram: I'm Ram Prakash from Accel Computers. You have been shortlisted for the first round of interviews. I need some more information from your side.
Gita: Oh sure, Mr Prakash. Please go ahead.
Ram: You have completed your MCA with high first class. Why did you apply for this job?
Gita: Market sources say, Accel Computers is among the front runners in computer education. I therefore thought it was the best place to start a career.
Ram: I see. But given your academic background, won't you be tempted to try for bigger and better prospects abroad? What kind of commitment can you give us?
Gita: I have no intention of going abroad, sir. I prefer to work for an indigenous company rather than faceless MNCs or foreign companies.
Ram: That's very interesting. When will you be available for employment?
Gita: Immediately, sir.
Ram: Great. I will get back to you in a couple of days through e-mail.
Gita: OK, sir. And thank you for your time.
Ram: You are welcome, Gita. Have a good day.
Gita: Thank you, sir.

PRACTICE EXERCISE E

Paraphrase the following passages:

Passage 1

'The twenties were the years when drinking was against the law, and the law was a bad joke because everyone knew of a local bar where liquor could be had. They were the years when organized crime ruled the cities, and the police seemed powerless to do anything against it. Classical music was forgotten while jazz spread throughout the land, and men like Bix Beiderbecke, Louis Armstrong, and Count Basie became the heroes of the young. The flapper was born in the twenties, and with her bobbed hair and short skirts, she symbolized, perhaps more than anyone or anything else, America's break with the past.[1]

[1] Extracted from Kathleen Yancey, *English 102 Supplemental Guide* (1989): 25.

Passage 2

'While the Sears Tower is arguably the greatest achievement in skyscraper engineering so far, it's unlikely that architects and engineers have abandoned the quest for the world's tallest building. The question is: Just how high can a building go? Structural engineer William LeMessurier has designed a skyscraper nearly one-half mile high, twice as tall as the Sears Tower. And architect Robert Sobel claims that existing technology could produce a 500-story building.'[2]

[2] Extracted from Ron Bachman, 'Reaching for the Sky', *Dial* (May 1990): 15.

FURTHER READING

1. SkillsYouNeed. https://www.skillsyouneed.com/ips/listening-types.html (accessed on 28 September 2018)
2. Effective CommunicationAdvice.com. effectivecommunicationadvice.com/barriers (accessed on 28 September 2018)
3. Hari Prasad, M., John Verghese, R. Kishore Kumar, Komali Prakash, and U. Saraswati Rao. *Strengthen Your Steps: A Multimodal Course in Communication Skills*. Hyderabad: Maruti Publications, 2013.
4. https://arrikurniawan.files.wordpress.com/2010/03/convversation.pdf (accessed on 28 September 2018)
5. https://www.easypacelearning.com/.../1207-job-interview-conversation-learning-engli (accessed on 20 August 2015)
6. www.improvespokenenglish.org/2011/06/telephone-conversation-between.htm (accessed on 28 September 2018)
7. https://opentextbc.ca/.../chapter-3-putting-ideas-into-your-own-words-and-paragraphs (accessed on 20 August 2015)
8. Madhukar, R. K. *Business Communication*, 2nd ed. New Delhi: Vikas Publishing House, 2005.

Answers to Practice Exercises

UNIT 1

Practice Exercise A

a. *am*-on both sides; amicable-peaceful
b. *circum*-around; circumspect-caution
c. *eu*-good; euphoric-happy
d. *eu*-good; eulogy-good praise
e. *mal*-wrong; maliciously-driven by wrong intention
f. *plac*-calm; placate-calm down
g. *plac*-calm; complacent- smug and self-satisfied
h. *omni*-all; omnipotent-all powerful
i. *carni*-flesh; carnivorous-flesh-eating
j. *trepid*-tremble; intrepid-unfearing
k. *termi*-end; interminable-endless
l. *contra*-against; contraband-illegal
m. *idi*-peculiar; idiosyncratic-marked by peculiarity
n. *ben*-good; benevolent-good
o. *turb*-disturbed; turbid-dirty
p. *tac*-be silent; tacit-silent
q. *sequ*-follow; obsequious-servile
r. *secr*-sacred; consecrated-having been made or declared sacred
s. *ris*-laugh; derision-ridicule
t. *ora*-plead; inexorable-unforgiving

Practice Exercise B

a. *in*-not; incorrigible-incurable
b. *im*-against; impregnable-impenetrable
c. *de*-remove; demythologized-remove mythical elements
d. *dis*-apart; disembark-get down from
e. *co*-with; cohabit-live with
f. *con*-with; concurrent-coinciding with each other
g. *trans*-across; transcontinental-across the continent
h. *ultra*-beyond; ultrasonic-beyond hearing
i. *intra*-within; intramural-within the group/party
j. *dis*-lack of; discord-lack of cordiality/harmony

Practice Exercise C

a. ballet
b. kindergarten
c. renaissance
d. café
e. rendezvous
f. faux pas
g. croissant
h. patio
i. waltz
j. entrepreneurs

Practice Exercise D

a. approval
b. usage
c. courageous
d. scholarly
e. argument
f. readily
g. excitement
h. greenery
i. reference
j. hurrying

Practice Exercise E

a. He will receive my ring tomorrow evening.
b. I replied to his letter yesterday.
c. Yesterday witnessed a lot of rains.
d. The corrupt politician is about to be exposed.
e. Quarrel with anybody should be avoided.
f. Calamitous rains destroyed the village.
g. She was accused of witchery.
h. The visitor gave the child a frightened look.
i. I'm headed to the coastal area this weekend.
j. She is enriched through her investments in the share market.

Practice Exercise F

1. Conversion
2. Conversion
3. Conversion
4. Process morpheme
5. Process morpheme
6. Process morpheme
7. Process morpheme
8. Process morpheme
9. Conversion
10. Process morpheme

Practice Exercise G

1. summary
2. satisfied
3. hungry
4. annihilate
5. sturdy
6. restraint
7. odd
8. profound
9. applause
10. elixir
11. spirited
12. keen interest
13. rash
14. macabre
15. uncommunicative

Practice Exercise H

1. kept suspended
2. deviation from normality
3. inactive
4. praise highly

5. ostentatious
6. call for repetition
7. abundant
8. interference in dominating way
9. expression
10. crushed
11. unmapped
12. show off
13. filled
14. monetary
15. circumspect

Practice Exercise I

1. plenty
2. indecisive
3. choke
4. divergent
5. concealed
6. sufficed
7. terminate
8. disappointing
9. unoriginal
10. familiar

Practice Exercise J

1. unclean
2. ameliorate
3. malodorous
4. orderly
5. feeble
6. contented
7. unhealthy
8. devoted
9. appreciate
10. courteous
11. adept
12. cowardice
13. careful
14. exciting
15. resolute

Practice Exercise K

a) e.g.
b) etc.
c) i.e.
d) St
e) St

Practice Exercise L

1. Teaching English to Speakers of Other Languages
2. Test of English as a Foreign Language
3. International English Language Testing System
4. Graduate Record Examinations
5. Acquired Immunodeficiency Syndrome
6. Light Amplification by Stimulated Emission of Radiation
7. Radio Detection and Ranging
8. National Aeronautics and Space Administration

Practice Exercise M

1. post-paid
2. untie
3. AIDS
4. intolerable
5. chauffeur
6. en masse
7. status quo
8. dutiful
9. clueless
10. organic farming
11. infotainment
12. flu

UNIT 2

Practice Exercise A

1. It is cool today.
2. It is a pleasant morning.
3. It is a pity that you can't attend the function.
4. It is an insult for the family.
5. It is shame on you to abuse your parents like this.

Practice Exercise B

1. It is not the way one should behave.
2. Charminar is a marvellous monument.
3. He is known to everyone.
4. It does not matter whether we win or lose.
5. You can change your attitude.

Practice Exercise C

1. Post the letter, will you?
2. Will/could you speak politely?
3. Will/could you take me to the principal?
4. Will/could you get me a glass of milk?
5. Will you keep quiet?

Practice Exercise D

1. I don't have much work to do./Do you have much work to do?
2. Not many people want to buy cars./Are there many people who want to buy cars?
3. There isn't much controversy about the language problem./Is there much controversy about the language problem?
4. The sea isn't far off./Is the sea far off?
5. Not much research has been done on the subject./Has much research been done on the subject?
6. Not much money has been spent on the project./Has much money been spent on the project?

Practice Exercise E

__X__ 1. Tom, **who is always late**, arrived late for his wedding.

______ 2. His bride was angry with him for arriving late.

__X__ 3. We replaced the window, **which we had accidentally broken with a baseball.**

______ 4. The broken window was in the living room.

______ 5. The cat with the injured paw limped on three legs.

__X__ 6. The cat **that won the fight** got injured.

__X__ 7. Irvin played on the team **that won the tournament last week.**

Practice Exercise F

______ 1. Yesterday I saw a man. The man was picking his nose.

__X__ 2. Yesterday I saw a man **<u>who</u> was picking his nose.**

______ 3. Yesterday I saw a house. The house was painted turquoise.

__X__ 4. Yesterday I saw a house **<u>which</u> was painted turquoise.**

______ 5. Yesterday I saw a woman. I knew the woman.

__X__ 6. Yesterday I saw a woman **<u>whom</u> I knew.**

______ 7. Yesterday I saw a dog. I chased the dog down the street.

__X__ 8. Yesterday I saw a dog **<u>which</u> I chased down the street.**

______ 9. Yesterday I saw a dog. The dog's collar was studded with spikes.

__X__ 10. Yesterday I saw a dog **<u>whose</u> collar was studded with spikes.**

______ 11. Yesterday I saw a man. The man's hair was green.

__X__ 12. Yesterday I saw a man **<u>whose</u> hair was green.**

Practice Exercise G

______ 1. Yesterday I saw a man who was picking his nose.

______ 2. Yesterday I saw a man that was picking his nose.

__*__ 3. Yesterday I saw a man was picking his nose.

______ 4. Yesterday I saw a house which was painted turquoise.

______ 5. Yesterday I saw a house that was painted turquoise.

__*__ 6. Yesterday I saw a house was painted turquoise.

______ 7. Yesterday I saw a woman whom I knew.

______ 8. Yesterday I saw a woman who I knew.

______ 9. Yesterday I saw a woman that I knew.

______ 10. Yesterday I saw a woman I knew.

______ 11. Yesterday I called a man whom I worked for.

______ 12. Yesterday I called a man who I worked for.

______ 13. Yesterday I called a man that I worked for.

______ 14. Yesterday I called a man I worked for.

______ 15. Yesterday I called a man for whom I worked.

___*___ 16. Yesterday I called a man for who I worked.

___*___ 17. Yesterday I called a man for that I worked.

___*___ 18. Yesterday I called a man for I worked.

______ 19. Yesterday a player made derogatory statements which he was suspended for.

______ 20. Yesterday a player made derogatory statements that he was suspended for.

______ 21. Yesterday a player made derogatory statements he was suspended for.

______ 22. Yesterday a player made derogatory statements for which he was suspended.

___*___ 23. Yesterday a player made derogatory statements for that he was suspended.

___*___ 24. Yesterday a player made derogatory statements for he was suspended.

______ 25. Insolence is a behaviour which I won't put up with.

______ 26. Insolence is a behaviour that I won't put up with.

______ 27. Insolence is a behaviour I won't put up with.

Practice Exercise H

1. a. The women took notes while being taught to cook. (This adverb clause describes when the women took notes.)
2. b. We will go to the game even if it rains. (This adverb clause describes a certain condition or a 'how'.)
3. c. You can put the package wherever you like. (This adverb clause denotes a place, even though that place is not specific.)
4. a. Since you have apologized, you will not be punished. (This adverb clause denotes a reason or a 'why'.)
5. d. She was so tired that she could not stand. (This adverb clause denotes a result of being tired or a 'how'.)

Practice Exercise I

1. Sentence: principal clause; in the east: prepositional phrase
2. Sentence: principal clause; by the collar: prepositional phrase
3. Coordinative clause
4. Principal clause
5. Adverbial clause
6. Gerund phrase
7. Adjective clause
8. Principal clause
9. Gerund phrase
10. Adverbial clause

Practice Exercise J

1. Interrogative sentence
2. Exclamatory sentence
3. Assertive sentence
4. Assertive sentence
5. Optative sentence
6. Imperative sentence
7. Exclamatory sentence
8. Imperative sentence
9. Imperative sentence
10. Assertive sentence

Practice Exercise K

1. We-subject; should-auxiliary verb; anybody-complement
2. Scholars-subject; love-main verb; books-direct object
3. Ram-subject; seems-main verb; happy-complement
4. It-subject; has grown-verb (past participle); dark-complement
5. She-subject; felt-copulative verb; brave-complement
6. Kiran-subject; is-helping verb; good player-complement; hockey-direct object
7. I-subject; ran-main verb; five-mile race-complement
8. He-subject; called-main verb; me-indirect object; liar-complement
9. The boy-subject; was beaten-verb; black and blue-complement
10. The uses of adversity-subject; are-helping verb; sweet-complement

Practice Exercise L

1. *Having learned his lessons,* he went out to play.
2. *Walking along the street,* I saw a dead cobra.
3. *In spite of being wealthy and educated,* he never made a name.
4. *Following my advice,* you will win your object.
5. *Driven out of his country,* he sought asylum in a foreign land.
6. A gypsy, *wandering across the fields,* found the baby.

Practice Exercise M

1. The old man was weak therefore he could not walk properly.
2. His father is poor but he is a contended man.
3. She must work hard otherwise she will not be successful in the examination.
4. Our teacher is diligent therefore he is popular among students.
5. He has faults otherwise he would have progressed immensely.
6. The traveller visualized a danger ahead and he became cautious.
7. The student must accept his fault otherwise he will be punished.
8. The culprit ran away otherwise he would have been arrested.
9. The children took off their clothes and jumped into the river.

10. You must not be late or you will not be allowed entry.

Practice Exercise N

1. Man is a wonderful piece of work.
2. I wish that I could fly high in the sky.
3. Is there any feeling greater than love?
4. Is this the way to talk to elders?
5. Nobody will forget those happy days spent here.
6. Unless you make hurry, you will be late in the office.
7. If you had not helped us we would have ruined.
8. Only a fool would trust him.
9. We had a very delicious food yesterday.
10. How pretty the child is!

Practice Exercise O

1. He is innocent in this matter and I am confident about it.
2. He must work hard otherwise he cannot pass the examination.
3. She may do as much hard work as she can but she cannot pass the examination.
4. He has stolen her purse and she is sure about it.
5. The shopkeeper quarrels with every customer therefore nobody likes him.
6. He must improve his behaviour otherwise he will lose all his friends.
7. The culprit must accept his fault otherwise he will not be spared.
8. She felt unwell today so she did not attend the office.
9. She had purchased a book and she has lost it.
10. You must attend the class otherwise you will not be allowed to sit in the examination.

Practice Exercise P

1. I shall talk to him when I reach my office.
2. The child is spoilt when the rod is spared.
3. The thief ran away when he saw the policeman.
4. She cannot attend her office today as she is feeling unwell.
5. The child started weeping because he felt hungry.
6. The news is too good to be true.
7. You will remain healthy if you eat less.
8. The old man is a miser though he is very rich.
9. Children went to see the fair after putting on new clothes.
10. You will repent if you do not keep quite.

Practice Exercise Q

1. We had a great time in France—the kids really enjoyed it.
2. Some people work best in the mornings; others do better in the evenings.

3. What are you doing next weekend?
4. Mother had to go into hospital: She had heart problems.
5. Did you understand why I was upset?
6. It is a fine idea; let us hope that it is going to work.
7. We will be arriving on Monday morning—at least, I think so.
8. A textbook can be a 'wall' between teacher and class.
9. The girl's father sat in a corner.
10. In the words of Murphy's Law, 'Anything that can go wrong will go wrong.'

Practice Exercise R

1. A grandparent's job is easier than a parent's.
2. It looks as if the sun goes around the earth, but of course the earth really goes round the sun.
3. He neither smiled, spoke, nor looked at me.
4. Long ago, in a distant country, there lived a beautiful princess.
5. It was my aunt who took Peter to London yesterday, not my father.
6. Ruth was invited to the party, but she was ill, so Jane went instead of her.
7. Sorry to disturb you—could I speak to you for a moment?
8. Is it any use expecting them to be on time?
9. John's going to sleep during the wedding was rather embarrassing.
10. Having lost all my money, I went home.

Activity A

1. I prefer folk music and on the contrary my girlfriend adores heavy metal.
2. Although he has received three threatening letters, yet he is continuing to investigate the case.
3. The referee blew his whistle to start the game; meanwhile, it began to pour with rain.
4. Her boyfriend is very good-looking, besides being a damn good cook.
5. She was absolutely exhausted in fact she has just finished her final exams.
6. You don't like him but at the same time you want that that job and then you'll have to be nice to him.

Practice Exercise S

Paragraph 1

The type of paper you choose for a poster or a sign depends on how it will be reproduced and how it is going to be used. For a lightweight poster or sign, you can use either offset book stock or cover stock. If you need to create a more durable poster or sign, or create packaging, bristol stock is your best choice. You'll probably have to take your publication to a commercial printer however, since bristol won't feed through most desktop printers or copy machines.

Paragraph 2

In general, Internet e-mail is considerably more reliable than the postal service. It's rare, but not unheard of, for mail to go astray. However, during 1997, AOL and Microsoft Network—to name just the big players—had severe mail outages resulting in delay, and in some cases loss, of e-mail. And many corporate mail servers have had growing pains too, experiencing holdups and the odd deletion. On the whole though, you can assume e-mail will arrive.

Paragraph 3

Different parts of the day, for example, are highly significant in certain contexts. Time may indicate the importance of the occasion as well as on what level an interaction between persons is to take place. In the United States, if you telephone someone very early in the morning, while he is shaving or having breakfast, the time of the call usually signals a matter of utmost importance and extreme urgency. The same applies for calls after 11:00 PM. A call received during sleeping hours is apt to be taken as a matter of life and death, hence the rude joke value of these calls among the young. Our realization that time talks is even reflected in such common expressions as, 'What time does the clock say?'

Practice Exercise T

Paragraph 1

Parasites exhibit four features that collectively identify them as such.

Paragraph 2

Still another aspect of pollution is that of solid wastes.

Paragraph 3

People of the Western world, particularly Americans, tend to think of time as something fixed in nature, something around us, and from which we cannot escape; an ever-present part of the environment, just like the air we breathe.

Practice Exercise U

Paragraph 1

Although new technology creates new kinds of jobs, it also usually makes many existing jobs disappear. For example, when trains started to be used as a primary form of transportation, many jobs that depended on horses and oxen started to disappear. Later, automobiles became the major form of transportation; as a result, railroad companies could no longer keep as many people employed. Another new kind of technology that is leading to job loss is the digital camera. Companies that make film are laying off workers because so many consumers are switching from cameras that use film to cameras that take digital photographs. In the same way, cell phones make public pay phones less profitable, so telephone companies no longer need to employ as many technicians to install and maintain pay phones. While it is true that technological change can produce new wealth and new jobs, new inventions also tend to lead to loss of jobs.

Paragraph 2

Mark loves to travel, but Amy doesn't, so they often argue about where to spend their vacation time. One summer, they decided to try something different. Mark went to Thailand, but Amy stayed home. Mark's brother, Alex, and sister-in-law, Jennifer, went with him. They knew that they could only spend one week in Thailand, so they had to decide what to do. They could all go scuba diving in Southern Thailand, or Mark could go by himself on an elephant trek in Northern Thailand, and Alex and Jennifer could meet him later in Bangkok. Mark chose the elephant trek, and he had an exciting time. Amy was also having a good time back home. Sometimes she went out with her friends at night, and sometimes her mother would visit her during the day. She also liked to spend time by herself practising her piano. Mark and Amy learned that they could spent their vacations separately, yet they both could have a good time.

Paragraph 3

Kamala lived alone in a small flat in Lawrence Enclave in the heart of the city. She liked the neighbourhood very much ever since she came to work in the city and had been living there two years ago. She usually missed her parents, brother, and sister sometimes a lot for she only went home every three or four months. Kamala worked hard from Monday to Friday but she relaxed completely and went out with her friends at weekends. One night, when she was reading quietly in her bedroom after dinner, she heard someone knocking on her door urgently.

Kamala ignored the knocking for a while, but it soon became much louder. She tiptoed noiselessly to the door and looked fearfully through the peephole. There was no one outside! But just with a sense of relief as Kamala turned back towards her bedroom, the knocking started again. Not able to bear it any longer, she opened the door angrily and ran out into the corridor, screaming loudly. Kamala stopped suddenly when she saw, much to her surprise, her family standing near the staircase, laughing uncontrollably.

Practice Exercise V

1. let down
2. carried away
3. come up with
4. going through
5. get on
6. picked at
7. go on
8. asking for
9. call off
10. work out

11. instead of
12. In spite of
13. In case of
14. on behalf of
15. On the whole

UNIT 3

Practice Exercise A

1. is
2. has
3. is
4. were
5. has
6. is
7. were
8. is
9. has
10. has

Practice Exercise B

1. Measles has broken out in the town.
2. The *Arabian Nights* is an interesting book.
3. The cost of all essential commodities has gone up.
4. Five miles is not a long distance for me to walk.
5. A pious man and a good neighbour has died.
6. Bread and milk is my only food for today.
7. The notorious dacoit with his followers has escaped.
8. The construction of these buildings has taken four years.
9. There are a bunch of keys on the table.
10. Sanjay as well as his brothers have gone home.

Practice Exercise C

1. Annie and her brothers are at school.
2. Either my mother or my father is coming to the meeting.
3. The dog or the cats are outside.
4. Either my shoes or your coat is always on the floor.
5. George and Tamara don't want to see that movie.
6. Benito doesn't know the answer.
7. One of my sisters is going on a trip to France.
8. The man with all the birds lives on my street.
9. The movie, including all the previews, takes about two hours to watch.
10. The players, as well as the captain, want to win.
11. Either answer is acceptable.
12. Every one of those books is fiction.
13. Nobody knows the trouble I've seen.
14. Is the news on at 5:00 or 6:00?
15. Mathematics is John's favourite subject, while civics is Andrea's favourite subject.
16. Eight dollars is the price of a movie these days.

17. Are the tweezers in this drawer?
18. Your pants are at the cleaner's.
19. There were 15 candies in that bag. Now there is only one left!
20. The committee debates these questions carefully.
21. We are going to go to the movies today after school.
22. Some of the boxes were opened and thrown in the trash.
23. Nobody near the trees likes the new game that they are playing.
24. Tilda seems to think that Tom was not at home.
25. Few of the apples are still hanging on the tree.
26. I disagree with the attitude of the author towards this new technology, 'the self-driving system'.
27. The best way to learn philosophy is to reflect on oneself every day.
28. The research is conducted to improve the lives of adolescents.
29. Pointing is one piece of evidence that indicates the ability of possessiveness and cognition.
30. In my home country, a lot of adults always tell children that they should have a good attitude for everything because it is good for their lives.

Practice Exercise D

1. book (common noun); table (common noun)
2. jury (collective noun); verdict (abstract noun)
3. oxygen (common noun); life (common noun)
4. love (abstract noun)
5. habit (abstract noun)
6. sea water (common noun)
7. girls (common noun); shy (abstract noun)
8. bravery (abstract noun); manhood (abstract noun)
9. will (abstract noun); way (common noun)
10. alcohol (material noun); health (abstract noun)
11. mankind (common noun); nature (common noun)
12. wool (material noun); sheep (common noun)
13. life (common noun); bed (common noun); roses (proper noun)
14. robbery (abstract noun); robbers (common noun)

Practice Exercise E

1. My friend gives me several pieces of advice regarding my future career.
2. The HMT factory has the latest machinery.
3. The beggar is begging alms./The beggar is asking for alms.
4. This scissors will not cut such a hard wire.
5. My hair has turned grey recently.
6. The magistrate has issued summons asking me to attend his court on Monday.
7. The magistrate has passed orders for his release from prison.
8. He has lost his entire luggage on his way home.
9. These scenery of Kashmir is beautiful.
10. Gold has been brought from South Africa.

Practice Exercise F

1. who
2. who
3. myself
4. herself
5. ourselves
6. Whom
7. Whose
8. whom
9. himself
10. that

Practice Exercise G

1. One should do one's duty honestly and sincerely.
2. I, he, and you are in the wrong direction.
3. The committee was divided in its opinion regarding this issue.
4. His problems are the same as mine.
5. My opinion is the same as yours.
6. Every teacher and every student should do his duty.
7. Those two companies always help each other.
8. Between you and me, the secretary is not a gentleman.
9. Only you and he can do the work fast.
10. Neither of the boys has submitted their records.

Practice Exercise H

1. When I reached the station, the sun came out.
2. The dog caught the stick which was thrown in the air.
3. Peeking through the window, I saw the trailer.
4. I was able to buy the house very cheap which was in a dilapidated condition.
5. The train roared down the track at 70 miles an hour smashing the stalled car.
6. When I was late again and running for the school bus, my book fell in the mud.
7. When I entered the doctor's office, a skeleton caught my attention.
8. When Joe decided to join the navy, the recruiter enthusiastically pumped his hand.
9. Though Martha was only 16 years old, the college accepted her application.
10. After I quickly changed into my hospital gown, the nurse told me to relax.
11. Standing on the balcony, we had a magnificent ocean view.
12. When I was a four-year-old, my grandmother taught me to knit.

Practice Exercise I

1. dangling modifier
2. correct
3. dangling modifier
4. correct
5. dangling modifier
6. dangling modifier
7. correct
8. dangling modifier

9. dangling modifier
10. correct

Practice Exercise J

1. B
2. A
3. B
4. B
5. A
6. B
7. B
8. B
9. A
10. B

Practice Exercise K

1. the
2. a
3. a
4. an
5. The
6. an
7. the
8. the
9. the
10. the
11. a
12. the
13. a
14. an
15. a
16. A
17. a
18. the
19. A
20. × (no article)
21. an
22. an
23. × (no article)
24. an
25. The
26. the
27. the
28. The
29. The
30. The

Practice Exercise L

1. an
2. The
3. × (no article)
4. a
5. The
6. × (no article)
7. an
8. the
9. a
10. the
11. × (no article)
12. × (no article)
13. An
14. The
15. a; a

Practice Exercise M

1. Beijing is the capital of China.
2. I first met your Dad at Walmart.
3. He has failed in English.
4. She died of malaria.
5. She is the best singer I have heard.
6. Rose is the sweetest of all flowers.
7. Man is mortal.
8. You are in trouble.
9. You are making rapid progress.
10. There is a vast scope for improvement.
11. Your words are not worth a penny.
12. Don't make a noise.

Practice Exercise N

1. to
2. to; at
3. of
4. at
5. with
6. in; for
7. for
8. for
9. on
10. across
11. for
12. from
13. at
14. since
15. at

Practice Exercise O

1. from
2. to
3. since
4. for
5. to
6. in
7. by
8. on
9. on
10. on
11. into
12. with

Practice Exercise P

1. at
2. by
3. of
4. on
5. of
6. about
7. By
8. in; in
9. on; on
10. in
11. for
12. in
13. for
14. of
15. of
16. from
17. in/with
18. about
19. in
20. at

Practice Exercise Q

1. Looking back, I can't remember a summer of my childhood when I didn't spend most of the day outdoors getting into trouble.
2. Justin is a friendly guy.
3. Mr James was introduced in the meeting.
4. The vote was completely unanimous.
5. We could see some ruins.
6. One of the twins says to the other, 'You are not fat.'
7. She herself has written her autobiography in just two weeks.
8. There is proximity between the two sentences.
9. Ravi decided to live in isolation.
10. Beauty products have an aroma.

Practice Exercise R

1. We need to cooperate.
2. This is a phenomenal piece of equipment …
3. A liaison officer responsible for …
4. 14 APCs …
5. With the proximity of …
6. The same number of soldiers…
7. Innovations will move our industry forward.
8. Let me summarize …
9. We also have ATMs inside the base.
10. Twenty-five companies have already expressed a desire to join the programme.
11. There is no need for further enhancement of the base.
12. The ministry is reviewing the memorandum.

Practice Exercise S

1. Helen is a smart woman./Helen is an intelligent woman./Helen is a smart and wise woman.
2. Our top student is ill today.
3. I will complete my research paper in a week.
4. John's stylish crocodile-skin boots cost him an arm and a leg.
5. Susan is a high-school chemistry teacher.
6. The student is writing an assignment for his English composition class.
7. The book on the table is a grammar book./The grammar book is on the table./There is a grammar book on the table.
8. Jennifer finished third in the 5,000-metre track event.
9. Her Italian purse was stolen yesterday.
10. Many people admire her lectures because the ideas are expressed so clearly./Many people admire her lectures because of the clear ideas.

Practice Exercise T

day and age
worth her weight in gold
works her fingers to the bone
washed over me
a bolt from the blue
the trials and tribulations
rotten to the core
leaps and bounds

jumped on the bandwagon
darted out
beat a hasty retreat to his seat
make a tempest in a teapot
Cool as a cucumber

Practice Exercise U

face the music: confront the unpleasant consequences
green with envy: jealous
sneaking suspicion: belief based on little evidence
as cold as ice: distant
vicious circle: continuing unpleasant situation
the pursuit of fame and fortune: endeavours to make it large in life

Practice Exercise V

1. Better late than never.
2. Every cloud has a silver lining.
3. Fall head over heels.
4. Breathe a sigh of relief.
5. All is fair in love and war.
6. When you have lemons, make lemonade.
7. As old as the hills.
8. Opposites attract.
9. All's well that ends well.
10. Sent a shiver down my spine.
11. All that glitters is not gold.
12. The apple doesn't fall far from the tree.
13. Ignorance is bliss, 'tis folly to be wise.
14. Better safe than sorry.
15. Like father, like son.

Practice Exercise W

Paragraph 1

1. My family *enjoys* scuba diving, so nearly every vacation, we go on a diving trip.
2. We have noticed that there *are* three completely different kinds of divers.
3. No change.
4. The people who we call 'nature lovers' enjoy getting in the water for a short swim to look at the rocks, seaweed, and underwater creatures, which *are* swimming around.
5. The 'pool guys', who wear the latest hi-tech equipment, *come* for a short while to have a swim and test how good their *equipment is*.
6. The 'seals', who wear only their swimsuits, dive in the water and disappear for what *seems* like hours.
7. Each of the divers *enjoys* the ocean in a different way.

Paragraph 2

1. My family *is* a combination of all three types.
2. All my brother wants to do *is* try out different kinds of equipment and see how deep he can dive.

3. As for my father, he is a 'seal': Swimming around and cooking his 'catch' *is* what he *enjoys* most.
4. My mother and I are 'nature lovers': Swimming with snorkels and fins is fun, but neither of us *has* any interest in diving 50 feet down or reaching under a rock to find a slimy abalone.
5. So we all enjoy our diving trips in our own *ways*.

Paragraph 3

1. The 'nature lovers' are the *ones* who enjoy snorkelling around for brief periods of time.
2. For example, their trash or garbage *is* always taken away.
3. No change.
4. Taking rocks and shells *is* something they would never do.
5. They are there to see but not spoil the beauty of nature that *is* underwater.

UNIT 4

Practice Exercise D

1. c. Using prepositions correctly in English is very difficult if English is not a person's first language. (Background statement that sets the context for the essay.)

e. Prepositions are small connecting words that do not necessarily exist in other languages, or may not have exactly the same meanings.

Issue. An explanation of the problem
a. Such language differences make teaching of this area very difficult.

Issue. Further explanation of the problem
f. One popular teaching method relies on students learning combinations of nouns and prepositions.

Issue. One solution
b. Another method takes a cognitive linguistics approach, in which prepositions are studied in relation to spatial relationships.

Issue. A second solution
d. The essay which follows gives a brief history of prepositional theory and compares the traditional and cognitive linguistics approaches, arguing that a cognitive linguistics approach helps students to understand the concepts underlying prepositions and so is more effective in helping students to use prepositions correctly.
(Thesis statement outlining what the essay will cover and what perspective the writer will take.)
2. d. This essay has argued that a cognitive linguistics perspective is more effective than simple memorization in helping students to remember noun and preposition combinations.
b. By studying spatial relationships, students appear to remember prepositions more accurately than they do using the traditional memorization method.

Restatement of main points and reaffirmation of thesis
a. Spatial relationships, however, may differ from one language to another, and so this method is not completely effective.

Restatement of main point and explanation that there may still be problems with it
c. Nevertheless, the cognitive linguistic approach appears to be useful for many students, and it is recommended that researchers study this approach further to see whether it is applicable for students with different language backgrounds and at different levels of language study. (Broad final statement relating to significance of argument)

UNIT 5

Passage 1

1. E
2. B
3. C

Passage 2

1. A
2. E
3. D

Passage 3

1. C
2. A
3. D

Passage 4

1. A
2. C
3. A

Practice Exercise A

Exercise 1

1. It is the lack of education which has resulted in the acceptance of mental slavery.
2. Joti's father was an uneducated man who observed old customs.

3. Joti left the procession and narrated the whole incident to his father with anger in his eyes.
4. Joti attended the marriage because his friend had invited him.
5. Joti was worried about the equality of human beings and was thinking about the caste system which was so deep-rooted. That's why he could not sleep that night.
6. The Brahmin was annoyed with Joti because he could not accept a low-caste boy walking with the Brahmins in the marriage procession.
7. Joti quit the marriage procession because he felt insulted.
8. The author highlights that caste system is so deep-rooted that lower caste people have accepted it. There is need to educate the marginalized sections of the society.

Exercise 2

1. The 'I' in the passage represents an ordinary man.
2. The ideal way of understanding a civilization is to study an ordinary day in the life of an ordinary man.
3. The complicated machine in the passage refers to an alarm clock which rings on the table by the bed of the author.
4. C
5. The kind of life experienced by the author represents that all of us are dependent on machines in one way or the other. From morning till evening many of the routine tasks are performed by the machines.

Exercise 3

1. The principle of weight training is that when the muscles are exerted against resistance, they are forced to adapt and deal with this extraordinary workload.
2. It is physical exercise which affects the nature of muscle fibres making them thicker and stronger.
3. During weight training, the heart is forced to beat faster and stronger in order to pump sufficient blood to the muscles being worked. As a result, the heart adapts to this extra workload by becoming stronger and more efficient.
4. The heart pumps more blood at the same number of heartbeats when exposed to excessive stress.
5. Due to physical exercise, our body becomes well-oiled and finely tuned piece of machinery.
6. The term 'well-oiled' in the passage denotes a healthy body which can carry out routine tasks easily.
7. Importance of Physical Exercise
8. In the present world, physical exercise is very important as the world is filled with stress and anxieties. In order to keep ourselves mentally balanced, physical exercise is a must.
9. The function of the heart is to pump sufficient blood to the muscles.
10. The above passage suggests that in order to keep ourselves healthy, we need to do physical exercise regularly.

Exercise 4

1. When the monkeys get irritated, they start beating their chests with their hands.
2. Lions are ferocious animals. That's why, they are kept in strong metal bars.
3. The chief function of the trunk of elephants is to drag heavy loads with ropes.
4. The children were afraid of riding on the elephant as the elephant seems an awkward creature when it moves along heavily with its legs covered with loose folds of tough skin and its trunk swinging from side to side.
5. An animal which has violent and furious energy is called a ferocious animal.
6. Elephants are awkward in appearance because their legs are covered with loose folds of tough skin and their trunks swing from side to side.
7. It is the long neck of the giraffe which makes it typical.

Exercise 5

1. We can recognize a smile by looking at the simple act of turning up the corners of the mouth.
2. An adult can convey his smile by a mere twist of the lips.
3. A
4. When a child smiles, it struggles to get in touch with its mother.

Exercise 6

1. If admissions are made far more selective, it can automatically help to reduce admissions.
2. The standards of education can be raised only when the teacher–student ratio is brought down to a manageable proportion, teachers are given refresher courses and trainings, and library budget is increased by the college managements.
3. The teachers can be helped to brush up their knowledge by providing them with refresher courses and training every summer.
4. C
5. The phrase 'vexed problem' means a difficult problem which causes disturbance.

Exercise 7

1. Through the passage the author wants to convey that hard work is the only key to success.
2. Constant work improving upon one's own findings progressively is necessary for effective work output.
3. A
4. According to the passage, the most important thing with regard to the work that we get involved in is that in whatever area we work we should perform our duty with utmost devotion and meticulousness.
5. According to the passage, the great nations have become stronger through their hard work and dedication to the cause of their country. There is no shortcut, no escape route. Hard work is the only way out.

Exercise 8

1. C
2. B
3. A
4. C
5. B

Exercise 9

1. The hardship caused by the smoker to the non-smoker is physical, while the hardship caused by the non-smoker to the smoker is spiritual.
2. According to the author, a smoker is not morally superior to the non-smoker because he has missed one of the greatest pleasures of mankind.
3. A man without any moral weakness is untrustworthy because his existence is too mechanical and his head always maintains its supremacy over his heart. According to the author, he is too correct, righteous, unemotional, and unpoetic a soul.
4. The author considers smoking a pleasure which he says is missed by a non-smoker.
5. Thackeray means to say that the pipe has dual purpose. A philosopher becomes more contemplative with the pipe, while a fool keeps his mouth shut while using the pipe.

Exercise 10

1. Our attitude to peace is that it is impossible to achieve it.
2. Man thinks peace is impossible to attain because we are gripped by forces we cannot control. This has made us believe that war is inevitable and mankind is doomed.
3. Peace as a concept is universal peace and goodwill of which some fantasts and fanatics dream. According to the author, it is unattainable. Peace as an attainable reality is practical which can be attained by concrete actions and effective agreements in the interest of all concerned.
4. Peace is a process because with each new generation there will be new problems which can be solved only with the capability of facing the challenges. The solution cannot be a static one. Hence the process of peace is ever evolving.
6. Practical Aspect of Peace

Exercise 11

1. Tagore, Radhakrishnan, Zakir Hussain, and Saiyadain were great teachers because they were committed to high ideals and superior academic norms. They made noble efforts for strengthening and enriching the educational curricula and programmes. They gave education a distinct personality of its own, and they were cultivated minds and integrated personalities.
2. They are known as great teachers and educationists because they were ready to work in the service of the nation.
3. They are known as cultivated minds because they were influenced by the high ideals of our great and ancient heritage.
4. Education can be used for building the nation.

5. Teachers have a great responsibility because they can mould the character of individuals and can shape the society itself.
6. The aim is to build up the nation in conformity with the lofty ideals laid down in our Constitution.
7. A. superior
   B. lofty
   C. sacred
   D. moral
   E. forward-looking

Exercise 12

1. The four reasons that made the author opt for hunting wild animals with a camera are:
   i. It is not a one-sided game.
   ii. Shooting with gun provides animals little chance to escape.
   iii. With camera the author can shoot the wild animals in their natural wild state.
   iv. He can also bring home some proof of what he had seen.
2. The author got more pleasure in this hunting than other kind of hunting because he could shoot without hurting, certainly without killing, and yet could get the trophies of the chase.
3. There was a risk while shooting ferocious animals as it can be life threatening.
4. When the author shouted at the rhinoceros, it did two things in reaction. It jumped with a remarkable speed and gave a horrid snort.
5. The author could not take the photograph because the pair had got his scent before he could spot them and being bad-tempered beasts they rushed at him.
6. A. going for pleasure
   B. wrong
   C. risky
   D. fortune
   E. interesting

Exercise 13

1. C
2. B
3. D
4. B
5. A

INDEX